D1510047

Healthcare Beyond Reform

Doing It Right
for Half the Cost

Healthcare Beyond Reform

Doing It Right
for Half the Cost

Joe Flower

CRC Press
Taylor & Francis Group
Boca Raton   London   New York

CRC Press is an imprint of the
Taylor & Francis Group, an **informa** business

A PRODUCTIVITY PRESS BOOK

MIX
Paper from
responsible sources
FSC® C014174
www.fsc.org

CRC Press
Taylor & Francis Group
6000 Broken Sound Parkway NW, Suite 300
Boca Raton, FL 33487-2742

© 2012 by Joe Flower
CRC Press is an imprint of Taylor & Francis Group, an Informa business

No claim to original U.S. Government works

Printed in the United States of America on acid-free paper
Version Date: 20120322

International Standard Book Number: 978-1-4665-1121-7 (Hardback)

Library of Congress Cataloging-in-Publication Data

Flower, Joe.
    Healthcare beyond reform : doing it right for half the cost / Joe Flower.
      p. ; cm.
    Includes bibliographical references and index.
    ISBN 978-1-4665-1121-7 (hardback : alk. paper)
    I. Title.
    [DNLM: 1. Health Care Reform--United States. 2. Costs and Cost Analysis--United States. 3. Delivery of Health Care--economics--United States. 4. Forecasting--United States. 5. Health Expenditures--United States. 6. Health Policy--United States. WA 540 AA1]

    362.10973--dc23   2012002158

Visit the Taylor & Francis Web site at
http://www.taylorandfrancis.com

and the CRC Press Web site at
http://www.crcpress.com

To my wife, Jenny, my inspiration and cheerleader and the best,
most thoughtful sounding board and critic for what I am trying to express

We are called to be the architects of our future, not its victims.

—Buckminster Fuller

Contents

SECTION 3   MAKING IT ALL WORK

Acknowledgments

It's been a long road. It has taken an inestimable amount of time, resources, and access to get me to a place where I can sit down and explain healthcare to you, dear reader, in a way that we can all understand better how it got here and what it takes to fix it. While I take all responsibility for the point of view in these pages, and any errors of fact or thought, there are so many to whom I owe real and constant gratitude for what I have been able to bring to this table.

Kathryn Johnson, during her years in the 1980s and 1990s as CEO of the Healthcare Forum, was my mentor and introduction to thinking of healthcare from a large, systemic, forward-oriented point of view. She and her editor at the *Healthcare Forum Journal*, Sue Anthony, sent me out to interview hundreds of healthcare executives and clinicians, as well as many of the top organizational and systems thinkers of our age. Johnson has reemerged, as well, to be the principal advisor to the Healthcare Beyond Reform Project. I thank as well Judy Berger, my first wife and mother of my children, and now a healthcare organizational consultant, for introducing me to Johnson and Anthony and the world of healthcare, and for working with me on the Healthcare Beyond Reform Project.

My editor at Taylor and Francis, Kris Mednansky, has given me enormous support and encouragement.

Economist and futurist Jeff Bauer not only has given me help and support over the years, but also gave me the introduction to Kris, which allowed this book to happen.

Over the years I have received great help and guidance from my fellow healthcare futurists and analysts, especially Jeff Goldsmith, Ian Morrison, Clem Bezold, Trevor Hancock, Sholom Glouberman, Leland Kaiser, and Leanne Kaiser Carlson.

At the same time, I take off my hat to the memory of two pioneers in the field, the late Russ Coile and the late "DocTom" Dr. Tom Ferguson, who pioneered the image of the electronically engaged e-patient in the dark ages of the 1980s.

I salute my colleagues in the "healthy communities" movement, such as Tyler Norris of the Community Commons, Deryk Van Brunt and Marcos Athanasoulis of the Healthy Communities Institute, and Michael Bilton of the Association for Community Health Improvement.

My thanks to Pam Strayer, my editor in the 1990s at HealthCentral.com, for her help and advice over the years. Ken Dychtwald, my coauthor on *Age Wave* in 1989, gave a leg up to my thinking about demographic and economic issues in healthcare.

My continuing thanks to Rick Hill, my editor at H&HN (Hospitals and Health Networks) Daily, the American Hospital Association/Health Forum publication, and his editorial director Mary Grayson, for providing an online platform all through the turbulent past decade.

Thanks to the Center for Health Design and its dedicated CEO, Debra Levin, for continuing my education in healthcare and giving me a window into the cutting edge of design in the built environment.

My thanks to Matt Holt, cofounder of Health 2.0, for his support and counsel, and to his editor at The Health Care Blog, John Irvine, for giving me a continuing platform in the rapidly growing world of change in healthcare.

My special thanks to the intelligent and rambunctious community on the Well, my online home for over 20 years, back into the Jurassic era of online social media, for their constant barrage of agreement, argument, stories, resources, references, criticisms, and updates. My special thanks to the Writers Conference on the Well—a stronger, warmer, more supportive backup no writer could ever hope for. And my special thanks to Well colleagues Dr. Alan M. Eshleman and Dr. Diane Brown, and health planner Andrea McKillop.

Finally, my deep mentors: Dr. Len Duhl, the inventor of the "healthy cities/healthy communities" meme, and a powerful force for good in the world, taught me much about what really creates health in the world. Stewart Brand, progenitor of the *Whole Earth Catalog*, one of the founders of the Well, and of the Global Business Network, has taught me much about creating tools for change in the world. My mentors in Aikido, as well: First, the founders of Aikido of Tamalpais, Richard Heckler (who dubbed me "the horse with the hard mouth"), Wendy Palmer, and the late and much missed George Leonard. And along with them the late and equally missed Terry Dobson, and Steven Seagal. The average reader may not easily make the connection between martial arts and building better healthcare, but if you wish to build a better healthcare you must deeply understand conflict, change, turbulence, and systems thinking. There is no better place to ground yourself in those subjects than in the dojo, where well-meaning people try to batter you with big sticks, and you learn to work with them anyway.

To all these, and many others whom I have missed naming or who would not want to be named, I owe thanks and gratitude. Strength and compassion to us all.

Joe Flower
Aboard the tug Owatonna
Sausalito, California

About the Author

Joe Flower is an independent healthcare analyst and futurist, a veteran of 30 years of studying, reporting on, consulting with, and speaking to organizations across the industry. His clients spread from the World Health Organization and the Department of Defense, to Fortune 100 pharmaceutical companies, manufacturers, and health plans, to local community hospitals, free clinics, physician groups, nursing associations, start-up companies, and small employers. He is on the board of the Center for Health Design, and on the speaking faculty of the American Hospital Association.

The Facts

In 1980, healthcare took no more of a bite in the U.S. than it did in other developed countries like Canada, Sweden, Denmark, and Germany—about 8% of the whole economy.

In 1983 the U.S. instituted the first cost controls. Did they work?

By 2000, healthcare cost the U.S. 50% more than its closest rivals, and twice as much as most other developed countries. Today it takes up 18% of all the resources in our struggling economy, even while many hospitals and clinics and doctors are struggling to stay in business.

There is something deeply wrong with this picture—and it's something we can fix. By 2020, we can be back to costing the same as any other country—half the current bite out of the economy. Here's why, and here's how we'll get there.

First, a Story:
Tom Johnson's Belly Encounters Healthcare as It Has Been

Tom Johnson's belly hurt. He sat on the edge of the bed and rocked, gripping his aching belly with both hands, grunting with the pain. This was getting worse. But there was nothing more he could do about it, unless it was bad enough to go to the hospital. He had insurance for the hospital.

Tom had never felt comfortable with health insurance companies. He remembered, and would recount with some vehemence whenever people argued about healthcare, an incident from the time when his wife was alive. When she got sick, she needed a particular type of respirator at home, so that she could sleep. The insurance company, the one that billed them $1,017 every month for the two of them, would not pay for it. A long call to the company finally got him to a supervisor who said that they only paid for things that Medicare would pay for. He went online and found a Medicare list—and the respirator was on it. Another long trek through telephone trees, and he finally talked to another supervisor. Oh no, he was assured, it wasn't the Medicare list that counted, it was the Medicaid list. He found that list online, and it too listed the respirator. A third long call, and this time the supervisor said the other supervisors were mistaken, they just don't cover that respirator. They cover a different kind of respirator, but the doctor hadn't prescribed that one, so they couldn't pay for that one either. In the end Tom just paid for it himself. Tom didn't like insurance companies one bit.

The pain in his belly was getting worse.

A month after his wife had finally died, a new monthly bill arrived from the health plan, listing him as the sole beneficiary, and increasing his monthly payment to $1,247. The bill did not explain why insuring one person in his 50s should cost even more than insuring two people in their 50s.

Tom had called his insurance agent, Bill Hackford. "Why, that's outrageous!" Bill said. "Listen, I'll get right on this. I'll find out what's going on. I'll call you back."

And he did. "Well, I talked to your health plan."

"Yeah, what did they say?"

"They said they were canceling your insurance."

"Why?"

"Didn't say why, really. I think they canceled you because you complained."

Tom sighed and sat shaking his head. He felt like he had been punched in the stomach. He had to have some insurance, but he couldn't afford much. He was a structural engineer, and his employer had cut back his hours in the building slump. So he told Bill to find him a policy that just covered hospitalizations, nothing else. It cost far less, but anything less than a hospitalization would come out of his own pocket.

The pain was getting very bad. Earlier in the evening, when his belly first started hurting, Tom had gone to see a doctor at a local clinic. The place was really for Medicaid patients and people like that, but he had heard that they would take cash, so he went. The place seemed well organized and welcoming. For his $50 he got a few minutes with a doctor who prodded, poked, asked a few questions, and told him to go buy some Pepto-Bismol at the drug store down the block.

The Pepto-Bismol had not helped.

Suddenly Tom bolted for the bathroom. The pink Pepto-Bismol and everything else came up. *All right,* he thought. *This is serious. It's a good thing I had Bill get me that hospital plan, because that's where I'm going.*

He felt light-headed, a little dizzy, it was hard to walk, and the pain in his gut was doubling him over. *I'll just call 911,* he thought. But does the insurance cover an ambulance ride? He wasn't sure.

So he drove himself to the hospital, Tradition Memorial.

He staggered into the busy emergency department and presented himself at the desk. He tried to explain what was going on to the woman at the desk, but he had a little difficulty talking. The woman waved at a section of hard plastic chairs in the corner and said, "Sit over there."

He did. He sat clutching his belly and moaning. A TV blared in the corner. He watched as a cop brought in a drunk, and the nurse waved to the same section of seats. He realized, *They think I'm just drunk.* He didn't know if he could talk any better now, but he pushed himself to standing, and started toward the desk when another wave of nausea hit him. He saw a rest room sign and headed for it.

He woke up on a gurney. He was in an ER room. He was still in serious pain. People were swarming around him. A nurse was pushing a needle in his left arm. Above him to his right was another woman. "Hi, I'm Dr. Hedley. I'm glad you woke up. But we're going to sedate you in a moment, and give you some morphine for the pain. You appear to have acute appendicitis. It may have ruptured already. We're going to operate as soon as we can get you in."

The nurse started undressing him. He could barely move to help her. Everything he did hurt. Someone was starting to shave his belly. The woman from the front desk appeared near his feet. "Mr. Johnson," she said, "I have your wallet here. May I look in it for your insurance card?" Tom nodded. The sedation was coming on, and he was feeling sleepy.

In the end, Tom Johnson would spend 12 days in Traditional Memorial Hospital recovering from the burst appendix and the six-hour open abdominal surgery to clean it up, and fighting the infections it brought on.

Recovery was tough, it was a hard fight, but in many ways his time in the hospital was tougher.

The first day he was heavily sedated and under strong pain medication. He drifted in and out of awareness. But that night the pain seemed to return. He pressed his call button. When a nurse finally appeared, he asked why it hurt so much.

"They are titrating your pain medication. They switched you from morphine to hydrocodone. You shouldn't need such a strong one now."

"But it really hurts. Can you put me back on the stronger stuff?"

"You'll have to wait until the doctor sees you in the morning. I can't just change the orders."

So he writhed in pain. *At least he might be able to sleep until morning*, he thought. But as soon as blessed unconsciousness came, it seemed, the nurse was shaking him awake. "Mr. Johnson, sorry I had to wake you up, but you were moaning and disturbing the other patient."

He looked over at the other bed, where a much older man lay on his back, eyes closed, not moving.

"Okay."

The pattern repeated all night long.

By the time morning came, Tom was exhausted. But finally the doctor bustled in. "How are we doing?" he asked briskly, lifting the sheet and probing at Tom's wound.

"We're hurting a lot. Ow! Could I go back on the strong stuff again for a while at least?"

"A lot of pain? Keeping you up?" He considered, made a note on the chart, and replaced it in the rack at the foot of the bed. "Okay, we'll do that."

After he was gone, a nurse he had not met before came in with a small paper cup with a syrupy dose in it. "Here you are, drink this down."

He took the cup, drank the syrup down, and said, "I'm glad to finally be getting something stronger for the pain."

"Stronger?" She looked at him quizzically. She pulled the chart out of its rack. "Oh. I see. Well, I can't give you morphine on top of the oral hydrocodone I just gave you. You'll have to wait another four hours."

After he got the morphine at noon, Tom once again drifted in and out of awareness. There was a TV screen near his bed. He watched old movies, but he could barely focus on them. The machines over his bed and his roommate's bed beeped softly.

That evening, the beeping from his roommate's bed was suddenly replaced by a steady electronic alarm that startled Tom awake. After some minutes a nurse poked her head in the door, glanced at the monitors, then left again. The alarm went on and on. The same nurse came back, peered at the monitors, and left again. In a while she returned with an older nurse, who glanced at the monitors, felt the man's neck, and said, "He's coding. Call a code blue." The younger nurse hurried out. There was an announcement on the PA system out in the hall. In what seemed only moments the room was bustling with doctors and nurses, barked orders, a rolling cart with equipment, but Tom was drifting back to sleep. He heard the young nurse say, "I thought the alarm was malfunctioning. Like it does, you know?"

When he woke the old man was gone. Tom never saw him again.

The next day Tom spent more time awake. Now he had a new roommate, a man about his age who seemed to be in pain a lot, like him.

Once, when the man seemed awake, Tom said, "So what are you in for?"

The man sighed heavily. "Brain tumor."

"Oh, wow. That's tough. They going to operate? They think they can help you?"

"Yeah, yeah. The doc says if they go after it right away, I have a good chance of making it. Bring in all the big guns, you know. Right now, real quick." After a long pause, he continued, "And I've got good insurance. I'm a professor over at the college. So at least I don't have to worry about that."

"Well, good luck, man."

Late in the afternoon, two women in business suits arrived in the room. They drew the privacy curtain around the professor's bed. But Tom could hear.

"Mr. Brennan, I'm Shelly, and this is Barbara. We're from the hospital finance office. I'm really sorry to tell you this. I have bad news for you. Your health plan has cut you loose."

"What?"

"They refuse to pay for your operation, and have rescinded your plan entirely. You are uninsured."

"Did they say why?"

"They said that you left some things off of your medical history the last time you re-upped—a possible aneurysm and being monitored for possible gallstones."

"My doc never told me either of those things."

"But apparently he made some notes in your medical record."

"Oh wow. Wow. Wow. So, wait, you're going to do the operation and I'll figure out how to pay for it, right?"

There was an uncomfortable silence. The other woman spoke. "Mr. Brennan, you are not at the moment in a life-threatening condition. The hospital has no obligation to treat you without knowing how it will be paid."

"But …"

"There are charity options we can explore, foundations, veterans groups, and such. But that will take some time to line up. For now, we are sending you home."

"But the doctor said …"

"I'm sorry, Mr. Brennan."

He was gone within the hour.

Two days later, Tom had another roommate. In the evening the man suddenly said, "I'm having trouble breathing. I think I'm having an allergic reaction to something they gave me. It feels like my throat's closing up."

"Well, hit your button."

He did. No one came. He hit it again. He whispered, "I can't breathe!"

Tom started hitting his own call button repeatedly.

His roommate staggered out of bed and toward the door. He managed to get his hand on the door handle and jerk the door open before he collapsed into the hall. There were cries in the hall. Two nurses came. Help arrived. Someone gave him a shot. They took the man away on a gurney. The next day he was back, breathing but shaken.

Tom was an engineer, with an engineer's interest in processes, in how things work together. As the pain medications were ratcheted down, and he began to think more clearly, he began to notice things and wonder. He didn't know much about medicine, but some things struck him as odd. Such as: The people treating him rarely read his chart. Those who did only glanced at the top page. And why was it a chart at all, in the twenty-first century? And: There was a washstand in the room. One nurse washed her hands every single time she came into the room, or even between dealing with his roommate and coming to deal with him. Others scrubbed now and then. Most doctors and nurses and orderlies seemed never to use the sink at all. It bothered him that the nurses could not see him from the nurse station. They couldn't see him at all unless they came into the room.

What was it about their work situation that made it so hard to get their attention?

After 12 days, Tom was discharged. He could walk, the pain was manageable with some vicodin every 4 hours. He even drove himself home. There was no one to care for him there. He didn't have a doctor to call his own. There was no home health nurse ringing his doorbell.

Two weeks later, two letters arrived on the same day, shoved through the door slot and landing on the beige carpet with all the drug store circulars and catalogs. Tom was still recovering, but he shoved himself out of his easy chair and walked slowly to the door to look at the letters. One was from the hospital. It included a bill for $47,378.24. The other was from the health plan. It informed him that his policy was rescinded, and that the health plan would not pay for his surgery and hospital stay. There was a box on the form giving a reason. The reason was an "undisclosed prior condition."

Under that was a box listing what the prior condition was. The box said "acute appendicitis."

Is this over the top? Is this fictional scenario a bit extreme, too absurd? Things like that don't really happen, do they? Or at least not often enough to worry about, right?

It certainly does not represent the average experience. It is a catalog of mistakes and problems. If most experiences in healthcare were that bad, we would all be dead or broke by now. But extreme? Over the top? Unfortunately, no. Unfortunately, these experiences have been far too common in healthcare the way we have traditionally run it in America.

This scenario is a fictional amalgam, but each separate element happened to me, or was reported to me by the person it happened to, or was pulled from testimony in lawsuits or before Congress. Each of them I recognized, from my 30 years of observing and analyzing the industry, as "business as usual."

Think about this: "Medical misadventure" is one of the leading causes of death in America. You won't often see it listed that way in "cause of death" tables. The victims of surgery accidents, drug dosing problems, hospital-acquired infections, and other medical "adverse events" tend to show up in some other column naming the syndrome they actually died from, such as "infectious disease" or "stroke," rather than how that happened. About 600,000 people die each year from heart disease in the United States, and close to 560,000 from cancer.* "Medical misadventure" or "adverse events" probably comes third, at between 100,000 and 200,000 premature deaths per year, according to the most thorough studies. These are followed by chronic lower respiratory diseases like emphysema and bronchitis at about 137,000, stroke at 128,000, and accidents at 117,000.

Stories like Tom's make me very angry. They are partly why I have chosen to come out of the relative privacy of my work consulting and speaking to groups inside the healthcare industry to make a more public statement about healthcare and how it can and must change.

I have been a healthcare analyst, a futurist, for over 30 years. It has been a long-term project in adult education—my education. I have consulted with governments and health systems in North America, Europe, and China; with the World Health Organization and the Department of Defense; with pharmaceutical companies, device manufacturers, health plans, and employers; with associations of doctors, nurses, physical therapists, psychologists, insurance brokers, healthcare architects—everyone involved in this sprawling industry. I work with organizations and leaders to work through the demographics, the economics, the technologies, and the systems dynamics of change, how they will affect their part of healthcare, their sector, their profession, and what they need to do tactically and strategically to survive and thrive and make healthcare better. I work with boards, sometimes for days at a time, working through the deep implications of these changes. I have helped train whole departments of large companies like Airbus, American Express, and GE Healthcare to think differently about what they're doing and to approach their customers in new ways. Over the years I have toured hundreds of hospitals, clinics, and laboratories; interviewed thousands of healthcare executives, board members, patients and family members, entrepreneurs, doctors and nurses; and interviewed and compiled the thoughts and approaches of 60 of the top thought leaders of our time on change and organizations, from Peter Drucker to Jim Collins. It's been a long search.

One of the things I learned over that time is the absolute necessity of listening to everyone, from the janitor in a hospital subbasement to the CEOs astride Fortune 100 corporations. The VP of quality can give you a whole PowerPoint stack about his or her "Lean manufacturing" principals and initiatives, but if the guy running the laundry can show you what he is doing to use less water and get better infection control at the same time, you know the company has something. The architect can talk about work flow patterns and walking distances and sight lines in the new wing; then ask the nurse executive whether nurses are vying to

---

* Kochanek, D., et al., "Deaths: Preliminary Data for 2009," *National Vital Statistics Reports*, Vol. 59, No. 4, March 16, 2011, Division of Vital Statistics, http://www.cdc.gov/nchs/data/nvsr/nvsr59/nvsr59_04.pdf.

work in the new wing or avoid it, and why. To understand a system this complex and complexly enmeshed, you have to see it through all eyes.

Borrow my eyes for a while, ask with me for a while the core questions that have informed all of this searching. I want to understand how we got here. How have we transformed the process of healthcare into a monstrous twin personality, one a remarkable world of thoughtful people in innovative organizations delivering miracles of healing, and the other a brutal machine for random cruelty, visiting massive unnecessary suffering, premature death, bankruptcy, and incurable poverty on millions of Americans, while imposing on the whole country an ever-growing burden of unnecessary cost?

I had to go through many phases—of fury, of study, of hope, of disappointment—until I arrived at the right level of analysis, the one from 30,000 feet. I had to abandon concern for my own career, for smoothing it over with the people who hire me to consult and speak. I had to confront the fact that publishing this book may mean that I retreat to that little place in Baja California Sur my wife and I bought years ago, because the smart money is not on speaking common sense about what works for the good of everyone.

The first point to understand is this: Despite its chaotic appearance and wanton destruction, healthcare is a system, a dysfunctional, chaotic, adaptive system. There are patterns at work that no one designed and no one would have designed if given the opportunity. We must deal with these patterns, and the institutions trapped in them.

Not an Easy Book

You may get angry reading this book. And I am going to ask you to bear with me. You may feel upset by my arguments, even dismissive. I'm going to ask you to stick around and think it through with me before you come to a conclusion.

Let me tell you why.

It has been a singular experience to write this book. People ask me what I'm working on—strangers, friends, people in the next seat on the plane. I say, "I am writing a book about how to make healthcare better and cheaper for everyone." Everyone, every single person that I have said this to, says encouraging things. They wish me well, they want to read it when it comes out, they hope it makes a difference. I have never encountered a single person who says, "Why? Healthcare is fine the way it is." No one. Everyone feels that healthcare is broken, and feels strongly that we need to fix it.

You probably have the same feeling. That's why you picked up the book in the first place.

The second singular thing is that almost everyone believes strongly not only that healthcare needs to be fixed, but that they know how to fix it. That opinion is almost always based on blaming one party or another—the greedy doctors or health plans, heartless behemoth hospital systems or overreaching pharmaceutical companies, overcharging device manufacturers or other healthcare vendors, vulturous malpractice lawyers or red-tape-happy regulators.

Everybody across healthcare has come in for their share of criticism, and a good case can be made in almost any direction. People's opinions usually revolve around removing the offending party from the equation, or strapping them down so tight that they can't make mischief anymore.

You probably hold some similar opinion. And you may well be right. I am not asking you to give up your opinion. I am asking you to hold it lightly while we think this through. Because blame is not enough. It will not fix healthcare. Removing any one group from the equation, or restricting them tightly, will not fix healthcare. Fixing healthcare means fixing the system.

The reality is that we have a system that rewards people all across healthcare for doing shoddy work at high prices, for ignoring what must be done and doing only what is profitable, for sloughing off the hard, years-long work of getting it right and instead concentrating on getting paid. We pay them to do this, and people will do what they are paid to do.

Most doctors and nurses are highly trained professionals who want to do nothing more than care for their patients in the best possible way—but they are caught in a system that rewards volume over quality, doing more things instead of doing the right thing, a system that overworks and distracts them while it squanders their time and skills. The incentives driving the decision makers of hospitals and health systems, of health plans, of pharmaceutical companies, and of medical suppliers have been similarly skewed. When they can see a better way to do things, they can usually also see that they would be penalized for even trying. Employers, who pay for much of the private side of healthcare, have not yet found a way to demand of healthcare providers the same constraints of cost and quality they would demand of any other suppliers to their businesses. And over the decades, the different segments of the industry have learned to protect themselves by skewing legislation, regulations, and payment systems even more in the direction of these perverse incentives, building up their sense of their own safety and stability rather than seeking solutions that are better for the whole system and for the hundreds of millions of Americans that they serve.

This $2.6 trillion industry is made of people—talented, good hearted, hard working, at desks, at bedsides, in laboratories, on the graveyard shift. They have spent much of their lives training and apprenticing for the work they do now. Some are in it for service, some are in it for money, but almost everyone I talk to feels the same way: trapped in their role, frustrated by knowing that the good they could do is in spite of the system, not because of it, that they are perpetually swimming upstream. It's a tragic waste of talent and hard work and treasure to have so many good people so hobbled by circumstances that no one intended.

After 30 years of working in the heart of healthcare, I believe that now is the best and only foreseeable moment when we can fix healthcare because healthcare as a system is more destabilized now than it has been in any of our lifetimes. It is at a tipping point. We are very close to being able to free the healing process and the people who are trapped inside this two-headed monster.

But here is the key: We now have the knowledge we need to make the change, to tip healthcare in the right direction. We have the evidence. We have done the pilots. We can see what works in real systems, with real clinicians and real patients in real lives. We can demonstrate the hard-won knowledge and experience that we will need in order to change healthcare. A clear framework for action has emerged, which I will outline in later chapters. And now, finally, we may have the momentum to make it happen. This is the moment.

Introduction

We could do healthcare better, for everyone, for half of what it costs today.

We in the United States, as a society, can provide better healthcare for all Americans for half the percentage of the economy (the gross domestic product (GDP)) that it costs today.

We can do this in more or less the system that exists today, without putting the whole healthcare system on the government payroll, or shifting Medicare and Medicaid into a private voucher system, or necessarily moving the entire system to a single-payer model, or implementing any other grand legislative scheme.

In fact, most of the changes we need are not political or legislative at all; much of the legal and regulatory support we need to make those changes is already there in the law as it exists now, or in the healthcare reform law now being implemented, or in the healthcare experiments happening in various states.

We can do this without rationing healthcare or restricting anyone's choice. In fact, the only way to make it work is by giving people more resources and options, smarter and sooner.

We know we can do this because it is already happening in places.

We know we can do this because across the landscape of health and healthcare we can easily see huge areas for improvement, vast opportunities disguised as intractable problems.

We know we can do this because we can see why we got into this mess of paying too much without getting what we want. We can see the mechanisms that drive down costs, and see examples where these mechanisms are already working.

We know we can do this because we have the technical tools that we never had before to track what works and what doesn't. We have done the pilot programs, the experiments, and the analyses. We have tested many new business models.

We know we can do this because if we look in the right places, it is obvious that we have learned an enormous amount over the last two decades about how to manage and pay for healthcare to get the best result. We can ignore all that we have learned, and end up with a system that is worse, more expensive, and less effective as every year goes by. Or we can notice what actually works, and shift our policies and business models to imitate what works. We can build a smarter healthcare.

It's the System

To make a whole system work better, you have to change how the system works, not just the people in the system.

Let me give you an example from outside of healthcare. Imagine that you were a young traffic engineer in, say, 1949. Imagine that you dreamed of making driving safer. What would you want to change to make driving safer?

The fact is, driving is much safer now than it was in 1949. In 2009, about 30,000 Americans died as a result of traffic accidents. This was the lowest figure since 1949. A nice outcome, but think of this.

Americans drove seven times as many vehicle miles in 2009 as they did in 1949. In 1949, 7.13 Americans died for every 100 million vehicle miles; in 2009, the figure was 1.09. So for every mile you drive, you are only one-seventh as likely to be killed in traffic as your grandfather was 60 years ago.*

Why? Are Americans more skilled behind the wheel today? Not particularly. Experts credit the mandated use of seatbelts and airbags; breathalyzers and tougher laws against driving under the influence of alcohol or drugs; graduated licensing for teenagers; antilock braking systems; crash barriers, rumble strips, median barriers, and other improvements in road and highway design; steel-belted radial tires that don't blow out; crumple zones, and better bumpers on cars. These are all system tweaks that actually work, that make it 10 times as hard for even a terrible driver to kill himself or you.

It's the system, not the individual actors within the system. We have only started on the thinnest little wedge of that kind of thinking about healthcare.

To understand how to make the system work better, we have to understand how it works now. We have to understand how we have ended up paying people vastly more than any other society and getting mediocre results. Once we understand that, it becomes easy to see why some system changes would give us much better results at much lower prices.

If we make some key system changes, just as traffic engineers managed to get seatbelts and airbags in cars and crash barriers on the highways, we can expect not just to "bend the curve" of healthcare inflation by a few percentage points, but to actually drive the cost of healthcare down in a virtuous deflationary spiral.

---

* Eisenstein, P., "U.S. Highway Deaths Plunge to Lowest Level Since 1949," Detroit Bureau, April 1, 2011, http://www.thedetroitbureau.com/2011/04/u-s-highway-deaths-plunge-to-lowest-level-since-1949/.

This will take many years and hard work at key leverage points in the system, but it absolutely can be done.

Most of that work will not be political. What is needed is mostly not grand new legislative schemes. Most of that work will be the efforts of people in healthcare, and people working for health plans, employers, and government agencies paying for healthcare, working together to build new business models and payment structures within the existing system—as many already are.

Systems Economics: Who Gets Paid? For What?

The core of the argument is about healthcare as an economic system. Understanding how systems work, and how the economics of healthcare drive the choices made by all the actors in the system, takes us a long way toward being able to see how healthcare got in this mess, and to find the points of leverage that will get us out of it.

Most of the focus of the vast ongoing discussion about how to reform healthcare has been on who pays for it: Should the government become the "single payer" for all healthcare, extending Medicare to all? Should employers continue to provide healthcare coverage for their employees? Does using private health plans bring the advantages of competition to the marketplace? Or does it simply put the consumer at the mercy of a faceless bureaucracy bent on its own survival?

These are valid questions. But they are obscured by the fact that the other side of the equation, who gets paid and what they get paid for, actually has a much greater influence on the dynamics of the system than who does the paying. Medicare, for instance, seems to be more efficient at allocating resources, requiring less overhead than private insurance companies, and less overhead by the clinicians making claims, and it usually reimburses the clinicians less than private health plans do. But this efficiency does not drive the system to be massively less expensive. Healthcare delivered under Medicare does not cost half as much as healthcare paid for by private health plans. There is no reason to imagine that extending Medicare to all would cause a massive drop in costs or increase in quality.

For that, we have to look to: Who gets paid? For what? Almost all of healthcare in the United States is paid for under one model: the commoditized, insurance-supported, fee-for-service model. That is:

Commoditized: The system pays as if every cardiac stress test is the same as any other, every replaced hip is the same as any other, which is clearly not true. There are wide variations on prices, but the variations have no relationship whatsoever to value. When the price has nothing to do with the value of what you are offering, the irresistible incentive is to offer the least value for the price.

Insurance supported: The person choosing to incur costs is separated from the entity paying for it. So at the moment of decision, cost has no influence. The incentive for the provider is always to use more, and for the patient is to demand more, since there is no other marker for value.

Fee-for-service: What is paid for is different from what we want. What we want might be a new hip, or treatment to heal us from an infection. What is paid for is a long list of items: therapies, tests, drugs. If you pay for items, you will get more items, whether or not the items move you toward what you really want.

This is why we don't get what we want and need out of healthcare: it's not just that there are for-profit health plans and pharmaceutical companies. Everybody works for a living, but no one is getting paid to deliver us what we need. Unlike any other industry, in healthcare nobody is making a market by delivering what we need, whether for profit or not, government paid or privately paid. If we don't pay for it, we will never get it.

Wherever we undermine, route around, subvert, or supplant this business model, suddenly we find all kinds of different opportunities to pay for what we want. That's what we will explore in this book.

The Reform Is Not the Change

It may be startling for many readers to delve into a book about reforming healthcare, and discover that there is very little in it about the federal healthcare reform law, the Patient Protection and Affordable Care Act (PPACA). This is by design. PPACA, passed in spring 2010 and still a major political hot button two years later, is a catalyst, a facilitator, and an accelerator of the change we are going through. It is not the change itself. It is not even the cause of the change, because the change is driven by much larger economic and demographic factors, especially by the sheer crushing cost of healthcare.

The PPACA reform law can help accelerate change in some ways, but it will not cause the change we seek—because it does not change the fundamental economics of healthcare. Repeal or defunding of PPACA would not make healthcare better and cheaper for the same reason: it will not change the fundamental economics. Even the more drastic government payment reform of a national single-payer system would not change the underlying economics, and would not by itself bring us better, cheaper healthcare for everyone.

How can this be? It seems counterintuitive, it seems wrong: How can the PPACA reform act be of so little importance to the real reform of healthcare, when the political sphere has been frothing at the mouth about it for 3 years already, and show all signs of continuing for years more? Surely it is of vast importance? Yes, it is. Healthcare is an incredibly large business, made up of enormous economic forces. Healthcare businesses are among the most profitable enterprises in the history of the human species. Why would they fight for more? In confronting such a question, it is well to remember a saying I made up: any population considering whether to have a third drink consists of people who have already had two drinks. You can lay good money on it: whenever any attempt is made to change the rules, those forces will bring out the long knives and fight in the political arena for their third drink. They are very good at it. That's what the fight is about. It is about economic forces trying to preserve their ability to make money the way they are used to, so every detail of the reform law is of vast importance to them. It is not of vast importance to us.

On balance the new law brings some good things, especially coverage of many who are now uninsured, and it catalyzes more good things. But it is not of epochal, life-changing importance to us, the consumers, the patients, the citizens, because it will not bring us better, cheaper healthcare for everyone. Nothing will do that until we change the fundamental economics.

Amazingly, that is what is beginning to happen right now. That's the good news. Actually, that is the incredible news. Despite these huge economic forces arrayed against common sense and doing the right thing, there is cause for optimism. Despite 30-odd years in these trenches, I am an optimist. Here's why:

As all these factors have come together, everybody in healthcare has come to believe that their usual way of doing business is crumbling under them. Doctors, hospitals, home health agencies, insurers, employers—everyone is desperate to find a new footing. And no one has found a certain footing yet.

That's why today, right now, we are at a tipping point in healthcare. Things are already changing, at every level and in every direction. Now, in this brief period before everything gels into its new shape, we have a window of opportunity to push the system in directions that will mean seriously better and cheaper healthcare.

From whatever place you have in the system, whatever influence you have over your part of it, whether as a citizen, a clinician, an executive in a healthcare system or a health plan or a supplier to healthcare (yes, I am talking to you), the time has come to do the right thing, to stand and deliver for the thousands and millions who depend on us. You: Make a difference. Now. Push it.

In This Book

In the first section of the book we will take a clear, unencumbered, serious look at the exact nature of the mess we are in and its underlying systemic causes.

In the second section we will go over the Healthcare Beyond Reform framework, the five major strategies that will change the dynamics of the system for everyone involved in it. In this section, I guarantee, there is something that can change the direction of your life and career, if you let it.

In the third section we will look at several other ideas that may make a huge difference in our health, our healthcare system, and its costs—an even bigger difference than everything we have talked about before. In the final section, I'll set out the clear actionable steps on the paths forward and offer materials for healthcare leaders, employers, voters, and people with bodies. We will see how the change will affect different parts of healthcare, what legislative changes are needed, and what the next healthcare might look and feel like.

We can do this. We can end the suffering.

The Goal

Healthcare: The best, highest-quality healthcare available.

For everyone: Because we are a compassionate people. Because it is necessary for life. Because we actually can afford it. And because it turns out that the only way to bring healthcare to most Americans cost-effectively is to bring it to everyone.

For less: Not just for a lower rate of inflation. For less.

For a lot less: For half the percentage of the economy it takes today (from 17% of GDP to 8.5%).

We Can Do This

This is possible. People are already doing pieces of it, or doing all of it for particular groups of people. It doesn't take caped crusaders or alien powers. It takes ordinary people looking at the problem a little differently and being willing to try new ways of doing things. We can do it. We must do it.

HOW WE
GOT HERE

1

Chapter 1

Half Off?

This seems like a bold assertion: We can do healthcare for half the cost. We have been struggling with the costs of healthcare for decades and have only succeeded in occasionally shaving a few percentage points off the inflation rate. We have never succeeded in driving that inflation rate below zero at all. Why would any sane person facing the available facts contend that we could actually drive the cost down by half?

Good question. There are, it turns out, lots of reasons to think this is true. The first is the experience of other countries.

Looking at Normal Countries

Look at other countries with major, advanced healthcare systems and this is what you see: whether you measure it by percentage of the economy (GDP) or in dollars per person devoted to healthcare, a few countries spend about two-thirds of what the United States does; the rest spend half or less.

And they apparently get more for their money. Leave aside such vague markers as life expectancy. Much of gross longevity may have little to do with the healthcare system and may have more to do with traffic fatalities, murder rates, diet and exercise, or economic stress. If we look mostly at markers that are better proxies for how well a particular national healthcare system serves its citizens—maternal and infant mortality, rates of diabetes treatment—and include especially surveys of how much its citizens and its doctors just plain like the system, the United States consistently ranks behind almost every other first-tier economy in almost every category.

For all the personal and national treasure that we pour into our system, we compete with countries like Malta and Fiji and Portugal in what we get back in health and satisfaction with our system.

This is not about "socialized" medicine either: though every other major country finds one way or another to cover all of its citizens, how they do it is all over the political spectrum. Several nations, such as the Netherlands and Switzerland, have completely private health insurance systems, with mandates that citizens buy insurance, and subsidies for the poor. Germany does without a single-payer system for older people like the U.S. Medicare system. Instead, it supplies its retired citizens with help to continue paying for the private health insurance they already carry.

Some argue that our system is more expensive because we have to support massive teaching and research facilities that are the envy of the world, but the data do not strongly support the notion that teaching and research make ours twice as expensive. Besides, such nations such as France and Germany, among others, are no slouches in the teaching and research department.

Similarly, some argue that our system costs more because it is, supposedly, the best in the world. They argue that the quality of healthcare in these other countries is obviously worse than ours. The results we get, ranking consistently behind other countries in the results of our healthcare system, argue otherwise.

We in the United States would not want to put up with the restrictions and delays that some systems, such as Canada's, impose on their citizens. Restrictions, delays, and outright denials of care permeate our system; they are just far more random than in Canada. The distribution of our wealth of medical resources is wildly uneven, with high-tech, expensive care often lavished on people whom it won't really help, and denied to people whom it would help—simply because of differences in their insurance status.

While the United States clearly leads the world in cutting-edge medical science and technology, there is little evidence that this prowess must of necessity cost us the more than $1 trillion extra we pay per year for our system. Much cutting-edge medical science these days arises in other countries, such as France, Germany, the UK, Israel, China, and India—and in some of those countries for far less than here.

Others argue that citizens of these other countries are groaning under much higher taxes, and Americans object to high taxes more than anything else. But both parts of this argument are misleading. The taxes of other developed nations only seem higher because those taxes include healthcare costs, and ours do not include private healthcare costs. If you add the amount we spend on private healthcare to the amount we pay in taxes, the total load is not that different from other advanced economies.* Polls show that a majority of Americans would

---

* Squires, D., "The U.S. Health System in Perspective: A Comparison of Twelve Industrialized Nations," *Issues in International Health Policy,* The Commonwealth Fund, July 2011.

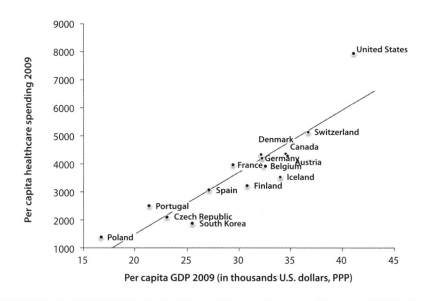

Figure 1.1   Per capita healthcare spending compared to per capita economic production.

be willing to pay higher taxes if their healthcare costs were reliably covered. For example, in a *New York Times*/ABC News poll conducted early in the reform debate, "sixty-four percent said they thought the federal government should guarantee coverage, a figure that has stayed steady all decade. Nearly 6 in 10 said they would be willing to pay higher taxes to make sure all were insured."*

One thing we could ask in looking at other countries is: "Okay, we spend way more than other countries on healthcare. But what do we spend more *on*?" The answer, it turns out, is "pretty much everything."

Most of the differences in spending per person on healthcare between different countries are just based on wealth: the pattern is, if you have more money, you tend to spend more money on healthcare. That's pretty straightforward. But the U.S. spends vastly more than other countries do, even more than its great wealth would suggest. In Figure 1.1, look how far above the trend line the U.S. healthcare economy lies.

That "extra" we spend runs all across healthcare. Even compared to our greater wealth per person, we spend more per person than other countries on hospital care, perform more procedures, and support more hospitals; we spend more on outpatient care; we take more drugs and more expensive types of drugs more often;

---

* Sack, K., and Connelly, M., "In Poll, Wide Support for Government-Run Health," *New York Times*, June 21, 2009.

we spend more on administration and finance; we spend more on public health and prevention, on research and development, and on new medical facilities. We pay physicians and nurses more compared to what other countries pay theirs, and also more compared to what we pay other American workers. We also have a greater percentage of specialists with higher incomes than primary care providers. We see doctors (and specialists) more often, pay our nurses more, and use more nurses per patient. The only areas in which we spend less are in home care and in durable medical equipment, from eyeglasses to walkers to surgical implants.*

Economists Behaving Badly with Smoke and Mirrors

Amazingly, you will find economists who will tell you that this is not so, that the United States does not really spend more than other countries do, given its much greater wealth. They call any such notion "unquestioned dogma"; they will talk about "opportunity costs" and "social costs,"† which is roughly equivalent to buying a mink coat on sale at half price, then buying a flat-screen TV on the money you "saved." The rationale is willing, but the arithmetic is weak. They will argue that, since every dollar amount paid in healthcare is influenced by something other than a pure, free-market price, when you add them up, "no one knows what the aggregate number really means"—somehow obfuscating the fact that the aggregate number means what it says it means: when you add up the actual amount of cash that we paid for healthcare, here it is. And it is really huge.

Economists of this bent will cherry-pick their analytical tools until they find one that makes it look like what the United States spends is somehow normal. Let me give you an example: the graph in Figure 1.1 is an example of linear regression analysis. Two factors vary together; in this case, the higher a country's GDP, the more it spends on healthcare. Put them on a graph, and they make kind of a line. You can make an actual line out of the average, and see how much

---

* Organization for Economic Cooperation and Development, accessed June 15, 2011, at stats.oecd.org.

McKinsey and Company Report, "Accounting for the Cost of U.S. Health Care: A New Look at Why Americans Spend More," November 2008, accessed June 15, 2011, at http://www.mckinsey.com/mgi/publications/us_healthcare/index.asp.

Carroll, A., "What Makes the US Health Care System So Expensive," September 20, 2010, accessed June 15, 2011, at http://theincidentaleconomist.com/wordpress/what-makes-the-us-health-care-system-so-expensive-introduction/.

Reinhardt, U.E., Hussey, P.S., and Anderson, G.F., "U.S. Health Care Spending in an International Context: Why Is U.S. Spending so High, and Can We Afford It?" *Health Affairs*, May/June 2004, p. 12.

† Goodman, J. "Do We Really Spend More and Get Less?" The Healthcare Blog, December 1, 2011, accessed at http://thehealthcareblog.com/blog/2011/12/01/do-we-really-spend-more-and-get-less/.

they each vary from the average. None of the countries seem very far off that line, except for the United States, which is way off the line.

If instead you use semi-log regression analysis, you will get a very curved line with a steep tail that, lo and behold, goes right up to the U.S. dot, so U.S. spending must in some sense be normal. Or at least, they argue, look, you get different results depending on what kind of analysis you use, so that linear regression graph is bogus.*

But what is semi-log regression analysis for? Why would you use it? It's for nonlinear correlations, that is, a relationship in which one term does not vary with the other term, but with its square or logarithm, like, say, generations of lemmings: Start with four lemmings, in one generation, you have 16. In two generations you have 128, in three you have 512, and in four you have 2,048. The relationship between generations and descendants is nonlinear. In other words, to use a semi-log regression is to assume that there is some reason why healthcare should not just cost more in a richer country, but vastly more than other countries that are nearly as rich. It's an argument that assumes its outcome.

The actual arithmetic is pretty straightforward: the United States not only spends more than other countries, but it spends about 50% more than its wealth suggests it should spend. When we encounter arguments that seem to say that 2 + 2 = 5, that suggest that the United States somehow spends less on healthcare than other countries "regardless of its reported spending,"[†] or that the United States is getting a great deal for its spending, it is reasonable to step back and wonder about the motives of people who would make such transparently strange arguments cloaked in dense mathematical language. There are trillions of dollars at stake in the discussion, and some professionals are willing to make any argument that might seem to sway the outcome, regardless of its intellectual integrity.

The Fairness Factor

Polls regularly show that while citizens of other countries complain mightily about their healthcare systems, they like theirs a lot more than we like ours.[‡] Equity is a big factor in those polls: If a health system is perceived as fair, people tend to like it; if it seems unfair, they don't. Most people consider bankruptcy

---

[*] Ohsfeldt, R.L., and Schneider, J.E., "How Does the U.S. Health Care System Compare to Systems in Other Countries?" presentation, American Enterprise Institute, October 17, 2006, accessed at http://www.aei.org/files/2006/10/17/20061017_OhsfeldtSchneiderPresentation.pdf.

[†] Goodman.

[‡] Commonwealth Fund International Health Policy Surveys, published annually in *Health Affairs*.

due to medical costs an indicator of unfairness; people feel that no one should have to lose everything because of an illness. Simply put, no Canadian or French citizen ever goes bankrupt because of medical costs, whereas more than half of all U.S. bankruptcies are attributed to medical costs. According to a 2009 study by Harvard researchers, 62.1% of U.S. bankruptcies in 2007 were mainly caused by overwhelming medical bills.[*] That study has been criticized by some (because it is arguable which debt is the one that breaks the bank), but bankruptcy attorneys and judges agree that medical bankruptcies in the United States are high and have been getting higher.[†]

It doesn't matter how many degrees you have, how hard you have worked, how organic your diet is, or how good a job you have. Even if you are well employed and well insured in the United States, you are one serious disease episode away from permanent poverty: Get cancer, become unable to work because of the disease, and you lose your insurance. You buy yourself some time by paying for the very expensive COBRA coverage (the temporary coverage made available by law to those who lose their jobs) out of your unemployment benefits and dwindling savings. If you don't fully recover before your COBRA period runs out, you will find yourself paying for your medical care out of your own pocket, selling any assets you have built up, until you "spend down" into poverty and qualify for Medicaid. The Medicaid world is an entirely different medical world, with sparse resources, inconveniences, and uncovered costs so huge that many people simply cannot afford the effort and money to get treated. They just die.

This is not an uncommon scenario at all. Think about your friends and acquaintances: most of us know at least one person whose life was permanently and drastically changed by disease in ways that go far beyond the physical ravages of the disease itself. Ours is a capriciously cruel system that may strike you down at any time, that will allow a virus, a tumor, or a bacterium to drive you into permanent poverty, extended suffering, and an agonizing death, alone, with no help.

Yet Americans seem immune to learning from other countries, as if being as smart as the Germans or the French about managing healthcare would somehow demean our great nation. And we are different, in significant ways. Simply adopting any other country's system wholesale would not bring us to the goal of better healthcare for everyone in this country for less money. Looking at other countries simply tells us that (1) it is possible, and (2) there may be some specific ideas we can learn from their system to import into ours.

At the same time, we can learn a lot just by looking at our own country.

---

[*] Himmelstein, D., et al., "Medical Bankruptcy in the United States, 2007: Results of a National Study," *American Journal of Medicine*, Vol. 122, No. 8, August 2009, pp. 741–46.

[†] Sack, K., "From the Hospital to Bankruptcy Court," *New York Times*, November 25, 2009.

The American Ways of Healthcare

Here's a fact I find astonishing: The least expensive place in the nation for a patient to be treated over the last two years of life? The Mayo Clinic, Rochester, Minnesota. Almost as inexpensive? The Cleveland Clinic. Both are consistently among the most highly regarded institutions in this country. The most expensive places? Other highly regarded institutions, such as Cedars-Sinai Medical Center in Los Angeles, UCLA Medical Center, and New York University Medical Center in Manhattan. They cost twice as much.* How can the best medical care in the world cost twice as much as the best medical care in the world?

The difference is clearly not quality of care. It has something to do with the way they are organized. Places like Mayo and the Cleveland Clinic make their living somewhat differently than places like Cedars-Sinai, NYU, or UCLA.

Over the years, the Dartmouth Institute for Health Policy and Clinical Practice has repeatedly analyzed statistics from the Centers for Medicare and Medicaid Services (CMS, the federal agency that runs those programs) to look at variations in healthcare spending around the country. These studies show that some specific areas of the country spend three times as many Medicare dollars per person every year as other areas. The studies divide the regions of the country by different hospital markets, and then rank them in quintiles (fifth, or 20%) from the highest-spending fifth to the lowest-spending fifth. The average difference between the highest- and lowest-spending fifths is 60%. In the higher-spending areas, patients are getting more services—more visits to specialists, more time in the ICU, more tests, more images—than in the lower-spending areas. But amazingly, patients' outcomes in highest-spending areas are no better than in the lowest-spending areas. In fact, some outcomes in the highest-spending areas are slightly worse, because the patients are getting more procedures and tests—and every procedure or test has a risk.

Economists struggle to explain these differences by showing that the people in one area are richer, poorer, sicker, better or worse educated, or of a different race or ethnic background from those in other areas, but when carefully analyzed, these factors do not account for most of the difference. Nor can the difference be explained by state policies, since major differences appear within states. Temple, Texas, spends half as much per person as Harlingen or McAllen, Texas.

In 2011, the Institute of Medicine (IOM) reworked the Dartmouth Center's analysis to take into consideration such factors as higher real estate or labor costs, or medical training, or the fact that, despite the common claims that "our patients are sicker," some people's patients really are sicker. After the IOM

---

* Pear, R., "Researchers Find Huge Variations in End-of-Life Treatment," *New York Times*, April 7, 2008.

analysis, the differences in spending were not so wide. But even with these variations in local costs accounted for, some parts of the country (such as Monroe, Louisiana, at $9,468) still spend twice as much per Medicare patient per year as other places (such as Honolulu, at $4,959), with no better results.

Why do different areas have such different habits in spending for healthcare? The map of these variations looks, to my eye, like a map of differences in organization. The less expensive regions are regions dominated or heavily influenced by systems that are differently and more tightly organized, systems such as Kaiser Permanente of Northern California, Group Health of Puget Sound, Peace Health in Oregon, the Billings Clinic in Montana, Intermountain Health in Utah and Idaho, Mayo Clinic in Minnesota, Cleveland Clinic in Ohio, Geisinger Health in northeastern Pennsylvania, and Scott and White in Temple, Texas.

But here is another wrinkle: the only thing that the differences clearly correlate with is the presence of healthcare resources, such as the number of specialists, ICU beds, and imaging systems per capita. A specialist in a locality is a specialist seeing patients, a CT scanner is a booked CT scanner, an ICU bed is a filled ICU bed.

This is a key point in understanding why the healthcare system we have does not work. It has to do with the feedback loop between supply and demand. The economics of unintegrated, commodified, insurance-supported fee-for-service medicine run counter to the expectations of classic economics in one crucial respect: supply pushes demand. Think about it: if your only way of making more money is to do more services, and if you have some control over what services are used, you will tend to do more services, whether or not that is exactly what the patient really needs. This is a conflict of interest at the core of healthcare. We will see how that unfolds from the day-to-day workings of healthcare into the extra $1 trillion we pay as the "American surcharge" for our expensive, wasteful system.

Possible Savings: Getting to Half

If all of the regions of the United States somehow practiced medicine the way they do in the lowest-spending fifth, the amount we would save across the system is about 30%. This year that would come to $780 billion. Remember the quivering, goggle-eyed awe with which politicians confronted the $1 trillion price tag of healthcare reform? That was $1 trillion over 10 years, $100 billion per year, about 4% of the $2.6 trillion we will spend this year alone.

A savings from within the system of $780 billion per year would be nearly eight times the cost of insuring all uninsured Americans.

There are a number of ways of estimating the waste in the U.S. healthcare system. Some look at variation and conclude that if you are paying more and not getting more, that's waste. Others aggregate numbers from specific types of identified waste, such as pharmaceutical waste, Medicare fraud, or common operations whose use is not supported by the medical literature. Others simply survey doctors to ask anonymously what portion of their practice is not truly medically necessary but done anyway to satisfy and keep the patient or to avoid malpractice concerns. Given the different methods, the consistency of the answers can be surprising: they all come in close to the same number, 30%.

But that 30% in possible savings does not come from doing healthcare in some revolutionary new ways. It only comes from cleaning up the waste and variation in the old-fashioned way. It only comes from imagining doing healthcare the way it is already done in Minnesota, or Utah, or Hawaii, or Seattle, or Temple, Texas, or any of the other low-spending parts of the country. Much of healthcare is stuck in a 1950s-style level of efficiency, without much of the digitization, automation, mobile technology, and new management techniques that have made other U.S. industries into models of productivity.

Since the inefficiencies are so large and blatant across healthcare, it is difficult to imagine that using these better management techniques and new technologies could not drive at least another 20% out of the cost. And once these changes begin to permeate healthcare, systemic effects will begin to kick in, as each sector of the industry affects the others, as we will see in more detail.

When we consider these factors, "better healthcare at half the cost" begins to sound like a reasonable, modest, conservative slogan, not a radical one at all.

Chapter 2

Waste

What are the biggest kinds of waste in healthcare—and therefore the greatest opportunities for savings?

This is a different way of asking the question about how to spend less on healthcare, a way that becomes more important as we burrow into the complexities of healthcare in search of real shifts in policy or economics or management techniques that will change the cost of healthcare.

There are three levels of waste in healthcare:

- Doing the right things in the wrong way
- Doing the right things in the wrong place
- Doing the wrong things—and not doing the right things

Level 1: Doing the Right Things the Wrong Way

This is about *working efficiently*, about questions such as: How can we avoid wasting the nurses' time with "foraging" for supplies, or refilling in data that have already been filled on other forms? How do we avoid wasting doctors' time with documentation and coding that could be done automatically through the electronic record? How do we avoid wasting the patients' time and effort by making them come back for additional appointments for things that could all be done in this meeting? And on and on through the million details of healthcare.

There are, of course, multiple tools in the kit for making healthcare more efficient and effective. As we shall see in later sections of the book, combining the right management tools with the right incentives can save significant money, time, effort, and frustration for everyone.

Level 2: Doing the Right Things in the Wrong Place

This is about *coordinating care*, about questions such as: How can we avoid duplication? How can we treat people at the right level in the system, whether that's an intensive care unit or a primary clinic? No matter how efficient we are at, say, doing a computed tomography (CT) scan on a patient, if the scan was a duplicate, the whole test is an unnecessary cost that does not help the patient. No matter how efficient our intensive care unit is, if we are treating people in the ICU that could be effectively treated in a general bed or at home, that is an expensive and unnecessary cost that does not help the patient.

Level 3: Doing the Wrong Things— and Not Doing the Right Things

This is about *avoiding* doing expensive and unnecessary things at all.

No matter how efficient your operating room team is or how well coordinated the care is, if you are doing an operation that will not really help the patient, then you are wasting money and time as well as putting the patient at risk. Healthcare burgeons with unnecessary tests and procedures. We are not only failing to properly treat millions of Americans, we are at the same time overtreating millions of Americans. This overtreatment not only costs hundreds of billions of dollars every year, it puts patients at risk. Dr. Elliot Fisher of the Dartmouth Institute has estimated that 30,000 patients each year die in unnecessary, unhelpful procedures.[*]

How Much?

So we have three ways of saving money in healthcare by doing it better:

- *Efficiency* (doing things with minimal waste)
- *Coordination* (doing things in the right context, without duplicating)
- *Avoidance* (doing what needs to be done, to avoid having to do expensive unnecessary things at all)

Which is the most important? Where will we find the greatest possible savings? What would the PowerPoint graph (the great arbiter of our civilization) look like?

---

[*] Brownlee, S., *Overtreated: Why Too Much Medicine Is Making Us Sicker and Poorer* (New York: Bloomsbury, 2007).

There is no way honestly, and with anything like precision, to put real numbers on the money that can be saved in each category. But we can think about the relative amounts to be saved and make a fantasy graph. If we were to actually come up with real numbers, the graph would look something like this:

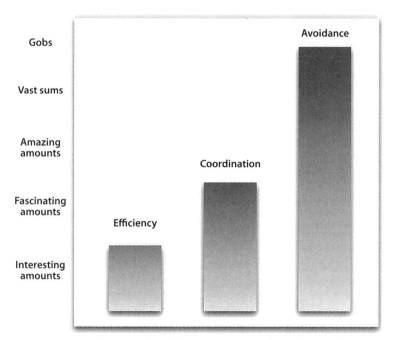

Contributions to the bottom line

We need to save money on healthcare in every way possible. But we can save far more money by not doing expensive unnecessary things than by being efficient. Efficiency can contribute something between "interesting amounts" and "fascinating amounts" to our savings effort; coordination can generate "amazing amounts," while avoidance can produce more than "vast sums," and even achieve "gobs" of savings.

For instance, amputating a foot because of diabetes can cost as much as $65,000 (not to mention the life-changing damage to the patient's body). If you treat the foot ulcer early and aggressively at a cost of $7,000 to $10,000 and avoid the amputation, you can save 85% to 90% of the costs of the amputation surgery.* Giving the patient with diabetes regular foot examinations and the

---

* "The Diabetic Foot: Amputations Are Preventable," position statement, the International Diabetes Foundation, May 2005, accessed June 20, 2011, at http://www.idf.org/position-statement-diabetic-foot.

health coaching he or she would need to avoid any foot problems at all would cost only a few hundred dollars per year—a cost savings of over 99% compared to amputation surgery. Doing better, smarter healthcare earlier saves gobs of money.

Where Are the Biggest Savings?

Looking for ways to save money in healthcare by doing it better is a lot like mining for gold or drilling for oil. A good geologist, some seismic soundings, and some test drilling can tell you where the oil is likely to be found or where the seam of gold ore lies embedded in the rock. In healthcare, the ore lies in four large, easily identifiable seams:

■ Inappropriate therapies
■ "Heroic" end-of-life treatment
■ Pharmaceutical waste
■ The acute results of untreated, preventable chronic disease

Let's spend a moment looking at each of these areas.

Inappropriate Therapies

We spend amazing amounts of money every year on therapies that don't work, or don't work any better than much cheaper therapies.

For example, consider *complex back fusion surgery* to relieve simple back pain. Surgeries to relieve back pain cost Medicare around $2 billion per year. That's a lot of money. Is the money worth it? Are we getting what we are paying for?

Let's compare surgery to what's called medical management, which is the use of nonsurgical interventions such as painkillers, weight loss, physical therapy, and exercise. Several studies have shown[*] that, in the short term, people who

---

[*] Wheeler, A.H., et al., "Low Back Pain and Sciatica," Medscape reference, May 16, 2011, accessed June 20, 2011, at http://emedicine.medscape.com/article/1144130-overview#a1.

Weber, H., "Lumbar Disc Herniation. A Controlled, Prospective Study with Ten Years of Observation," *Spine (Phila Pa 1976)*, Vol. 8, No. 2, March 1983, pp. 131–40.

Atlas, S.J., Keller, R.B., Robson, D., Deyo, R.A., and Singer, D.E., "Surgical and Nonsurgical Management of Lumbar Spinal Stenosis: Four-Year Outcomes from the Maine Lumbar Spine Study," *Spine (Phila Pa 1976)*, Vol. 25, No. 5, March 1, 2000, pp. 556–62.

Atlas, S.J., Keller, R.B., Chang, Y., Deyo, R.A., and Singer, D.E., "Surgical and Nonsurgical Management of Sciatica Secondary to a Lumbar Disc Herniation: Five-Year Outcomes from the Maine Lumbar Spine Study," *Spine (Phila Pa 1976)*, Vo. 26, No. 10, May 15, 2001, pp. 1179–87.

suffer from lower back pain are more satisfied and pain-free as soon as they recover from surgery than those who use medical management. But talk to them a year, two years, or four years later, and the difference disappears: people who had the surgery are no better off than those who didn't. Surgery is a temporary fix at best.

But the story is actually worse. Those studies mostly compared medical management with spinal decompression, the simplest type of back surgery. A major study published in 2010 in the *Journal of the American Medical Association*[*] compared decompression (microdiscectomy, or microdecompression, and laminectomy, or open decompression) with simple and complex back fusion surgery. The study showed that between 2002 and 2007, complex back fusion surgery for Medicare patients increased by 15 times, despite the fact that there was no evidence that complex back problems had increased that much in six years, or that new techniques had made the more complex surgeries any more effective than decompression. These complex surgeries cost nearly four times as much as decompression, produced twice as many patients who had to be readmitted to the hospital for complications, twice as many deaths, and three times as many life-threatening complications. On the other hand, the complex surgeries certainly make more money for the surgeon, for the institution, and for the medical vendors. The surgeon's fee (which is only a fraction of the overall charges) for a simple decompression is about $600 to $800, while the fee for a complex fusion surgery may be 10 times as much. The more complex surgeries often involve implants, which themselves may cost more than $50,000.[†] Does this make sense for the patients? For most of them, clearly not. Does it make sense for the payers (health plans, Medicare, Medicaid, and such)? Most of the time, clearly not. Does it make sense for the surgeon and the institutions where the surgeon does the work? Absolutely.

Now let's compare two other kinds of surgery: *kyphoplasty* and *vertebroplasty* are two procedures to fix the spines of people with vertebral compression fractures by injecting acrylic bone cement into the fracture. The cost

---

[*] Deyo, R., et al., "Trends, Major Medical Complications, and Charges Associated with Surgery for Lumbar Spinal Stenosis in Older Adults," *JAMA*, Vol. 303, No. 13, 2010, pp. 1259–65.

[†] Centers for Medicare and Medicaid Services, "Physician Fee Schedule," accessed at http://www.cms.gov/physicianfeesched/.

Cahill, K.S., et al., "Prevalence, Complications, and Hospital Charges Associated with Use of Bone-Morphogenetic Proteins in Spinal Fusion Procedures," *JAMA*, Vol. 302, No. 1, 2009, pp. 58–66.

Levin, D.A., et al., "Comparative Charge Analysis of One- and Two-Level Lumbar Total Disc Arthroplasty vs Circumferential Lumbar Fusion," *Spine (Phila PA 1976)*, Vol. 32, No. 25, 2007, pp. 2905–9.

(including the magnetic resonance imaging (MRI)) ranges from around $3,000 to $14,500.* There has been some research showing the benefits of vertebroplasty, but these studies were faulty. The research patients often knew what treatments they were getting, which probably influenced their treatment response and the results of the study. Patients in the control group knew they were not getting the real treatment, but just painkillers. However, in two good randomized single-blind studies (in which patients are "blind" to the treatments they're getting) researchers compared vertebroplasty to a sham treatment dressed up to look and feel like vertebroplasty. There was no real effect of the surgery[†] at all; the fake treatment worked just as well as vertebroplasty. Yet Medicare still coughs up for the majority of the funding for the thousands of these procedures done every year at a cost in 2008 (the latest year for which data are available) of $907 million.[‡]

Heartburn surgeries have a profile similar to that of back surgeries. Studies show that if you have chronic heartburn, over-the-counter drugs called proton pump inhibitors (such as omeprazole (Prilosec) or esomeprazole (Nexium)) work just as well as surgery to relieve your problem.[§] But U.S. surgeons still perform thousands of antireflux operations every year to relieve chronic heartburn. The drugs can cost as little as $12 per month and cause few problems. The hospital charges for the surgeries run from $10,000 to $25,000, of which roughly $3,000 is the surgeon's fee. Health plans typically will not pay for the over-the-counter drug, but will pay for the surgery if the doctors think it is indicated.[¶]

---

* Goodman, B., "New Studies Raise Doubts about the Benefits of Vertebroplasty," *Arthritis Today*, August 5, 2009.
  Brown, D., "Comparative Effectiveness Research Tackles Medicine's Unanswered Questions," *Washington Post*, August 15, 2011, accessed at http://www.washingtonpost.com/national/health-science/comparative-effectiveness-research-tackles-medicines-unanswered-questions/2011/08/01/gIQA7RJSHJ_story.html.
† Buchbinder, R., et al., "A Randomized Trial of Vertebroplasty for Painful Osteoporotic Vertebral Fractures," *New England Journal of Medicine*, Vol. 361, No. 6, 2009, pp. 557–68.
  Kallmes, D.F., et al., "A Randomized Trial of Vertebroplasty for Osteoporotic Spinal Fractures," *New England Journal of Medicine*, Vol. 361, No. 6, 2009, pp. 569–79.
‡ Redberg.
  Elshaug, A.G., and Garber, A.M., "How CER Could Pay for Itself—Insights from Vertebral Fracture Treatments," *New England Journal of Medicine*, Vol. 364, 2011, pp. 1390–93, accessed at http://www.nejm.org/doi/full/10.1056/NEJMp1101475.
§ Galmiche, J.P., et al., "Laparoscopic Antireflux Surgery vs Esomeprazole Treatment for Chronic GERD: The LOTUS Randomized Clinical Trial," *JAMA*, Vol. 305, No. 19, 2011, 99. 1969–77, doi: 10.1001/jama.2011.626, accessed June 22, 2011, at http://jama.ama-assn.org/content/305/19/1969.abstract.
¶ "Laparoscopic Treatment for Reflux Disease (GERD)," accessed June 22, 2011, at http://www.lapsurg.org/reflux.html.

Implanted defibrillators that shock a heart back into a normal rhythm can be lifesavers for those who need them. But a major recent study[*] in the *Journal of the American Medical Association* found that 22% of Americans who get them don't need them—they don't fit the profile of patients who would be helped and not hurt. Implanting the device is a major, invasive operation that involves sticking wires into your heart. It's expensive at an average cost of about $40,000 for the device, the hospital charges, and the surgeons. It's common, at about 100,000 operations per year. If 22% are not needed, they represent an unnecessary expense of about $880 million—nearly $1 billion per year for one common, unnecessary operation that, by the way, puts the patients at risk, as any operation does. And for unknown reasons, the percentage varies enormously from place to place. In some institutions, more than 40% of the implanted defibrillators end up in people who don't need them. And again for reasons unknown, the rate of unnecessary defibs is significantly higher in black and Hispanic patients.[†]

Coronary stents, tiny wire-mesh tubes that look somewhat like the springs in ball-point pens, are lifesavers for some patients who have a lot of heart pain due to unstable heart disease that might kill them at any moment. Interventional cardiologists use long, steerable catheters to snake the stents up the arteries to the spot where a heart artery is blocked, then open the spring to push the blockage open. They call the process a percutaneous coronary intervention (PCI). For those patients, stents cut heart pain rapidly and greatly reduce the chance that they will die or have a second heart attack. But large-scale studies[‡] have shown that many of these stents are put in people with no heart pain who have lower-level, stable heart disease. For them, the PCI combined with a cocktail of heart drugs works no better than the drugs alone. Medicare spends about $1.6 billion per year on catheterizations to put in stents,[§] of which as many as half may not be needed or helpful. If we add in the number of unnecessary stents put in people not on Medicare, here we have another approximately $1 billion wasted in the system.

Cesarean sections and induced labor are both continuing to rise at a faster pace than the births warranting them, suggesting that many of them are performed

---

[*] Al-Khatib, S.M., et al., "Non-Evidence-Based ICD Implantations in the United States," *JAMA*, Vol. 305, No. 1, 2011, pp. 43–49, doi: 10.1001/jama.2010.1915, accessed June 22, 2011, at http://jama.ama-assn.org/content/305/1/43.abstract.

[†] Grady, D., "Many Defibrillators Implanted Unnecessarily, Study Says," *New York Times*, January 4, 2011, accessed June 22, 2011, at http://www.nytimes.com/2011/01/05/health/05device.html.

[‡] Boden, W.E., et al., "Optimal Medical Therapy with or without PCI for Stable Coronary Disease," *New England Journal of Medicine*, Vol. 356, 2007, pp. 1503–16, accessed July 7, 2011, at nejm.org.

[§] Redberg, R., "Squandering Medicare's Money," *New York Times*, May 25, 2011, accessed July 7, 2011, at http://www.nytimes.com/2011/05/26/opinion/26redberg.html.

more for convenience than for medical reasons. About one in three U.S. births are by C-section, far above the 5% to 10% rate considered necessary by the World Health Organization studies. Studies show that healthy women with good prenatal care should see about a 4% C-section rate. C-section is major surgery, with all the risks that implies. Cesarean section approximately doubles the cost of a normal birth to around $7,000.

Let's do the math. The difference between 5% or 10% of deliveries problematic enough to need C-sections, and 33% of the approximately 4 million births in the U.S. every year, means that we do 800,000 to 1 million extra C-sections. Multiply that by the approximately $3,500 extra cost, and it seems that we spend about $2.8 billion to $3.5 billion per year wasted in unnecessary, unhelpful C-section surgeries.[*]

Excessive CT scans not only cost us vast sums, they are building a likely plague of tumors into our future. Medical imaging is a $100 billion per year industry, doing close to 100 million scans per year in hospitals and clinics and in free-standing imaging centers. Experts who study the problem estimate that 35% of all those scans are unnecessary. This includes multiple scans for a single problem, scans used when some less expensive and less risky diagnostic technique is available, scans that are repeated just because of lack of coordination and communication between different parts of the system, scans done not because they help the patient feel better but because they help the doctor feel better about malpractice exposure, and prophylactic whole-body scans peddled to the public just to take a look in case there's something wrong in there. No professional society endorses the whole-body scans, and the FDA has warned for years that there is no demonstrated medical benefit to them, whereas there is demonstrated medical risk. A CT scan dumps about 100 times as much radiation into the body as a typical x-ray does. The increased risk of cancer from any single scan is very small, but the 100 million scans a year have in aggregate pushed the risk from CT scans ahead of all other sources of natural or industrial radiation as a cancer risk. Estimates of the number of future cancer deaths that will arise out of each year's scans run from 10,000 up.[†]

---

[*] Multiple studies cited in "Why Does the National U.S. Cesarean Section Rate Keep Going Up?" *Childbirth Connection*, accessed July 8, 2011, at http://www.childbirthconnection.org/article.asp?ck=10456.

[†] LaPook, J., "Too Many Unnecessary MRIs and CT Scans?" CBS News, September 25, 2009, accessed July 9, 2011, at http://www.cbsnews.com/stories/2009/09/24/eveningnews/main5337931.shtml.

Maugh, T., "Overuse of CT Scans Will Lead to New Cancer Deaths, a Study Shows," *LA Times*, December 15, 2009, accessed July 9, 2011, at http://articles.latimes.com/2009/dec/15/science/la-sci-ct-scans15-2009dec15.

Numerous cites at the website of Dr. David Brenner of the Center for Radiological Research at Columbia University: http://www.columbia.edu/~djb3/.

So 35% of a $100 billion per year industry comes to $35 billion per year wasted on unnecessary scans.

Computer-aided mammography sounds like a great idea: have a computer program help the radiologist pick out the problem areas in those cloudy, fuzzy breast x-rays. Anything to fight breast cancer, to find it and treat it earlier, right? Except that it doesn't work. A group of doctors published a massive study[*] in 2007 in the *New England Journal of Medicine*. They had set out to find how much better the computer assist had made cancer detection, comparing tens of thousands of cases at 43 mammography centers, and the answer surprised them. What they found was that computer assistance brought out many more suspicious spots to be looked at, many more callbacks for the women to get a second look, many more biopsies. But extra cancers? None. For all that expense, all that extra trouble and worry for the patient, zip results. Overall, computer-assisted diagnosis does no better than the regular readings of skilled radiologists. Yet the percentage of mammograms that are done using computer assistance keeps climbing, and is now around 40% of all mammograms. The authors of the study found that, counting the extra fees for the computer assistance, plus all the extra work in the unnecessary callbacks and biopsies, and converting the entire system to computer assistance would cost an extra $550 million per year. At 40%, that comes to $220 million per year wasted on computer-aided mammography.

None of these figures are precise. They are studies, extrapolations, readings of the data. Their details are disputable. But the overall picture they paint is hard to deny, their logic is clear, and the gross numbers give us a feel for the scope of the problem.

What is going on here? Are these doctors choosing to do risky and remunerative procedures on their patients with reckless disregard for their health? Some probably are. But it appears that many doctors are unaware of the differences in efficacy for many of these treatments.

At the same time, device manufacturers and other companies that have an economic stake in these medical decisions can seriously influence the debate. To take one example, in 1985, Congress created a new federal bureau called the Agency for Health Care Policy and Research (AHCPR). This new agency was given three rather sensible tasks: fund studies on the effectiveness of various medical procedures, create evidence-based clinical practice guidelines that physicians could follow for what was the best way to treat particular conditions, and recommend which procedures, drugs, and devices Medicare and Medicaid should cover.

---

[*] Fenton, J., et al., "Influence of Computer-Aided Detection on Performance of Screening Mammography," *New England Journal of Medicine*, Vol. 356, 2007, pp. 1399–409, accessed July 9, 2011, at http://www.nejm.org/doi/full/10.1056/NEJMoa066099#t=articleTop.

In 1993, the AHCPR asked a panel of 23 medical experts to come up with guidelines for treating back pain. Looking at all the studies available, the panel concluded that surgery was not the leading best practice for reducing simple back pain. In response, a number of back surgeons formed a group called the Center for Patient Advocacy. Combined with the resources of Sofamor Danek, a company that makes the plates and screws used in complex back fusion surgery, they set out not just to overturn the findings of this expert panel, but to destroy the agency that commissioned the panel.

They nearly succeeded. In the 1994 mid-term congressional elections, the Republicans took over the House. Under the aggressive new speaker, Newt Gingrich, they targeted 140 federal agencies for destruction. At the urging of lobbyists for Sofamor Danek and the back surgeons who were members of the Center for Patient Advocacy, the AHCPR was put on the list. The American College of Physicians, the American Hospital Association, and the American Medical Association all went to bat for the AHCPR, but it was doomed in the House. Eventually the Senate saved it from destruction, but it was renamed the Agency for Healthcare Research and Quality, its budget was cut 25%, and crucially its teeth were pulled: the AHRQ was not allowed to make recommendations about what Medicare and Medicaid should cover.*

How Big Is This Waste?

Let's look at it this way: Remember the discussion above about the searing debates we had over the horrific cost of covering all Americans? The added costs were said to amount to the mind-boggling sum of $1 trillion, a cost the opponents of reform said we clearly could not afford. Notice that $1 trillion was a 10-year estimate; that is, the yearly estimate was $100 billion, or 4% of our yearly total healthcare cost of $2.6 trillion. So $100 billion per year is a good yardstick by which to measure these wasteful practices: that is the number that was deemed so huge and overwhelming that we could not possibly afford it, if that's what it took to cover all Americans. Yet we waste more than that every year in the system.

Our list of unnecessary procedures is far from a comprehensive survey of the healthcare industry. It is a casual list of some of the most obvious problem areas. And it is a list only of unnecessary procedures. It does not begin to cover wasted drugs, or unnecessarily high costs of drugs or devices, or myriad other sources of waste in healthcare. Yet in this one casual list, we end up with numbers like

---

* Deyo, R., and Patrick, D., *Hope or Hype: The Obsession with Medical Advances and the High Cost of False Promises* (New York: Amacom, 2005).

$1 billion to $2 billion in unnecessary back surgery, hundreds of millions for heartburn surgery, nearly $1 billion for unneeded defibrillators, $1 billion for unnecessary coronary stents, $3 billion for unneeded C-sections, $220 million in computer-assisted mammography, and $35 billion in unnecessary scans. Right here, in the system as it exists today, in the normal course of doing medicine as it is done now, is enough obvious, documented waste to pay for nearly half of the added cost of covering all Americans.

Heroic End-of-Life Treatment

We spend even more amazing amounts of money every year on therapies that don't work, aren't necessary, and aren't even helpful—because the patient is dying.

This is not a matter of "let's pull the plug on Grandma." This is "let's stop torturing Grandma. Let her have some peace and dignity at the end."

This is not about establishing "death panels" to toss people on the trash heap when they have become too expensive to treat. This is about learning to have the compassionate conversation, to tell the truth to patients and families when the end is near, and to ask them what they want that end to be like.

This is not about guessing how long, say, a cancer patient has to live, and yelling, "So long buddy!" when they cross some line like a 50% chance of 90-day survival. We can all cite stories of people who beat the odds.

This is rather about the other stories we can all cite, about parents or grandparents in unspeakable agony from end-stage cancer or slipping away due to multiple organ failure being subjected to one surgery after another, one massive drug regimen after another, kept alive by tube feeding and ventilators long past the point where there is any real hope of recovery, all on institutional reflex, all without any real decision on anyone's part to submit this poor dying patient to this painful, useless medical barrage.

The most common death scene in America is no longer the peaceful, dignified image from the old movies, the family gathered at the bedside, the dying person saying their goodbyes or slipping away in their sleep. The most common death scene is now the operating table, or the ventilator in the intensive care unit, the vital signs monitor finally flatlining, the digital pulse count reading 00.00.

The extraordinary waste of money is almost an afterthought compared to the extraordinary violence done to life's final passage. But here we are talking about the waste of money. How much do we waste on end-of-life care that is not helpful, is even hurtful (and often, if truth be told, not even wanted)?

The great majority of medical care takes place in the last six months of the patient's life. But not all of that is spent on clearly terminal patients; much is spent in personal battles against disease that might have been won, or on care for someone who would have been expected to live if it weren't for the catastrophe that brought them down (the heart attack, the stroke, the drive-by shooting, the failed parachute). That is "catastrophic care" that was unsuccessful, and the patient died. End-of-life care, on the other hand, is the treatment of terminal illnesses, usually the endpoint of long-term chronic disease. These two categories obviously have a lot of overlap between them. But some very significant portion of risky, costly medical intervention is lavished on people who are clearly not going to make it this time.

Often the patients, and the families who speak for them as medical advocates, don't even want heroic care. "Better treatment" and "more treatment" at the end stage may be quite different things, and studies* from the Dartmouth Institute for Health Policy and Clinical Practice show that most people understand this. Surveys find higher satisfaction from the dying patients and their families when the treatment is less invasive, involves fewer procedures and less time in the hospital. And the one group least likely to get heroic care, most likely to understand when the time has come to seek palliative care, get their affairs in order, and gather the family around them for a peaceful death? Doctors.†

Doctors less often refer to "heroic care"; more commonly they call the last-minute rush to throw every ounce of medical technology into the breach by the more realistic name of "futile care." They understand better than most of us how such futile care can enormously add to the pain, suffering, and loneliness of life's final weeks, days, and hours. The morbid joke among doctors about cancer specialists runs: "Why do coffin lids have nails? To keep the oncologists out."

It is estimated that we spend some $60 billion to $80 billion per year on this type of terminal care.‡ How much of that would we save if we had a more

---

* Wennberg, J.E., and Cooper, M.M., eds., *The Dartmouth Atlas of Healthcare in the United States*, 1999. The Health Forum, American Hospital Association, Chicago IL.
Fisher, E., et al., "The Implications of Regional Variations in Medicare Spending, Part 1: The Content, Quality, and Accessibility of Care," *Annals of Internal Medicine*, Vol. 138, No. 4, 2003a, pp. 273–87.
Fisher, et al., "The Implications of Regional Variations in Medicare Spending, Part 2: Health Outcomes and Satisfaction with Care," *Annals of Internal Medicine*, Vol. 138, No. 4, 2003b, pp. 288–98.
Wennberg, J.E., "Variation in Use of Medicare Services among Regions and Selected Medical Centers: Is More Better?" Lecture at the New York Academy of Medicine, January 24, 2005, accessible at http://www.dartmouthatlas.org/lectures/NYAM_Lecture_FINAL.pdf.
† Murray, K., "How Doctors Die: It's Not Like the Rest of Us, But It Should Be," Nexus, Zocalo Public Square, accessed at http://zocalopublicsquare.org/thepublicsquare/2011/11/30/how-doctors-die/read/nexus/.
‡ Farrell, D., et al., *Accounting for the Cost of U.S. Health Care: A New Look at Why Americans Spend More*, McKinsey Global Institute, December 2008, p. 109.

compassionate way of dealing with terminal illness? That's a hard question, but it could well be as much as half—$30 billion to $40 billion per year, approximately a third of what it would take to cover all uninsured Americans.

Insurance Waste

How much more does it cost us to run this amazingly fragmented payment system than it would to run a streamlined, efficient payment system? Let's just consider payment for the moment, not how efficient the care is, or how inefficient it is that some people have a payment system and some don't.

Think of your credit cards and debit cards. There is certainly a lot to complain about, but let's focus on the efficiency and effectiveness of the consumer credit system. You go to the store, whip out your credit card, pay for the groceries. You go to Mexico or Tahiti, same thing, same credit card. How often is your credit card statement wrong, due to a fault of the system rather than fraud or theft? Almost never. How often is your card wrongly denied, or a payment not made? It's certainly not an everyday occurrence.

For physicians and hospitals, troubles with insurance payments (such as wrongly denied claims, disputed diagnostic codes, mistakes, impossibly byzantine appeal processes) are a much more than everyday occurrence. Physicians' offices and hospitals have whole departments that do nothing else but process claims and argue with the insurers.

A study from the University of Toronto compared the costs and clerical time of U.S. physicians submitting claims to multiple payers with different forms, rules, and bureaucracies, to those of Canadian physicians submitting claims to one payer. They found that U.S. physician offices spend nearly 10 times as many hours per physician wrestling with payment (21 hours per week, compared to 2.5 in Canada). The extra cost to the U.S. healthcare system? $27.6 billion dollars per year,[*] a quarter of what it would cost to insure all Americans.

Keep in mind that this amount is solely the waste in extra processing costs, solely on the providers' side. The number does not include the vast amount spent on processing costs on the insurer's side, or the side effects of our insurance system on driving up the cost of clinical care. These amounts are undoubtedly far greater, but are far more complex and harder to estimate. We will revisit the subject in later chapters.

---

[*] Yahoo News and Agence France-Presse, "Simplifying US Health Care Could Save Billions," August 4, 2011, accessed August 4, 2011, at http://news.yahoo.com/simplifying-us-health-care-could-save-billions-study-042711819.html.

Pharmaceutical Waste

We waste enormous amounts of money every year in our use of drugs.

Leaving aside, just for the moment, the substantial arguments about whether we are overusing pharmaceuticals (or underusing certain classes of drugs), consider this question: How much would we save if everyone just took the drugs that they have been prescribed, at the prescribed dose, in the least expensive formulation, bought in the least expensive way that is convenient?

Seems like an odd question. Isn't that what most people do—go to the doctor, get a prescription, buy it the cheapest way that they know how to, and take it? Apparently not, for the answer to the question is startling: according to a study by the pharmacy benefit manager Express Scripts,* we waste $163 billion every year in the fundamental mechanics of the way we use drugs, approximately 1.6 times what it would cost to cover all uninsured Americans.

There are three parts to this huge number. The first two are simple waste: Americans spend $6 billion more than they need to by buying their drugs at a retail pharmacy instead of getting them through the mail. We spend $51 billion buying branded drugs when a cheaper generic would do just as well. Fifty-one billion dollars is more than half of the extra amount it would take to insure all now-uninsured Americans, and it is wasted just in the way we buy drugs.

The third part is more complex: When people with chronic disease fail to continue the prescriptions they have been given, it costs both them and the system less in the short run because we are not paying for those drugs. In the long run, though, it costs the system much more, as the chronic disease overwhelms them and they end up in hospital emergency departments, surgical suites, and intensive care units. The difference? One hundred six billion dollars, as part of our fifth and biggest category of waste: untreated chronic disease.

Chronic Disease

Chronic disease is huge. In fact, it's most of healthcare. Chronic diseases cause 70% of all deaths in America. Just three of these diseases—heart disease, cancer, and stroke—cause half of all deaths.† Chronic diseases (and the acute

---

* Miller, S., et al., "2009 Drug Trend Report: Solving for America's $163 Billion in Pharmacy-Related Waste," *Express Scripts*, April 2010, p. 6.

† Kung H.C., Hoyert, D.L., Xu, J.Q., and Murphy, S.L., "Deaths: Final Data for 2005," *National Vital Statistics Reports*, Vol. 56, No. 10, 2008, available at http://www.cdc.gov/nchs/data/nvsr/nvsr56/nvsr56_10.pdf.

episodes that spring from them) account for 75 to 85% of all medical costs in our system.*

Most chronic disease is preventable. When it has not been prevented, most chronic disease is manageable and treatable. The opportunity to save money—and to prevent vast amounts of suffering and poverty—is larger in dealing with chronic disease than in anything else in healthcare. In fact, that opportunity is larger than anything else our nation could save in any field for anything.

Let me repeat that: The largest money-saving opportunity available to our entire nation lies in the prevention, management, and treatment of chronic disease. If we imagine that we could reduce by half the amount we spend on untreated or poorly managed chronic disease, that would mean a reduction in healthcare costs of 40%, about $1 trillion per year. In all the discussions of trimming the federal budget or finding new sources of revenue, from cutting defense spending to raising the age of Medicare eligibility to raising taxes on the extremely rich, no single idea comes anywhere close to that figure.

In a nation swimming in debt, mad for ways to save money, desperate to slash costs, chronic disease dwarfs very other opportunity to save, and we are doing almost nothing about it.

Cynical sorts have been known to say, "Well, yeah, but everyone is going to die of something. Keeping people from dying of any particular chronic disease just pushes their death off a little further. So why bother?"

This is true enough, in a limited way. The cheapest deaths are sudden and traumatic, such as death from sudden cardiac arrest, the most common single natural cause of death in the United States, taking some 325,000 people per year. But the way we treat (and fail to treat) chronic disease pushes the cost and the suffering to the maximum. The Agency for Healthcare Research and Quality estimates that as many as 60% of all hospital admissions of people over 65 are avoidable "with the delivery of high-quality outpatient treatment and disease management." Those hospital admissions happen when a chronic problem gets out of control, and they can account for as much as 80% of the cost of care for one of these diseases.† Treat chronic disease early, often, and well, that is, manage it, and the costs plummet—and so does the suffering.

The larger savings, though, lies in prevention. The majority of chronic disease has its origin in behavior and environment. We eat the wrong things, smoke too

---

* Lynn, J., Straube, B.M., Bell, K.M., Jencks, S.F., and Kambic, R.T., "Using Population Segmentation to Provide Better Health Care for All: The 'Bridges to Health' Model," *The Milbank Quarterly*, Vol. 85, No. 2, 2007, pp. 185–208.

† Quoted in Nucci, C., "Insurers Curbing Hospital Admissions, Remotely," *HealthLeaders Media*, January 13, 2011, available at http://www.healthleadersmedia.com/content/MAG-260996/Insurers-Curbing-Hospital-Admissions-Remotely.

much, drink too much, are exposed to too many toxins and carcinogens, and don't get off the couch enough. Why? As the Buddha pointed out 2,500 years ago, life is "dukka," unsatisfactory. Life hurts. Far too many of us are depressed, anxious, and in pain—so we self-medicate with another super-sized serving, a few more beers, or another pill, all to stave off the pain for another few hours.

The cynical (who are always with us) can be counted on to say, "But what can you do about that? You can't force people to change the way they live. They won't change."

But the real attempts to help people change their behavior show that at least some good portion of people want to live healthier lives, and actually can get healthier with the right help. We can now assume that people who smoke have heard that it is bad for them, for instance, but many of them don't really know how they could stop. You and I might think that they should know, but they don't. People aren't depressed because they want to be. Most people who are obese don't like being obese, don't know how they got that way, and don't really see a realistic path to losing all that weight. Again, we might think that we could tell them what to do, but they don't actually know what to do (and most of the time, we would be wrong about what would actually work). Assuming that people with behavioral problems could just correct them if they wanted to is not a realistic or fruitful way to frame the problem.

If we are not going to just tut-tut disapprovingly and cast people out into the cold because we think they have caused their own problems, then we end up treating them. What's the cheapest way to treat them? As early as possible. In fact, the absolute cheapest way to treat them is to prevent the behavior from causing a medical problem in the first place, by getting very engaged with them as early as possible, at the primary care level, and in the schools, in the work-place, and in the community. So the answer to "Why do we have to pay so much to take care of people who won't take care of themselves?" turns out to be: Because we have been in denial about the problem. If we truly want to spend as little as possible taking care of people, we need to build better systems for engaging with them earlier, stronger, in their language, on a voluntary basis, when they want the help, and before they have despaired.

Applying smart healthcare to chronic conditions in a major way across society could save vast sums of money while avoiding enormous amounts of suffering and poverty.

The chief actuary of Medicare estimates that we waste 15 to 30% of every Medicare dollar.* Dr. Donald Berwick, the pediatrician the President Obama named as his first head of Medicare and Medicaid, estimated the amount of

---

* Foster, R., "The Financial Status of Medicare," presentation for the American Enterprise Institute, May 16, 2011.

waste in healthcare at 20% to 30%. When he left the job in December 2011, Berwick told the *New York Times*, "Much is done that does not help patients at all, and many physicians know it."[*]

As large as those percentages sound, these are not wild guesses, but conservative estimates. Most other surveys and estimates put waste at 30% of all healthcare spending, which in 2011 would come to nearly $800 billion per year,[†] eight times the extra cost it would take to insure all uninsured Americans. We spend enormous amounts on inappropriate therapies, on wasteful drug-buying habits, on unneeded and unwanted heroic end-of-life treatment, and by not being smart and active about preventing and treating chronic disease.

We could do far better than this. But how?

To answer this question, we must first look at the context: How is the world around healthcare changing? Then we have to look at the weird economics of healthcare, to understand why they are so different, and what would actually cause them to change radically.

---

[*] Pear, R., "Health Official Takes Parting Shot at 'Waste,'" *New York Times*, December 3, 2011, accessed at http://www.nytimes.com/2011/12/04/health/policy/parting-shot-at-waste-by-key-obama-health-official.html.

[†] Kelley, R., "Where Can $700 Billion in Waste Be Cut Annually from the U.S. Health Care System?" White paper, Thomson Reuters, September 27, 2009.

Chapter 3

Trends: Opportunities

Healthcare is knit into the fabric of the nation, not only because it is the largest business sector, but because it is a must-have for everyone. We all have bodies, sometimes they break, and eventually they fall apart completely. And we all pay for this enormous system in one way or another. So the healthcare problem does not exist in isolation. Any solution lives or dies in the context of the stuttering economy, the changing demographics of the patients and the workforce, changing disease profiles, new technologies, reform legislation, and changes in the insurance market. Perhaps the most important of all these trends is the growing realization among policy makers, healthcare executives, employers, and the public that the way we have done this all these years is not working anymore, that this boat is sinking, this train is careening off the track, this platform is burning—that we are running short on metaphors and clichés vivid enough to capture the caliber of disaster we are facing. Too many people are dying, too many are suffering and are being driven into bankruptcy and poverty, too many companies are burdened and slowed by the cost—and all because of a problem that we could actually fix.

What are the trends that make up this context?

The Economy

Millions out of work, the housing market cratered with millions of homes still scheduled to reset their mortgages to higher rates, banks hesitating to lend, business hesitating to expand: this is not temporary. The political sector seems incapable of producing a vigorous response and consistently puts other issues ahead of getting the economy back to full vigor. Income disparity continues its decades-long march to third-world levels,* with the aggregate income of almost all Americans essentially flat in constant dollars for over three decades.† Job security, pensions, and retirement healthcare coverage even in the public sector continue to evaporate, and the economic infrastructure (from roads and bridges to education and research) is aging and eroding.

We can expect the economy to improve, but jerkily, spasmodically, and with wide regional and sectoral variations. We can expect second and third dips over the coming few years. We cannot expect steady growth or anything like full employment throughout this decade. These bumps and twists will affect different regions and sectors of the economy differently, but the job market will be especially hard on the age cohort that is just preretirement, the pre-Medicare cohort that has the most difficulty paying for healthcare.

Healthcare, of course, has been the one bright spot in the current debacle, creating new jobs, spawning new businesses, and throwing up new buildings at an astonishing pace. But the health of the healthcare industry will increasingly depend on its ability to offer real solutions to the denizens of a limping and anemic economy.

Rampaging Geezers

The leading edge of the baby boomer generation has just turned 65, and has begun filling out Medicare forms. This massive cohort is beginning its long transition from the years of racquetball and kung fu through its years of Viagra and pacemakers, on the way to its years of walkers, hearing aids, and Depends. Its needs would swamp the system even without all these other compounding factors.

It's important to notice the myriad ways in which these "new elderly" are different from preceding cohorts, different especially from their parents, the "greatest generation" of Depression and WWII survivors, now disappearing from the scene. Compared to their parents, the booming geezers are far more active, and more active in their healthcare, more discriminating and demanding, more skeptical of mainstream healthcare, but more willing to experiment with alternatives, and far more engaged with their Blackberries, iPhones, and iPads. Facebook, Twitter, and Google are terms of everyday life for them. And

---

* Saez, E., summary tables, University of California at Berkeley, available at http://www.econ. berkeley.edu/~saez/TabFig2008.xls.

† Congressional Budget Office, figures and tables, available at http://www.cbo.gov/publications/ collections/tax/2010/all_tables.pdf.

they are far less willing to age anything like gracefully. They hate aging, and won't do it if they can help it—so they are far more ready to engage with anyone who looks like they are going to really help them with their health.

When Dr. Ken Dychtwald and I wrote *Age Wave*[*] in 1989, we learned through our research that the early boomer cohort, born between 1946 and 1954, had already had a strangely different experience of life from other generations. Their parents' experience was that big things happened to them, massive nation-changing historical events like the Depression, the Second World War, and the Cold War. The early boomers' experience was that their universe bends to them, that the specific gravity of their demographic heft changes their world.

A personal example: My brother John was born in 1946, the first year of the boom, the first year that the mass of demobilized soldiers and sailors and their spouses, in a burst of postwar optimism, produced over 4 million babies in one year in the United States. John's experience as one of those 4 million was that every school he ever attended was old and overcrowded. Despite years of warning, the school systems were not ready for the influx when that wave first broke over them. I was born four years later, in 1950, at the peak of that first wave of the boom. In those four years, the education system had awakened to the demographic wave and learned to surf. Every single school that I attended, from kindergarten through university, was brand new or expanded, with new books and supplies and freshly minted teachers (some still working on their credentials). It was not until I had children of my own that I realized that most schoolbooks are reused year after year, or that there might be a shortage of them.

Similarly, just about the time John came of early dating age in the late 1950s, rock and roll music was invented, with Elvis Presley and Buddy Holly and Bill Haley topping the charts. When I came of dating age in the early 1960s, the Beatles and the Rolling Stones blasted out of the UK and played to stadium-filling audiences. Just about the time that I got old enough to drive, cars got really interesting with the introduction of "youth cars" such as the Mustang. The civil rights movement was driven by an earlier generation, men and women born in the 1920s, such as Martin Luther King Jr. and Malcolm X, but 1963's March on Washington and King's "I Have a Dream" speech helped galvanize the boomer generation into an era of mass protests. The anti-Vietnam War protests gave the boomers the truly new experience, that peaceful mass protests could actually bend the shape of history—an experience that has ramified through American and world politics, both liberal and conservative, ever since.

As popular music came to dominate the cultural landscape, the technology of personalizing music shifted rapidly, from vinyl LPs to eight-track players to

---

[*] Dychtwald, K., and Flower, J., *Age Wave: How The Most Important Trend of Our Time Can Change Your Future*, Jeremy Tarcher, Los Angeles, CA, 1989.

cassettes, to the Walkman, to CDs, to iPods. Just about the time that I got far enough along in my career that I could afford to buy a desktop computer that cost a few thousand dollars, someone invented them and built out an industry based on them—specifically, people of my cohort, such as Steve Jobs and Bill Gates, both born in 1955.

At every stage of our lives, the commercial, technological, and political worlds have notably reshaped themselves to the needs and desires and points of view of this notably larger cohort. At the time Dr. Ken Dychtwald and I wrote *Age Wave*, we were both approaching 40. We predicted that this trend would continue, that as we aged the systems of aging would change. In our writing and talks at the time, we predicted specifically that the concerns of boomers as our parents entered their elderly and frail elderly years would drive healthcare reform, that such reform would be a major political issue in the 1992 elections as it never had been before. Bill Clinton was a cipher as we wrote, a barely known regional politician from a minor state. But we predicted that whoever won those elections would take a stab at changing healthcare—and that healthcare would change whether the attempt succeeded or not. We were correct.

Over the years, we have continued to be correct in predicting that as boomers approached Medicare age, healthcare reform would resurface as a major political issue despite its drubbing in the early 1990s. The problems of aging, of financing healthcare in our 50s and 60s and beyond, of re-creating the healthcare system so that it actually works, and works at a sustainable price, would drive massive political and economic change until satisfactory solutions arose.

History does not support the notion that "Whatever boomer wants, boomer gets." But the notion that we will go through the coming decade and more, ignoring the concerns of the aging boomer, and failing to solve the healthcare conundrum, flies in the face of history. The record of the past decades clearly supports the notion that whatever boomer wants becomes deeply important to our nation and our economic system. Solutions—probably multiple—will be found.

I guarantee you this: when I get to be 85, we are going to have kick-ass convalescent homes in this country.

Aging Clinical Workforce

Boomers make up as big a chunk of the clinical workforce as they do of the healthcare market. Just as tens of millions of boomers will be entering their peak years of needing diabetes care and cardiovascular care, many of the endocrinologists, cardiac surgeons, and other clinicians that they need will be ready to start chasing the marlin in Baja. Already, a 2010 survey showed 40% of all physicians planning to get out of patient care within the next three years alone.[*] Nearly a third of all of today's physicians plan to retire completely by 2020.[†]

A quarter of the RNs in the United States are already out of the field, while another quarter are planning career moves in the short term that will take them away from direct patient care. Every study[‡] that looks at the question shows that the current nursing shortage will grow enormously over the next decade, pushed by the confluence of boomer nurses retiring, boomers aging into the prime healthcare years, and millions of newly covered patients arriving at the doors of healthcare institutions.

A limping economy, boomers aging into the Medicare years, major shortages of clinicians: even leaving aside the staggering cost of healthcare as we do it now, all of these point to a need for the healthcare system to go through a major phase change to wholly new levels of efficiency and effectiveness and to do it quickly. If it does not, no matter how sincere, how hardworking and dedicated the doctors and nurses and healthcare managers are, our system as it exists today will simply and quite spectacularly fail to provide the care that we need.

Chronic Disease

Add chronic disease to the picture, and the future looks even more dire. But at the same time chronic disease offers the greatest opportunity for improvement.

Chronic disease is on a long upward trend. One marker of this future might be seen in the growth of obesity. Obesity is one good marker for the future of chronic disease for three reasons:

■ Obesity is apparently a factor of many chronic diseases, including not only the obvious ones, such as diabetes, cardiovascular disease, and stroke, but also less obvious ones, such as Alzheimer's and many types of cancer.

■ Obesity can be easily measured.

■ Obesity tends to be a lifelong problem, and has a lag time of decades in its effects. Measurements of today's obese population can tell us something about the trend in chronic disease in decades to come.

---

[*] Physicians Foundation, survey, released November 18, 2010, available at http://www. physiciansfoundation.org/PressReleaseDetails.aspx?id=250.

[†] Association of American Medical Colleges, survey, released September 30, 2010, available at aamc.org.

[‡] A fact sheet linking to and abstracting dozens of studies of the nursing shortage is available from the American Association of Colleges of Nursing at http://www.aacn.nche.edu/ Media/FactSheets/NursingShortage.htm.

Obesity has been growing at a shockingly rapid pace over the last two decades, especially among the young, African Americans, Hispanics, and Native Americans. This growth in obesity has tracked neatly with the growth of diabetes, and with the growth of the use of sugars (including sucrose, fructose, and high-fructose corn syrup) in the American diet.[*] Today, nearly a third of all Americans register a body mass index (BMI) higher than 30. In this small picture, the dark gray states are those with more than 25% of the population with a BMI over 30. The darkest states have more than 30%.[†]

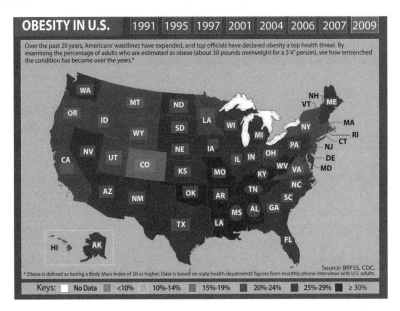

Our healthcare system is simply not set up to deal with chronic, maintenance, and preventive problems; both the payment system and the expectations of practice are set up to deal with acute episodes in isolation from the underlying problem that produced them. We deal with chronic disease so poorly that it could almost be said that we do not deal with it at all. We need to direct far more attention and money into, for instance, programs to effectively manage such conditions as diabetes, congestive heart failure, asthma, congestive obstructive pulmonary disease (COPD), alcoholism, and clinical depression. This is the heart of any campaign to make healthcare cheaper by making it better. Every initiative

---

[*] Taubes, G., "Is Sugar Toxic?" *New York Times*, April 13, 2011, research funded by the Robert Woods Johnson Foundation, accessed May 26, 2011, at http://www.nytimes.com/2011/04/17/magazine/mag-17Sugar-t.html.

[†] Centers for Disease Control, "U.S. Obesity Trends," accessed July 17, 2011, at http://www.cdc.gov/obesity/data/trends.html.

that has achieved that cheaper/better combination is focused on preventing and managing chronic disease. Cutting the cost and suffering associated with chronic disease by any significant fraction would make an enormous difference.

Computerization and Automation

Healthcare will computerize and automate rapidly over the coming years, but the process will be more expensive and difficult than most people expect. Computerization and automation can help drive huge efficiencies in healthcare. But the gap between the possibility of those efficiencies, and the understanding of how to use information technology to drive toward them, remains wide and deep, among both healthcare executives and technology vendors. But automation will and must come to this most backward industry.

We have a cultural resistance to automating healthcare. People say things like "I'm not a car" or "I'm not a credit card." They see automation as a depersonalization of the process partly because they are mostly unaware of the systems operating in the background. They picture healthcare as that moment of personal counseling face-to-face with the doctor in an examining room, and they imagine being deprived of that moment. But the vast majority of all transactions, interactions, and steps in healthcare are not between the doctor and the patient, and many of them are dysfunctional and inadequately thought through as processes in a larger system. There's the nurse foraging for a particular catheter fitting, and not finding it because there is no inventory system; there's the tissue sample making its way through a laboratory by hand through 14 different steps, at every one of which there could be a simple human mistake; there's the radiology tech instructed to repeat a scan unnecessarily, because the first set of images from the freestanding imaging center across the street can't be accessed by the hospital.

Count up the billions of daily transactions, encounters, and handoffs in the everyday business of delivering healthcare, examine each one, and we can easily see that 99% or more would be accomplished better and cheaper by machines, robots, computers, and electronic communication systems. A fully automated and computerized system would not deprive clinicians of face time with the patient, or of the information that they need to render good medical judgment. It would give them more of each. A computerized system can deal with more patients, faster, more accurately, while giving doctors and nurses more actual time with each patient and more real information on each case.

Computerizing healthcare is not just, in some vague way, an effort to drag it into the twenty-first century. Computerizing healthcare is absolutely essential to improving it, because healthcare is irreducibly complex, in every aspect from the clinical to the administrative to the financial. A system in which the data live in scattered, incomplete, unconnected paper files filled with illegible scrawls is opaque. If you want to change a system, you must be able to see its inner workings. If the chief of nursing sets out to end deaths from adverse drug reactions, she will need to know, for instance, if someone on the second shift on the fifth floor is habitually resetting the recommended limits ("soft bumpers") on the drug perfusion pumps, or ignoring the timing of drug administration orders. If the laundry operators want to make their operation more efficient, they need to know how much water they use for each operation and what's happening to all those missing sheets. If you can't get your hands on real data about what is actually happening in healthcare, who is doing it, how it's working, how they are getting paid to do it, every detail, and have a way to drill down into that data, to see it in different ways, to ask questions and test hypotheses, you have no hope of making it work better, faster, and cheaper.

Data mining is to the healthcare system today as the microscope was to germ theory in the nineteenth century. At the very moment when we need to be able to see into healthcare in order to change it, we finally have the tools to do that.

Reform and Insurance

The reform is not the change. The Patient Protection and Affordable Care Act of 2010 is not the change that healthcare is going through, it is not forcing that change, nor is it the cause of that change. It catalyzes the change, enables it, accelerates it in some ways, and could deter it in other ways. But it is not the main driver of the change. The change is far larger and deeper than any piece of legislation. The main drivers of change in healthcare are demographics, economics, and the sheer overwhelming costs of the system as it exists today, along with the technology that allows us to analyze the system, to see how it is failing and change it.

The change will not stop if the reform act goes away. Actually repealing the act would be politically very difficult. Ending it or crippling it through litigation, though, has about a 50/50 chance of succeeding. The Supreme Court is fairly evenly divided between conservatives and liberal-centrists, with no true progressives on the left. When the cases winding their way through district and appellate court reach the Supreme Court, we can reasonably expect four votes to strike the law down and four votes to uphold it. Justice Anthony Kennedy holds the unpredictable swing vote, and at this writing we have no hint of which way he will vote.

There are roughly five specific findings that the Supreme Court could rule on:

■ The court has the power to rule on the individual mandate (the part of the law dictating the individuals must have health insurance or pay a fine) before it takes effect in 2014. Or it does not.

■ The individual mandate is constitutional. Or not.

■ If the individual mandate is not constitutional, the rest of the law can survive without it. Or not.

■ The law's demand that states expand the eligibility for Medicaid, as well as their share of the funding, is constitutional. Or not.

■ Other parts of the law, such as the provision that health plans must take all comers regardless of their health status, are constitutional. Or not.

Reversal on any of these points will have different effects on healthcare. But none of them will have profound world-changing effects on healthcare. If the reform act is struck down, the changes that are rapidly ramifying through healthcare will not suddenly reverse course. They will be slowed somewhat, and reshaped somewhat in unpredictable ways, but they will continue.

The main actual effect on healthcare of the continuing political struggle against the reform act (as well as continued talk of Medicare cuts, and frequent, actual Medicaid cuts) is to inject continuing uncertainty into healthcare markets.

If the reform act survives, it will bring tens of millions of new people into the healthcare system, widening the covered conditions, and mandate that all preventive and maintenance care be covered from the first dollar. All three of these shift the incentives within healthcare deeply.

At the same time, the reform act enables, funds, and provides incentives for various experiments in different payment designs that begin to chip away at the core fee-for-service economic structure of most of healthcare, which is in fact the root of the problem. I'll get into the specifics of these experiments later.

Brute Force Cost Reductions

The middle A in PPACA stands for *affordability*, but there is little in the act that will lower healthcare costs or even slow their rise forcefully or soon. The deficit in the federal budget continues and will continue to be at the center of ferocious political fights—and healthcare costs account for one-fifth of that budget. The same fights are mirrored in every state legislature. As of this writing, the super-committee charged with coming up with a grand plan to reduce the deficit has failed, which means that 2% across-the-board reductions in Medicare payments automatically kick in beginning in 2013. We cannot expect any other major reductions to happen in 2012, since it is an election year. But come spring of 2013, we can brace ourselves for far greater cuts, and increasing demands from payers for big changes in how healthcare institutions are paid, and for what.

Physicians are already facing their own drastic reductions, even sooner. The 1997 Balanced Budget Act contained a sustainable growth rate (SGR) provision that tied the growth in physicians' reimbursements under Medicare and Medicaid to growth in the economy. Every time it has threatened to actually come into play, Congress has put in a temporary fix, letting the doctors slide for another year or so—for 14 years. The latest deadline (as of this writing) is January 1, 2012. Congress may once again patch the hole for a while. But a "permanent doc fix"—repealing the SGR—would cost an estimated $300 billion to $350 billion of the $1 trillion in savings that were supposed to fund the PPACA. In a time of ferocious deficit reduction fights, that is not likely to happen.

People who are leading healthcare organizations are facing an increasingly dire future. They are and will be increasingly ready to try new ways of doing business because the old way of doing business is forcing them out of business. In the biz-speak cliché, they are on a burning platform.

Let's step back for a moment from the mechanics of reform. In order to understand the scale and complexity of the problem that healthcare must tackle, we need to burrow into the economics of healthcare and see what makes it so different from other sectors of the economy.

Chapter 4

Healthcare Economics 101

U.S. healthcare is unbelievably vast. How big is it? If U.S. healthcare were a country, it would be the sixth largest national economy in the world:

United States	$14.3 trillion
China	$8.8 trillion
Japan	$4.1 trillion
India	$3.5 trillion
Germany	$2.8 trillion
U.S. healthcare	**$2.6 trillion**
UK	$2.2 trillion
Russia	$2.1 trillion
France	$2.1 trillion
Brazil	$2 trillion

The vastness of healthcare is one reason it is so hard to understand, let alone change. It is extraordinarily large, unfathomably complex, and it seems to operate by different rules from those of other industries. Take a look at its peculiar economics, to tease apart its internal rules and begin to understand why it works the way it does. Healthcare is truly a foreign land.

Ahmed Buys a Rug

Ahmed wakes up one morning and finds a stain on the rug in the foyer, some red wine that a guest spilled during last night's party. The rug was old anyway, so he decides that today is the day to replace it. He gathers up the old rug, to make sure he gets the size right, and heads to the bazaar.

In the street of the rug sellers at the bazaar he finds a dozen merchants hawking their wares. He can see the rugs on display, feel their weave, read what the labels claim about what they are made of and where they come from. He can read the prices on the tags, listen to each merchant try to outdo his neighbors with their "fabulous discount, just for you, Ahmed, since you are such a long-time customer and dear to me and my family." He can judge the character of the merchant, and have some idea how much each will stand behind their product. He selects a rug that is the right size and color for his foyer, haggles over price, pays the man, and carries the rug home on his shoulder.

But this story is a bit like the movie *Groundhog Day*. The next morning he wakes up again (or maybe he only wakes up in a dream) in the same situation: there is an old, stained rug in the foyer he must replace. But this time it's a healthcare rug. He dresses and shaves, gathers up the old rug, and heads out to the healthcare bazaar. Instead of a street full of merchants, there is only one. In some versions of the dream, there are two, but they are so alike they and their booths might as well be twins. In this version of the dream, there is only one healthcare rug merchant, and he has no rugs on display.

"You sell rugs?"

"Yes, that's what the sign says. I sell rugs."

"But where are they?"

"You can't see them."

"How can I choose one?"

"Trust us. We will send a team to examine your situation. There will be a charge of course for the examination. But once it is done, you can be assured that we will choose and install the perfect rug for you. You will see it once it is installed, and you will be very happy with it. Trust us."

"Oh. Okay, if that's the way it is, I guess. So how much will all this cost?"

"That depends on many factors that are yet to be determined."

Ahmed considers this. "Such as how nice the rug is, whether it is silk of wool, whether it is hand or machine woven?"

"Yes, and also what your arrangement is. The rug may actually cost you nothing at all. It may cost you a few silver drachmas. It may cost you everything you have set aside in your special rug-buying fund plus a sackful of gold florins. It may cost you everything you own, your house, your job, all your savings, all you can earn for the rest of your life, and the patrimony you hoped to leave your children. Maybe. We can't tell just yet."

"That's nuts! If that's the way it is, I'll just do without a rug! I don't have to enter into such a crazy transaction with you or anybody!"

"Actually, you do. You actually do have a stained and tattered rug. It's right there on your shoulder. It must be replaced. The penalty for not replacing it is death—and a slow, agonizing death at that."

Shocked, Ahmed wakes from his nightmare, and rushes to the foyer, gratified to see the nice new rug he actually bought yesterday.

The Convoluted Economics of Healthcare

How do we awake from the nightmare?

First we have to recognize its parts.

Classic economics is based on the interaction between a buyer and a seller, like Ahmed and the rug sellers. Both sides have competition: there are typically many sellers and many buyers. Both sides have information, but not complete information. The seller has more information about his product, what he paid for it, how it was really made, by whom, and where, and what its competitors are. The buyer has more information about his or her own needs, the resources available to fill those needs, and his or her willingness to part with those resources. The seller's resources matter, as well. If the seller has a lot of resources, and a lot of commitment to this market, the seller might be willing to sell at a loss to gobble up a larger share of the market and sell other products into it.

In this constantly imbalanced and fluid interaction between buyers and sellers, reasonable prices are born. Competition keeps prices as low as possible, and perceived value as high as possible—which creates more buyers, and more willingness to buy. This is why prices for new cars and plates of scrambled eggs vary over a range but not outside the range: you have never once in your life seen either a plate of scrambled eggs or a new car advertised for $1,000.

Yet we see absurd prices for items in healthcare all the time, charges that drift by an order of magnitude, possibly two orders of magnitude, from one supplier to another and from one buyer to another. The identical item that costs $750 in one transaction may cost $7,500 in a different one, between different providers and different payers. To take one example, head-and-neck computed tomography (CT) scans that routinely are priced at $1,000 to $1,500 in the United States are compensated in Japan at a government-mandated rate of ¥11,400, or $146 at current exchange rates,* an order of magnitude less. As in the United States, freestanding imaging facilities are run for profit. Yet $146 must be enough, since imaging continues to be a robust sector of the healthcare economy in Japan, which is certainly among the most complex and high-cost economies of the world.

The problem of prices that have no firm basis in reality exists throughout the healthcare value chain. For instance, a hospital might charge $40,000 to implant a pacemaker in a patient—of which $20,000 is for the device itself, for which it paid the manufacturer $5,995.† The top retail price for the same device in India is about 60,000 rupees, or a little over $1,000. Think this through with me: How much do you think it cost the manufacturer to make that pacemaker? I don't know how to make a pacemaker, and the manufacturers don't tell you how much it actually costs them. But think about what a pacemaker is: it's a tiny electronic timer attached to a long-life battery, some sensors, and some capacitors to deliver a minuscule shock to the heart, manufactured to a high degree of reliability with a case and leads that can survive years in the body, and then exhaustively tested. Do you have an iPhone? An Android? A Blackberry? These are vastly more complex devices. The manufacturing costs of an iPhone 4S (that is, the amount paid by Apple to its manufacturer, Foxconn) are estimated by industry analysts to be $192.‡ It is difficult to believe that the actual incremental cost of manufacturing a pacemaker is (or needs to be) more than that.

Competing solutions to an identical problem may vary even more, as we have seen in the examples of waste in healthcare. A solution to back pain that costs a few hundred dollars often competes directly and unsuccessfully with solutions that can cost $50,000 to $75,000.

When you can move the decimal point on a transaction left or right and still find a place in the healthcare economy that the transaction will work, something very drastically strange is going on.

Similarly, a few years ago I was invited to work with a global pharmaceutical marketing group. In the discussions, I asked the executives I was talking with

---

* Ikegami, N., and Campbell, J.C., "Japan's Health Care System: Containing Costs and Attempting Reform," *Health Affairs*, Vol. 23, No. 3, 2004, pp. 26–36, doi: 10.1377/hlthaff.23.3.26, accessed at http://content.healthaffairs.org/content/23/3/26.full.
  Also cited in Reid, T.R., *The Healing of America: A Global Quest for Better, Cheaper, and Fairer Health Care* (New York: Penguin, 2009).

† Prices are average, from conversations with patients and insurance brokers and analysts.

‡ P.K., "Slicing an Apple: How Much of an iPhone Is Made by Samsung?" *The Economist*, August 10, 2011, accessed at http://www.economist.com/blogs/dailychart/2011/08/apple-and-samsungs-symbiotic-relationship.

to explain how drugs are priced in the real world, since we so often see drugs marketed for $4 a bottle in one context, and $50 or more in another. There was an audible sighing noise on the other end of the conference call and one of them said, "We have it all in a document. We'll send it to you." They did: 45 pages of dense prose. I studied it and still couldn't understand, really, how a given dose of a given drug comes to its price. When I told one of the executives that I still didn't understand drug pricing, he replied, "Nobody does."

Extreme examples are easy to find. For instance, getting stung by a scorpion is no picnic. Some varieties can be deadly to children. Luckily, there is an anti-venom available for it: Anascorp, manufactured for years by the Instituto Bioclon in Mexico, and approved for use in the United States by the Food and Drug Administration in August 2011. Get stung while waiting in the pedestrian line in Nogales, Mexico, to cross the border into the United States, and Anascorp will cost you $100 per vial, and you may need as many as six. But imagine that the scorpion hitched a ride on your shoe, and stung you after you crossed the border into Nogales, Arizona: the very same Anascorp, manufactured by the same company, will cost you from $7,900 to $12,467 per vial, depending on which Arizona hospital you end up in.*

Then there's the drug 17p, FDA approved and used for years for treating disorders of the adrenal glands or the ovaries. Then doctors discovered that for some pregnant women it could help prevent premature births. Doctors started to prescribe it "off label" for this use, a National Institutes of Health paper commented that it seemed to help, and some insurance and managed care companies and Medicaid programs started paying for it. At $15 per dose (sometimes as little as $5) for the 15 to 20 shots needed, covering it was no big deal—and the premature births it helped prevent cost an average of $51,000 each.

Then the drug company KV Pharmaceutical decided to try for FDA approval for this use and, under the "orphan status" program, asked for a monopoly on the drug that it planned to rename Makena.

In March 2011, KV was granted the FDA approval and orphan status monopoly on Makena, and started selling it—for $1,500 per dose, 100 times the former price. After public outcry and shaming in the media, it reduced the price to $690 per dose. Even at that price, a full 20 shots would cost the pregnant mother or her insurer, or Medicaid, nearly $14,000, instead of $300.†

---

* Staton, T., "Scorpion Antivenom's Price Stings AZ Patients," FiercePharma.com, November 15, 2011, available at http://www.fiercepharma.com/story/scorpion-antivenoms-price-stings-az-patients/2011-11-15.

† Doyle, J., "KV Boosts Prenatal Drug Price 100-Fold," *St. Louis Post-Dispatch*, March 10, 2011, available at http://www.stltoday.com/business/local/article_55dbaf88-4ab0-11e0-ad73-0017a4a78c22.html.

Competing Influences

We want to trust our doctors. The most important part of that trust is that their judgment is uninfluenced: we trust that when they render a judgment about our health and our bodies, they have no other consideration in mind than what is the best thing for our health, for this body in front of them. If they recommend something more expensive, we need to trust that the more expensive route is the better, more effective route to health. Yet the convoluted economics of healthcare often run at cross-purposes to that trust.

Doctors are the most prominent decision makers in medicine about whether to operate or go with "medical management" (using drugs, dietary changes, and physical therapy, for instance, to deal with a problem). Or whether to use brand X knee implant or brand Y, which may be twice as expensive. Or this suture or that suture. Or a branded drug or a similar, much less expensive generic version.

Doctors are continually tempted in their judgments by concerns beyond the clinical facts in front of them—and consciously or unconsciously, many of them routinely succumb to that temptation. They are tempted by the "I'm a hammer and you look like a nail" syndrome: doctors will tend to diagnose and treat in line with the tools at their disposal (and for which they get paid). An orthopedic surgeon is far more likely to recommend surgery, while another doctor might recommend nonsurgical medical management. Doctors are more likely to refer patients for imaging that they can perform in their own office, for which they can charge (and which is an exception to the Stark laws against self-referral). Doctors on workers' compensation referrals, if they can manage it, will tend to diagnose problems with simpler, less expensive solutions, because the referrals from employers are a nice source of income, and employers don't like having to pay for complex problems caused on the job.

Or there is the matter of "detailing," a little known but pervasive practice. When a drug company comes up with a new drug, the company must conduct years of expensive testing in controlled situations. When the drug is finally approved for use by doctors, the company still must follow up on how it is used and whether there are side effects. How does it do that? It invites doctors to log on to a website and fill out a form for each patient listing the diagnosis, the dosage, any problems, and so forth. Doctors are busy, so to get them to do this faithfully, the drug company pays them a fee. Now, this is valuable information. Surely we do want to know how a new drug actually performs and whether, like Vioxx, it turns out that it's giving people heart attacks. But look at the process by which the information is gathered: doctors have to use the drug to get paid the fee, and they are not paid a fee for any rival drug they might have otherwise prescribed. Doctors, in effect, are paid to prescribe the new drug.

Beyond individual decisions in the clinical moment, doctors also help make major decisions about technology investments for whole systems. When hospitals and health systems decide to buy, say, the millions of dollars of new equipment that it takes to equip a modern operating or imaging suite, or when they try to save money by settling on one brand of joint implants and getting a package deal, they consult the people who will be using these supplies: their doctors, meeting in formal recommendation committees. The peer reviewers who advise medical journals whether an article should be accepted or rejected are prominent doctors with expertise in the area being discussed. And of course the panels of the Food and Drug Administration that approve or disapprove a drug or device are made up of physicians, and by definition they are experts in that particular area of medical technology.

Are doctors ever bribed to make one decision or another?

It would be great to be able to say flatly no. But the reality is far more complex than that. A doctor recommending that a hospital use a particular device, or speaking at a physician education conference about a particular medicine, or peer reviewing an article, or sitting on an FDA panel may well have been paid by the pharmaceutical company or a device manufacturer as a consultant, or may have accepted substantial speaking fees from them. Looked at through one lens, this is not shocking: If you are developing, say, a kidney drug, what outside advice would you legitimately seek? That of the most prominent nephrologists, of course. If you are developing an improved knee implant, you would need the advice of top orthopedic surgeons. If you are an orthopedic surgeon attending a conference, and you are attending a session in which a new knee implant is being discussed, you would want to hear from the surgeons who are most familiar with it, that is, those who helped develop it. If you were a consultant to the company that helped develop the product, you are of course inclined to say it's a great product. You're going to talk about how you helped improve it.

Device manufacturers and pharmaceutical companies distribute such consulting and speaking contracts widely through the specialties that they want to influence. Doctors are supposed to disclose the sources of their income when they review a paper, give a talk, or serve on an FDA panel, or work for the National Institutes of Health, but the enforcement of these restrictions is spotty, and numerous egregious cases have surfaced. In 2004, the *Los Angeles Times* ran a series of investigative articles detailing hundreds of thousands of dollars in unreported payments to top medical experts on the NIH payroll from drug and device companies that they also served as consultants.* Rules have been tightened in the last eight years, but it cannot be said that the problem has disappeared.

So prices are phantom prices that are not even vaguely a marker for quality. And we cannot simply rely on physicians to tell us whether it is worth it to use a particular test or therapy, or to go a more expensive or less expensive route, or what is really necessary for our health. Further, it turns out that one of the many reasons healthcare providers have difficulty putting a real price tag on something is that they usually have no idea what it costs them to produce it.

No Cost Accounting

I came to healthcare writing from business reporting. So in my very first investigations, back during the Carter administration, I asked the healthcare executives I interviewed about pricing, reimbursement, and the cost basis of their products, normal business questions that translate to: How do you make a living? I was astonished to find that healthcare executives whose organizations produced products such as a gall bladder removal or a bone fracture repair could not say how much it cost them to produce that product. Their cost accounting did not work that way. They calculated costs for each clinical department (such as cardiovascular or radiology), then added in such items as nursing services, housekeeping, security, and plant maintenance. How much of each of these really added up to producing a cholecystectomy? Who knew?

In the twenty-first century, more healthcare institutions are beginning to be able to do product cost accounting. But many healthcare institutions are not there yet—or they may think they are there but are fooling themselves. Much of healthcare still cannot tell you realistically how much it costs to produce a given outcome.

Unlike people who run organizations that produce cars or scrambled eggs, the people who run the organizations that produce healthcare's products and

---

* Willman, D., "The National Institutes of Health: Public Servant or Private Marketer?" *Los Angeles Times*, December 22, 2004, accessed at http://www.latimes.com/news/nationworld/nation/la-na-nih22dec22,0,7519657.story.

Willman, D., "Firm's Research Stalls as Cancer Experts Work for Rival," *Los Angeles Times*, December 22, 2004, accessed at http://www.latimes.com/news/nationworld/nation/la-na-liotta22dec22,1,2069837.story.

Willman, D., "Public Pays for Blood Expert's Advice, and So Do Firms," *Los Angeles Times*, December 22, 2004, accessed at http://www.latimes.com/news/nationworld/nation/la-na-klein22dec22,1,7519640.story.

Willman, D., "$508,050 from Pfizer, but No 'Outside Positions to Note,'" *Los Angeles Times*, December 22, 2004, accessed at http://www.latimes.com/news/nationworld/nation/la-na-sunderland22dec22,1,7074780.story.

services can tell you with great precision and at great length how much they can get for those products and services, but they can rarely tell you exactly what their products' true competitors are or might be in the future or what a "real" price would be. They don't know—because the way healthcare is structured they can't know. There is no way for the market to give them the value information they would need to truly answer such questions.

This is why healthcare costs so much, and yet we are still not satisfied with it. "You get what you pay for" is such a truism that we rarely notice how bold the assertion is. Do we get what we pay for in healthcare? As consumers, as payers, as healthcare executives, nobody knows. And nobody really knows how we could know. That's the puzzle at the heart of the healthcare conundrum: Do you get what you pay for? How would you know?

Split Buyers, Split Sellers

Let's get back to the basic buyer-seller interaction, like Ahmed and the rug seller:

Buyer <=> Seller

Let's look at this through the lens of the feedback loop, perhaps the most important single concept in understanding any kind of system. Picture a thermostat in a room: The room cools off, the thermostat senses the cooling, and turns the heater on. The room warms up, the thermostat senses the warming, and turns the heater off. This is a negative feedback loop: any trend kicks off a reaction that counters the trend. When negative feedback loops predominate, the result is stability and predictability: the room stays more or less at the temperature the thermostat is set to, with small variations.

Now picture a bank in a small town: If rumors begin that the bank is running low on funds, some depositors panic and withdraw their money. Now the bank is even lower on funds, so more depositors panic and withdraw their money, which makes the situation even worse, and so on until the bank fails. This is a positive feedback loop: any trend kicks off a reaction that increases the trend. When positive feedback loops predominate, the result is a rapid escalation of processes, and a devolution into chaos and destruction of the system, until something outside the loop steps in to interrupt the process and rebuild stabilizing negative feedback loops (such as the Federal Deposit Insurance Corporation taking over the bank and paying the depositors).

Between Ahmed and his fellow buyers and the rug seller and all his colleagues there are a number of negative feedback loops that serve to determine and stabilize the price of rugs. A seller can lower his prices to sell more units, but the lower the price the less profit per unit, so he won't go too low. He can raise the price to get more profit, but will sell fewer rugs, so he can't raise it too much. Or he can sell higher-quality rugs at higher prices, but at some price level he still runs out of buyers. The buyers can bargain hard for ever-lower prices, forcing the sellers into a price war and cutting into their profit, but sellers will tend to drop out of the market if they can't make a profit. When there is only one seller left, and the buyers have no alternative without going to another town, that last seller can raise his prices back to a profitable level.

Both the buyers and the sellers are making choices based on information about how good the rugs are, what other sellers are charging, where else rugs are for sale, and other factors. This flow of information makes the stabilizing negative feedback loops possible.

Now let's imagine a typical clinical decision driving the use of healthcare resources, such as the decision to get a hip replacement, take a certain drug, or have an image taken, and see how that decision is different from Ahmed dickering with the rug seller. In an insurance-supported fee-for-service healthcare system, something strange happens: the buyer splits into a chooser and a payer:

Chooser
<=> Seller
Payer

One party chooses the necessary product or service, and another party pays for it. The payer (such as a health plan, employer, or government program) has only limited insight into the actual transaction, and limited control over it but is committed to pay for it. Already the buyer <=> seller feedback loop is becoming confused.

But there is another conundrum buried within this diagram: Who is the chooser?

Patient
Provider
<=> Seller
Payer

So the chooser is actually two parties: on the one hand the patient, and on the other the provider (usually a physician or a nurse practitioner, working in a private practice or for some institution). One of these, the provider, has almost all the information and almost all the resources; the other, the patient, takes almost all the personal risk. The doctor will not die or suffer years of pain or disability if the decision is wrong. At the moment of transaction, the patient depends upon the doctor's judgment about how to avoid death, pain, and disability. If the patient and the provider have somewhat different incentives, then the feedback loop is further obscured.

But wait, there is yet another confounding element: Who is the seller?

> Patient
> Provider
> <=> Provider
> Payer

It's the provider (or the provider's employer). The same entity is doing most of the choosing ("We'll need to do a biopsy on this") and selling the product being chosen.

This does not mean that the choice is necessarily wrong, or the product overpriced or unnecessary. It does mean that there is a conflict of interest: the provider as chooser has the incentive to buy the product because he will profit from the decision as the seller. And as the seller he has an incentive to sell it for as high a price as he can get, but as the chooser, the price plays no role, since he is not paying for it.

Almost as bad, or perhaps even worse, any knowledge that the market might gain from this transaction is lost. The buyer <=> seller feedback loop has become so obscured and convoluted that it has become a black hole of value: no real value information leaks out of it to inform the marketplace. We simply don't learn what was worth how much, to whom. Do you get what you pay for? Who knows?

Why did the manufacturers of the old Soviet Union and East Germany make cars of such legendary poor quality? Is it because of the failures of a centrally planned economy, as the conventional wisdom would have it? Sure, but what was the nature of the failure? Why does central planning fail? It was a failure of exactly this kind of feedback of economic information. Imagine that you are chairman of the executive planning committee of the manufacturer of the Trabant, the East German car often considered the worst car ever made. The market gives you no information about what it wants in a car, because you have no real competitors. Your market can't easily choose a different car by another manufacturer. It gives you no information about price, either, for the same reason. Prices are set by an allocation committee of the government, so who knows what would be the "right" price? You, in turn, give no information to your suppliers through any kind of shopping behavior, because the steel, rubber, and glass are all allocated to you according to quotas based on what you need to produce this year's quota of cars. If, despite this lack of any real market information, you determined that your factory would produce much higher quality cars, and with years of work you succeeded—what would that get you? Nothing. Less than nothing, because you would have irritated your suppliers, your workers, the people on the government allocation committees, everybody who had influence over you and your factory. The most likely outcome is that you would get fired for even trying.

Such a system without real market feedback pushes the people caught in it to make themselves as comfortable as possible, and as part of that to make everyone involved in the system as comfortable as possible. There is simply no payback for investing a lot of time and energy in trying to do the thing better, or cheaper, or more efficiently.

Feedback loops of economic information guide a market toward value for both buyer and seller. When those feedback loops become sclerotic, obscured, and tangled, strange things start to happen. Unlike the rug seller, the providers of healthcare goods, whether a hospital or a maker of CT scanners or a pharmaceutical company, are not guided to the right level of price and quality that the market needs. They are guided by the reimbursement, that is, by what they can get out of the buyer. The reimbursement, set for most of the market by various committees for generations, has come unhooked from any reference to a real market. The only reference is what the item cost last year, or what Medicare is paying in another city. Unlike Ahmed at the bazaar, the patient considering a back operation cannot get any real information about what is the best solution for him or her at the best price. Since the price doesn't affect him or her, in the absence of any other information about what is best for him or her, he or she opts for "more." Since the only real choice a patient can make in most situations is to take his or her business to another doctor, doctors have to provide the customer more if they want to keep the customer—and doctors are not affected by the price either. In traditional insurance-supported fee-for-service healthcare, the only actors affected by the price are not present in the decision to buy. And the payers for healthcare, since they have little control over how people choose to consume healthcare resources, fall back on trying to control the price for each item. They try to control costs, which doesn't work.

Why the Ever-Popular "Cost Controls" Do Not Control Costs

If we hope to steer healthcare toward a better, cheaper future, we have to wrap our minds around this conundrum: simply slashing spending does not necessarily improve the bottom line of the system as a whole or even of parts of the system.

Let's look at that system as a whole first.

Governments in Ireland, the United Kingdom, and a number of countries have come up hard against this conundrum in recent years. They have faced soaring deficits due to the economic downturn because their tax revenues have fallen at the same time that their costs for unemployment and other kinds of social support have risen.

So they did what might seem like the sensible thing: they attacked the problem by cutting spending in the professed belief that such a move would also increase the financial markets' confidence in the future, and thus pump up the economy, reduce unemployment, reduce the interest the government has to pay on its debt, and increase tax revenues.

Result? Their deficits have grown ever larger. Why? Because of what economist Paul Krugman likes to call "the confidence fairy"; she never showed up. The austerity measures dragged their economies down even further. Firing a lot of people, it turns out, means more people out of work. That drives unemployment numbers up and tax revenues down. The worsening debt picture increases the cost of borrowing. Many U.S. states are headed down the same path right now, slashing spending in order to slash deficits, and the U.S. Congress is famously and forever wrangling over the same formula.

This is a pattern that repeats in one way or another at all economic levels:

■ A government cuts spending drastically, lays off workers, cuts salaries and restricts unemployment benefits, and finds that there is a drop in income to the economy as a whole, the very economy on which the government depends for its tax revenues and its borrowing ability.

■ A state finds its austerity spending program helps drive down its tax revenues, and drives up the number of people applying for Medicaid and other support programs.

■ A business faced with a fall in sales lays off workers and cuts back investment in new equipment and inventory, as well as its sales force, and therefore finds that sales decline even further. Meanwhile it has narrowed its own ability to respond with new products, more efficient and innovative production, or new revenue streams.

■ A national health system faced with cutbacks reduces its support for poor and elderly populations and lowers its level of reimbursements and subsidies. As a result, those populations increasingly shift away from regular preventive maintenance and management of their chronic conditions, and toward showing up in the emergency department with full-blown acute crises, which cost the system far more. As individual hospitals and medical systems within the system respond with the same simple tactics to cuts in reimbursement levels, and to a payer mix shifting away from private payers to the more abstemious Medicare, and way more abstemious Medicaid and public general assistance, they lay off people and cut back on new investment. If that is their only response, they may find that they have actually decreased their efficiency, increased costly mistakes, and cut their ability to respond with new initiatives and new revenue streams.

Health Systems: More Complex

The cost situation in medical systems has always been much more complex than other businesses, and has traditionally been drastically different, for one simple reason: healthcare providers have been able to pass on their excess costs to customers and payers, to "decant" the costs to all their payers the way a lab tech pours a solution into different vials.

Medical reimbursements are set based on various formulas. When major players like health plans negotiate those medical reimbursements with health providers the numbers are based on a variety of factors, including vague ideas of how different items generally are priced in a given market, what they cost last year, how much should be allowed for system overhead, and how able the payer is to beat up on the provider. These negotiated reimbursements have not been based on any actual accounting of the cost of producing the service in a given setting. In fact, in the past, most systems have been incapable of producing any such realistic cost accounting. They have not been organized in a way that they could really answer those questions. And there has been little real competition of the type that would demonstrate how efficiently a particular product or service could be delivered.

Hospitals and health systems always complain that the reimbursement is far too low; the payers that it is too high. Providers have dealt with the reimbursement squeeze in three ways:

- Cutting costs in general
- Moving strategically to get a different mix of payers (by building facilities in growing suburbs and closing facilities in poor areas, for instance, so that they have more paying customers with private insurance and Medicare, and fewer on Medicaid or with no coverage at all)
- Performing more well-reimbursed procedures and fewer poorly reimbursed ones

Overall, though, since health systems have continued to survive, we can conclude that the reimbursements have included the cost of their inefficiencies. If they did not, if payers were only paying for what a service would ideally cost in some ideally efficient system, providers would all have closed their doors long ago.

No More Cost Decanting

That's changing. Healthcare providers (physicians, hospitals, clinics) can no longer assume that they can decant their costs to the payers. Let's take a look at how, exactly, that is changing.

Remember the three ways to cut costs in treating a given patient? The techniques of efficiency, coordination, and avoidance each have quite different effects on the provider's bottom line.

Efficiency relates to unit costs, that is, how much does it cost to administer a given procedure or test (such as foot amputation for a diabetes patient)? In a fee-for-service system, the more efficient you are at delivering a service, the more services you can perform and therefore the more money you can make. Whether the service is really necessary or helpful to the patient or not, or even whether it damages the patient, does not show up on the balance sheet. What shows up is whether you can produce the service for less than the average reimbursement received from your mix of payers.

Here's the economic strategy that hospitals have followed for years: they determine which outcomes they are already delivering at a cost substantially below the reimbursement and do more of those, and they do less of the ones that they deliver at a loss. That's a lot easier than doing the hard work of becoming steadily more efficient at all your processes.

Saving money through efficiency has always been a good idea for the provider. Efficiency lowers the actual cost and increases the profit margin of each test or procedure.

Coordination relates to bundled costs. How much does it cost to produce not just a procedure or test, but all of a particular solution to the problem (such as the entire foot amputation bundle, from intake and diagnosis, through imaging, anesthesia, operation and post-op care, through discharge and maintenance care)? Can we deliver this solution at the right level of acuity, treating coughs and colds in a primary care clinic rather than an emergency department, for instance? Can we avoid duplicating services, doing the same imaging work over and over, for instance?

In a traditional fee-for-service world, saving money through coordination can be less profitable than not saving it, because the hospital, doctor, or clinic could have been reimbursed for all those items that they managed not to do.

Avoidance relates to solution costs and system costs. Solution costs answer the question: How much does it cost to solve the whole problem, including all possible solutions (such as aggressive early treatment of the foot abscesses to avoid the need for amputation)? System costs answer an even wider question: How much would it cost to prevent the problem in the first place (through aggressive management of the diabetes, including regular foot exams)?

In a fee-for-service world, saving money through avoidance is always less profitable for the provider. The provider is in the business of providing services. If they help avoid the need for those services, they lose money on those lost services.

We have seen how much money is wasted and could be saved in a range of different ways across our system. But traditionally, these are not wasted costs for hospitals and doctors. In a fee-for-service system, they are decanted to the payer. The only costs that really matter to the provider are their costs per reimbursable item: Can they get reimbursed for this? Can they get their costs of production significantly below their reimbursement? If an extra CT scan, or the whole operation, is not strictly necessary, they're still fine as long as they can get reimbursed for it under the right code.

Cost savings through coordination and avoidance save money for the customers, for the payers, and for the system at large, but in a fee-for-service system the money the customers are saving would have been the providers' money. The providers could have charged for the inefficiencies, the unnecessary scans, the avoidable surgeries. A number of schemes have arisen to reward doctors and hospitals for doing the right thing, coordinating care, and avoiding unnecessary care, including the "accountable care organizations" embedded in the PPACA reform law. But as long as these schemes exist within a strictly fee-for-service system, the invitation to healthcare providers is simple: "Save us costs by driving down your own income. We'll give you a little of that back as a bonus."

We are entering a world with a host of new business models and strategies, such as bundled purchasing, value-based purchasing, mini-caps (such as disease management contracts), and full capitation. We'll get into the details on these later, but all of these are deviations from a strict fee-for-service model that bring the other ways of cutting costs to the fore because they put the provider, at least partially, at risk for the costs. If you are a hospital in a strictly fee-for-service system, every avoided test or procedure is a hit to your bottom line. If you are at risk for those costs, saving them turns into profit.

It's About to Get Really Complicated

This is about to get really complicated for most providers. Organizations like Kaiser, the Veterans Administration, and Group Health of Puget Sound are "fully capitated" for most of their users; that is, they get a set amount of money for each customer per month, plus a little whenever the customer uses the system.

For organizations like these, the calculations are complex, but they have a simple basis: How do you deliver the best possible health and healthcare at the lowest possible cost?

Most doctors, clinics, and hospitals are not in that situation. Most of them are in a fee-for-service universe, and they are not going to become another fully capitated Kaiser any time soon. But over the next few years they will find themselves easing out of a strictly fee-for-service environment into a much more complicated situation with a mix of risks. Providers will be taking on various types of risk-based contracts and competing for value-based purchasing contracts, in which they get paid for better results, not just for more medical activity. They will be coming to count on pay-for-performance bonuses as a major revenue stream. (These are payments linked to specific performance measures, such as having all of your diabetes patients in a patient registry and contacting them regularly.) They will be offering more bundled products (such as a complete gall bladder removal, from diagnosis to rehab). Each of these flips the incentives in some ways with some of their customers and changes the relationships between the providers themselves.

Inflexible Systems

In the face of this vastly more complex price picture, healthcare executives are starting to realize that they are driving systems whose very complexity makes them relatively inflexible. A car company, for instance, can design a cheap-as-dirt car for the Indian market, say, and a range of products from basic pickups to a line of luxury sedans for the U.S. and world market. No problem. But a health system with some users on risk contracts and others on fee-for-service finds those patients intermixed through all their facilities. And the fee-for-service patients from different payers come with different levels and kinds of incentives in their copays and deductibles, and different pay-for-performance and value-based purchasing incentives from their plans. It can become very difficult to tell whether any particular avoided cost helps or hurts the bottom line.

Redesigning the system to avoid unnecessary costs is hard enough. Designing it to avoid some costs for some patients and not for others is impossible. Kaiser of Northern California, for instance, has a medically sound, guideline-based program that helps steer patients with knee problems away from unnecessary and unhelpful MRIs, operations, and total knee replacements. This saves Kaiser a lot of money and helps the patients improve their knees. If another medical system put such a program in place, would it save them money or just cost them reimbursements? This can become extremely difficult to tell.

Most healthcare executives haven't been trained for this. Their training and experience is in a different universe. They are just feeling their way forward.

Unit Costs vs. System Costs

At the time I first started writing about healthcare in the early 1980s, the big discussion was about the coming of the dreaded diagnostic-related groupings (DRGs) by which Medicare planned to control costs. They were the first true effort at cost containment, and were soon adopted with modifications by all the payers.

Over the past 30 years, we have seen more and more such cost containment schemes adopted. They have all had one thing in common: they control unit costs. They set a fee for, for instance, an office visit, a limb x-ray, or a cholecystectomy. Every one of them was promoted as an attempt to control the rapidly growing costs of the system, but none of them actually made any attempt to control system costs (such as the overall cost of cardiac care for a given patient), only unit costs (such as the cost of a cardiovascular stent).

Think of fuel efficiency: Increasing fuel efficiency does not cause people to use less fuel. If you double the miles per gallon that the average car gets, you have, in effect, halved the cost of fuel and made it cheaper to drive. So people drive more.

Every time there is a spike in the price of gasoline, people cut back on driving for a while. But over time, they tend to shift toward more fuel-efficient cars and the number of miles driven creeps back up until people are spending the same amount as before on fuel but driving further. Reducing the cost per mile does not reduce the overall cost of the system, it just enables its growth.

Think of it this way: Imagine you are in the consumer electronics business, selling TVs and stereos and iPods. Imagine the market has depressed the price you can get for one of your product lines, cutting deeply into your profit margins. What do you do? Do you simply sigh and say, "I guess we'll have to make less money and shrink our business"? No, you adapt your strategy in one of three ways or all three at the same time: You cut your price to the minimum margin and make up the difference on volume. ("Yes, we're blowing out the doors! At these prices you're crazy not to buy!"). Or you get out of that line of business entirely. ("We can't make a good margin on boom boxes anymore. They're so yesterday. Let's stop selling them.") Or you upsell. ("You're interested in a flat-screen TV? Let me show you what a lot of people are going for these days: A full five-way home entertainment system with an HD plasma screen and Blu-ray disc.")

We tend to think of healthcare providers as simply providing what the patient needs to regain health. But if we look at how the whole system has responded to cost-cutting measures over the last 30 years, it looks like doctors and medical systems have adopted all three of these strategies. As reimbursements for each particular item have been capped, they have struggled mightily to do more of them, to spend less time with each patient, to do more scans and surgeries, to increase "throughput" every way that they can. They have backed away from poorly compensated services (such as nutritional counseling for diabetes and wellness programs), and they have introduced increasingly complex procedures, often performing them in the absence of evidence that they helped the patient more than simpler approaches.

These strategies to keep up providers' revenue have worked. But there is no evidence that all these unit-cost-cutting efforts have actually slowed the growth of healthcare spending at all. They simply haven't worked. They haven't worked because they were not designed to do the one thing they were supposed to do: control the costs of the system.

The Two Core Rules of Economics

All of this is intricate and complex beyond belief, layer after layer, wheels within wheels, feedback loop twisting through feedback loop. But under it all we need to remember the two core rules of economics:

Rule 1: People do what you pay them to do. That's obvious to us in any other part of our economy. But when it comes to healthcare and medicine, other concerns distract us. When we talk of the Hippocratic Oath, of for-profits vs. not-for-profits, of the proper role of government, we lose track of the fact that there are underlying economic incentives in all sectors and aspects of healthcare. Whatever we believe actors in the system "should" do—that doctors should spend more time with their patients, pharmaceutical companies should charge less for rare drugs, hospitals should not divert non-paying patients to other institutions—our belief in these "shoulds" just doesn't make the difference in results, even if those actors themselves share our beliefs. The actors don't do what they should do because they cannot afford to do it. Even the Red Cross has a business model. Mother Teresa had a business model. Anything important that you want to do as an organization has to have some form of economic support or you can't do it. To ignore that is economic suicide.

Rule 2: People do *exactly* what you pay them to do. Think about your job. You know, at work, just what would get you fired and what would get you promoted. You know this in great detail and with great precision. The same is true of companies and organizations. They pay exquisite attention not just to doing their job, but to all the ins and outs of surviving and thriving in the many-faceted economic ecology in which they exist. If they are doing something, it's either because they see profit in doing it, or because they will see big costs—litigation, fines—in not doing it. If they are not doing something, it's because they don't see anything in it for them, neither profit nor safety.

Financial incentives are not the only reasons why people work or why organizations do what they do. People work for many other reasons. Most doctors really want to be doctors, they want to do something special, they want to help people. Most nurses have a dedication to nursing that is profound. If this were not so there would be many healthcare careers, such as independent primary care, that would be pretty much empty by now because the financial incentives are so poor. Although those career choices are not empty yet, they are starting to empty as practitioners flee them to the safety of a salary on staff to a medical system, and as new graduates of medical or nursing school pick safer, less angst-ridden, and more reliably remunerative careers.

Incentives do make a difference. For individual practitioners, the right financial incentives do not force the right behavior; they allow it. They make it possible for people to survive by doing the things we deeply need done. For organizations, the right financial incentives shape, guide, and facilitate the performance of the functions we deeply need performed.

When we contemplate the healthcare system and see some part failing to act in the way we would want it to act, the question to ask is not: "Why aren't they doing what they should?" The question is rather: "In what way are we paying them to do what they are doing? In what way are we penalizing them? What other way of paying them would produce what we are after?"

The economics of healthcare are intricate and complex and they are rapidly shifting. It is only by understanding the economics of healthcare that we can understand what will work, and why some solutions are already working, to bring down the cost of healthcare by making it better.

WHAT MUST BE DONE

2

Chapter 5

The Five Strategies

Healthcare seems like an enormous tangle of problems. Yet it also presents a vast array of opportunities. It is, in fact, an enormous opportunity disguised as an intractable problem.

For all of its seemingly insurmountable hurdles and tangled ways, the healthcare problem actually has a number of enticing and encouraging features. There is plenty of money in the system already to do everything we might hope to do. The amount we spend in the United States is almost off the charts compared to other sophisticated national systems of healthcare. Whether measured in dollars per person, or as a percentage of the economy, we spend 50% to 100% more than would seem absolutely necessary. The vast amounts of waste in our system stand as much more than opportunities for us to be outraged, to stand aghast, to mop our foreheads with our hankies and say, "How dare they!" They stand, actually, as multiple veins of ore, each far richer than any gold seam ever discovered on the planet. The waste in our healthcare system is this nation's greatest untapped natural resource. For our future and our children's future, we must mine it.

Then we ask, "But how?" And we find, to our surprise, that in fact there are many examples of "how" already in place: emerging business models, different methods of organizing healthcare, new technologies, and proven management techniques. Some of these are pilot programs, suggestive experiments, or merely proposals. But most of them are actual working examples serving real populations in real American cities and towns, bringing them better health for less money.

We can study these examples and ask, "Okay, so how do we do that? What can we imitate in other parts of the system? What's really working here? What's the enduring, transportable principle, and not just a fad or a quirk or a cultural pocket?"

When I started asking those questions 30 years ago, I did not yet know what I have come to see now:

First: There is no one way to make healthcare work better, no single business model or government program that fits all situations. Nor, apparently, is it necessary to find one overarching model for everyone everywhere. When I speak around the country, when I have conversations about healthcare with experts, with people in the industry, and with nonexperts as well, I find we all have a tendency to reach for a single, simple, overarching solution to this highly complex situation, whether it is "single payer" or "more competition" or "mandates" or "the free market." Yet none of these answers, and no single answer of any kind, can solve the whole problem. In fact, no single, simple solution even solves a single slice of this complex, highly interconnected system. Blunt instruments cause unnecessary damage.

What's important to recognize is that healthcare is a complex dynamic system. You can't operate on one part of the system without reckoning with the impact on the rest of the system. At the same time, because of healthcare's complexity, no one solution will fix the whole system.

Now, we all prefer simple solutions. It will be difficult for many people to settle for anything less. Bear with me, though, because I will show you what I mean in the following sections.

Second: While no one system is right for all, we do find that the examples that work—that actually produce better healthcare and better health for more people at lower cost—have certain elements in common. In one way or another all of these usually new and successful projects incorporate all of the key elements. Drawing on my research on complex systems, the experimentation of courageous healthcare organizations, and the successes and failures of many, I have deduced five core strategies that we must adopt to rebuild the entire healthcare system. These are:

Explode the business model. In one way or another overturn, subvert, supplement, or rework the commodity-based, insurance-supported, fee-for-service model that dominates the healthcare market in the United States. Share risk in much more measured ways across healthcare, putting some financial risk on the customer, and some on the medical provider, not all of it on the payer.

Build on smart primary care. Every example where healthcare works better and cheaper is tightly organized around smart, efficient, well-incentivized primary care.

Put a crew on it. Every example that works in every part of healthcare is a true team effort, not part of the siloed, blinkered, uncommunicative past of medicine.

Swarm the customer with help, information, advice, resources, hand-holding, early, often, and as close as possible. Target special help for those who are costing the system the most.

Rebuild every process. The processes of most parts of healthcare are still archaic. Every process must be rebuilt—and the data to drive it must be derived from a fully digitized and transparent healthcare that is ready to become the most massive learning organism in history.

We need all five, but we need only these five. These five strategies are interdependent. Each one of them, on its own, brings a measure of success. Each one of them works better if combined with other strategies. Some of them cannot be implemented alone. All five of them working together will create a synergistic, virtuous spiral, an intertwined set of positive and negative feedback loops that will greatly improve results, drive down costs, and widen access for everyone.

If every organization in healthcare, or even most organizations in healthcare, rebuilt themselves on these five principles, healthcare in the United States would cost far less than it does today, and work far better. It would deliver better health and longer lives, and exact far less pain, suffering, premature death, bankruptcy, and poverty from the American people in the process.

Chapter 6

1. Explode the Business Model

Try this thought experiment: Imagine for a moment that we had a fee-for-service insurance-supported automobile service system. Imagine that, because of the enormous complexity of modern auto systems, we relied on each mechanic's individual judgment for every detail of the car's "treatment." The mechanic could order any test, diagnostic procedure, replacement part, or full overhaul he deemed mechanically indicated, as long as it had a proper reimbursement code and fit the diagnosis of the car's presenting condition. Oh, and let's imagine that the mechanic could get sued and his entire business destroyed if he missed a step or put in an inferior part.

We'll stipulate that most mechanics in this system are honest and that they are just trying to do the best thing for your car while surviving in business. What might we imagine would happen to the auto service industry, to our cars, and to our wallets under such a system? We might imagine that cars would be very well cared for—as long as their owners had the right kind of auto maintenance insurance. New tests and procedures that could be done on your car might proliferate despite minimal evidence that they would actually help the car last longer. Your old Yugo might end up with a Ferrari exhaust manifold. And a new muffler might cost $4,000. Those who did not have the right car maintenance insurance would be seriously out of luck as car maintenance prices spiraled out of control. It would be the "bus, bicycle, or walk" solution for them. Given how important cars are in our society, who got car maintenance insurance, for how much, and under what conditions would become a massive social and political question.

The End of Fee-for-Service Healthcare?

Most of healthcare is run on a single business model: fee-for-service. I do a service, I get a fee. I do two services, I get two fees. What's not to like?

There are some good reasons to pay for some healthcare on a fee-for-service basis. There are no good reasons to pay for all healthcare on a fee-for-service basis.

Hire a lawyer to deal with a complex, multifaceted, unfolding problem, and the lawyer will not quote a flat fee, simply because the lawyer has no idea what kind of work will be required, or how much, for how long. You have to pay the hourly rate plus fees for specified services, such as research by assistants, or copying and mailing briefs, and hope for the best.

On the other hand, if you hire a lawyer to draw up a will or vet a contract, or hire an accountant to do your personal taxes, they will likely quote a set fee for everything it takes to produce a set outcome: A filed tax return, a completed legal will, a well-vetted contract. They have done hundreds of these before; they know how long it will take them, they know how likely it is that extra problems will arise, and they recognize that a flat fee is less intimidating to clients making the choice to hire them.

A doctor dealing with late-life multisystem failure, or a spreading cancer, or a multiple trauma victim rushed to the ER, has no idea what services, tests, resources, or procedures will be needed, or how long the effort will take, or whether the case will be successful. He or she needs to be able to do whatever it takes (the services) to save the patient and let his or her organization bill (the fees) for all those services afterwards. Until we can learn enough about these contingencies to standardize them, these treatments must be either performed on a fee-for-service basis or bundled into some much larger structure that can absorb the risk of all that variation.

A surgical team replacing a mitral valve, on the other hand, has done hundreds of identical procedures before, and knows within a pretty good range how long this one will take and what resources it will consume, from diagnosis and imaging through anesthesia and blood plasma to recovery and rehab. They also know their failure rate, and how much those failures cost in dollars and lives. There is no reason the procedure cannot be sold as a package, or as part of a larger package. The same can be said of most of the millions of transactions and encounters that make up day-to-day healthcare, from diabetes care to mammograms to annual physicals to strep throat: the processes are self-contained, well-defined routines that take up a defined amount of resources.

Often, we operate a fee-for-service system out of habit and for the convenience of healthcare institutions, not because it gives us the best, most effective health and healthcare possible.

But what business model would work better than fee-for-service? That depends on what we are buying.

What Are We Buying?

In the auto industry, what's the product? The main product is an obvious, clear-cut unit: a car. We have whole distribution networks and financing networks built around selling one car at a time to one customer at a time. Sometimes, though, the unit that the customer is buying is different: not a single car at a time, but fleets of cars or trucks for taxi companies, rental companies, and delivery companies. These have very different business models, pricing structures, and distribution systems. For very high-end vehicles, such as business jets, there are business models (fractional ownership) that permit you to buy less than one whole unit. The business model that works best differs depending on what you buy.

When we pay for healthcare, what are we buying?

The ultimate customer, of course, for healthcare, is the individual. Healthcare is about our bodies, and we have precisely one to a customer, neither more nor less. If you're rich, you can buy lots of shoes, houses, cars, or oil wells. You cannot buy a six-pack of extra bodies to switch to when your original body has problems. Rich or poor, well insured or not, we all have precisely one body's worth of potential troubles to fix. All other "customers" of healthcare, such as families, health plans, employers, and governments, certainly have their own interests, but they are mainly proxies and payers for the ultimate customer, the individual with his or her one body.

So it is worth it to ask: What do you want to buy, as a customer of healthcare? Most of us want four things:

1. When I am sick, fix me.
2. If you can't fix my problem, help me manage it.
3. When I am not sick, help me stay well.
4. Be there when I really need you.

Each of these has its own shape and might be better supplied using different business models.

What's Wrong with Competition?

Many of our top economists and analysts of business competition have asked a very interesting question: Why doesn't competition work in healthcare? Most of them (such as Clayton Christensen,* the inventor of the term *disruptive innovation*;

---

* Christensen, C., et al., *The Innovator's Prescription: A Disruptive Solution for Health Care* (New York: McGraw-Hill, 2009).

Michael Porter and Elizabeth Teisberg*; and Regina Herzlinger†) make variations on the following argument: competition does not work in healthcare because it happens at the wrong level, over the wrong stakes, and in the wrong business model to bring about the best healthcare for the ultimate customer at the lowest price. You can watch this happen: put two healthcare systems in direct competition, and what they do is add services that are reimbursed well enough to make money, add specialists, jack up utilization as much as possible, and avoid as much uncompensated service as possible. Done this way, competition between health systems helps drive the cost of healthcare up, not down.

Christensen and his coauthors argue, in *The Innovator's Prescription*, that medicine comes in different flavors. Some diagnoses and some therapies have no settled pathway, and truly call for the intuition, experience, and judgment of the best clinicians who, ideally, work in teams bringing a blend of skills to bear on the same problem. Think migraines, depression, multiple sclerosis, and most types of cancer, examples of illnesses for which there are no agreed-upon solutions. Call this intuitive medicine. On the other hand, there are broken bones, strep throat, type 1 diabetes, cataracts, and hip and knee replacements: conditions for which the diagnosis is certain and the clinical pathway quite clear. Call this precision medicine.

These two types of medicine have completely different "pathways to value" (economic shorthand for how we find our way to the most cost-effective method of delivering the result). We will never be able to find that value until we separate them, each with their own business model. Intuitive medicine calls for a "solution shop" model, in which the right resources are gathered to look at your particular problem. Examples are M.D. Andersen for cancer; National Jewish in Denver for pulmonary disease, particularly asthma; the Texas Heart Institute; or the Heart and Vascular Institute and the Neurological Institute of the Cleveland Clinic. Unless it is in the context of a much larger structure, intuitive medicine must always be billed as fee-for-service because both the level of resources needed and the outcome are unpredictable.

Precision medicine, on the other hand, calls for a value-added process model, much like a factory. A factory gathers raw materials, then adds value to them by processing them into a product. You do one thing over and over and get really good at it. You can predict fairly well what kinds of value you can add, how much it costs to add them, and how you can price the result so as to make a profit. For treating a fracture, a myocardial infarction, multi-drug-resistant tuberculosis,

---

* Porter, M., and Teisberg, E.O., *Redefining Healthcare: Creating Value-Based Competition on Results* (Cambridge, MA: Harvard Business School Press, 2006).
† Herzlinger, H., *Who Killed Health Care? America's $2 Trillion Medical Problem—and the Consumer-Driven Cure* (New York: McGraw-Hill, 2007).

or a host of other presenting situations, there is a clear path to diagnosis and a standard, recognized treatment plan. The project is well defined, the outcomes highly expectable, and the variations well managed. Such processes can be bundled into products that, for healthcare, would mean a soup-to-nuts treatment program starting with diagnosis and ending with rehab, including along the way imaging, pharmaceuticals, and counseling as necessary. The bundle is given a price tag and warranty. The bundle can be billed on a fee-for-outcome basis, as the outcome is fairly certain. Repeating and honing the process, the healthcare provider can get both rapid clinical improvement and lower costs.

Christensen and his coauthors cite Ontario's Shouldice Hospital, which does only hernia repair, as a four-day in-patient process on a country club-style campus—and still charges 30% less than the U.S. CPT 49560 outpatient hernia repair reimbursement. The results are clearly better: U.S. hernia repairs average 10 to 20 times the Shouldice's 0.5% complication rate.

The distinction between intuitive and precision medicine is just one way of looking at healthcare business models. If we shift our perspective, we can start to recognize business models all around us organized around who the patient is and what he or she is seeking:

- Urgent care
- Primary care
- Mothers and children
- Chronic disease management
- Major acute management
- Major body refurbishment
- Managing aging
- Late-life multiple system failure

We can immediately see the reason for these subdivisions; the people and needs fall into groups requiring different kinds of care, over differing periods of time, quite different technologies and skill sets.

In fee-for-service medicine, we treat all these different types of medicine as if they were all one type in which the diagnosis, the work flow, and the path to treatment are all unknown, variable, intuitive, and subject to judgment and trial. But well-baby care, for instance, and chronic disease management are not like that at all. Some hospitals can now say, "Mrs. Smith, here's the price if you have your baby here in an uncomplicated birth, and here are our patient satisfaction scores, and our medical quality scores." The hospitals that do this have a huge competitive advantage. Can you imagine how much better, faster, and cheaper healthcare could be in the United States if all hospitals adopted this model?

Emerging Business Models

Because the traditional fee-for-service model does not fit much of the actual need for healthcare, many other models for healthcare delivery are already emerging, including guided patient networks (for patients with chronic conditions), the medical home, and clinical well-care. On the simple end, we are seeing an enormous growth in urgent care clinics (largely small, doctor-owned operations), which are essentially primary care operations that have extended hours and take walk-in traffic. Despite the current recession, the number of urgent care clinics has grown 7% since 2007. Now the first franchise chain of locally owned clinics has popped up—Doctor's Express, based in Towson, Maryland.

Retail clinics, mostly large chains associated with Wal-Mart or chain drug stores such as CVS/Caremark or Walgreens, are expected to resume their rapid growth in the coming years. Retail clinics do a strictly limited menu of primary care items, such as coughs and colds and cut fingers, for set prices, and they often take no insurance. We are beginning to see retail clinics help people manage their chronic disease as well. For instance, CVS/Caremark's Minute Clinics are launching an aggressive program of supporting customers with diabetes by doing A1C (average blood sugar level) tests on demand, as well as showing them how to test their own blood glucose levels and administer insulin.

Both of these business models not only save the customer costs on each encounter, but they save system costs as well, because many patients come into the clinic rather than going to an emergency room, which would cost vastly more. A RAND Corporation study published in *Health Affairs* in September 2010 showed that some 17% of all ER visits in the United States are for conditions that could be treated in retail or urgent care settings. If they were, that one shift would save the system $4.4 billion.[*]

But how do you shift people into thinking about the consequences of their choices so that they consciously choose the better and cheaper option? One way is to make enough of the cost come out of their pocket that they will pay attention and try to keep the cost down. The trick is to make their bill just enough of the overall expense, and only for the right part of the cost.

The Safeway Experience

Until 2004, Safeway was having a common experience for employers in America: healthcare costs that rose at 10% per year or more. For a Fortune 500 company with

---

[*] Pitts, S.R., et al., "Where Americans Get Their Acute Care: Increasingly, It's Not at Their Doctor's Office," *Health Affairs*, Vol. 29, No. 9, 2010, pp. 1610–29.

nearly 200,000 employees, these annual increases were huge. Since 2005, though, Safeway's healthcare costs under a new plan have been essentially flat, through a period when most healthcare costs and premiums have risen by about 50%.

What made the difference? In 2005, the self-insured grocery company instituted a new healthcare plan. The new plan had two parts that worked together: "skin in the game," and resources to help employees to get healthier.

For employees on the new plan, the company would fully pay for a specified set of primary and preventive care visits and tests. Plus it put $1,000 in a health reimbursement account that employees could use for their medical needs. The next $1,000 was out of their own pocket. For the next $2,000, the employee would pay 20%. Beyond that, the company paid everything.*

Now that they were actually involved in shopping for healthcare value, employees treated even that first $1,000 as if it were their own money, since if they used it up quickly, the next $1,000 would come out of their own pocket. Suddenly employees were eager to find out how much healthcare services actually cost, and where was the best and least expensive place to get them. For instance, one company survey found that prices for a routine colonoscopy within a 30-minute drive of Safeway headquarters in Pleasanton, California, varied from $700 to $7,000.

The other half of the plan helped them find those values, and helped them make changes in their lives that would improve their health and lower their costs. CIGNA managed Safeway's self-funded plan. The insurer used claims data to fill databases connected to a website with information about how much different items, from aspirins to new knees, actually cost. Safeway employees could enter their zip code, or even the route of their commute, and get actual, recent prices for everything they might need—from prescription drugs and checkups to stress tests and hernia operations.

The coverage and shopping information are linked to the voluntary Healthy Measures program: Sign up, go through an intake that includes some basic measurements, such as smoking, weight, blood pressure, and cholesterol. Set some goals with a health counselor, and if you meet them, you get a discount on next year's premium, up to $1,560 total per year per family. If you don't meet them but show improvement, you still get a partial discount. As a result, Safeway employees on the new plan (according to the company) have smoking and obesity rates 30% lower than the rest of the population.

Some critics say that such premium discounts amount to discrimination against smokers and obese people that will be struck down in the courts under the Americans for Disabilities Act. But the 1996 Health Insurance Portability and Accountability Act specifically permits employers to differentiate premiums

---

* "Mr. Burd Goes to Washington," *Wall Street Journal*, June 19, 2009.

based on behaviors. Though the shift in plan was greeted by disagreement and some strikes from the company's union employees, union leaders have since come to cautiously accept it, as it has become clear that the plan does not simply "cut benefits." The company claims that 80% of the nonunion workers who participate in the plan give it positive ratings as good, very good, or excellent.[*]

CIGNA's Choice Fund

Bill Antonello, a CIGNA vice president, says, "We conducted a blind focus group last year [2010] in Miami that was typical. Among the questions that the facilitator asked was, 'What health insurance carrier is actually improving people's health?' They literally laughed at him. They said things like, 'Great story! Great game! Send out brochures! But get real!' Nobody believes that anyone is actually doing that."

CIGNA clearly believes it is doing just that. CIGNA markets its Choice Fund, similar to the Healthy Measures plan it designed and implemented for Safeway, to employers across the country. For an extra fee, CIGNA helps the employers design their own package of deductibles and incentives built around a high-deductible consumer-directed health plan (CDHP), then builds in masses of information resources. These resources are designed to be as accessible to the customer as possible. CIGNA has run large-scale studies and focus groups to find what words people respond to and which turn them off. It turns out, for instance, that customers don't like to be called "members." "It's not a club," one said. "You don't get voting rights." They don't know what an explanation of benefits (EOB) actually is, and typically can't understand one when they read it. The answer to many questions on the website might be: "Call your provider." The customers thought that meant: "Call the people who provide your health plan, that is, your insurance company." The insurance company meant: "Call your doctor, hospital, or clinic—your medical provider." Such language barriers only add to the distrust most people feel for a health insurance carrier.

Similarly, some people prefer to get their information from a website, and never read printed material. Others need to talk to someone on the phone. Some are willing to be called, others feel it is intrusive for the insurance company to call them. CIGNA has worked to build its resources in ways that people will actually hear, understand, and use them.

At the same time, CIGNA researched the effect of incentives: How big an incentive will help people change behavior? How does it relate to salary level

---

[*] Burd, S., "How Safeway Is Cutting Costs: Market-Based Solutions Can Cut the National Healthcare Bill by 40%," *Wall Street Journal*, June 12, 2009. Steven Burd is the CEO of Safeway.

and type of job? How big a health account should the employer provide? How big should the "hole" be in which the employee is responsible for all costs? What should be on the list of preventive measures that the employer pays for directly?

CIGNA publishes the results of its Choice Fund every year, and the results are both consistent and surprising. The latest survey, for instance, looked at nearly 900,000 customers in nearly 500 groups across the country. It compared the 318,000 in a voluntary CIGNA Choice Fund program with the 579,000 using the more traditional HMO and PPO plans in the same employer groups. Those in the Choice Fund plans didn't go to the doctor less; in fact, they used 10% more preventive care services, and 9% more of the services that they need for their chronic conditions, including the appropriate drugs, according to the guidelines of evidence-based medicine (standardized medicine based on industry-wide clinical guidelines backed up by the best data that medical science can provide). But they spent 13% less on emergency care, 14% less for pharmaceuticals, and 15% less overall—and were just as satisfied as those in the traditional plans.*

CIGNA is far from the only health plan offering such programs, but it seems to have the deepest experience to draw from when we begin looking for winning formulas.

Formula One

The formula here (in the Safeway and CIGNA cases) is fairly simple:

- Pay for all preventive care.
- Give people skin in the game, financial incentives to shop for their medical care, to look for real value—and give them every resource they need to find that value.
- Give people a financial incentive to improve their health markers, such as weight, cholesterol, and smoking—and give them all the help they need to improve them.
- Talk in language they can hear, in ways that they can accept.

This tweaks the fee-for-service business model in interesting directions. Suddenly the providers of medical care are forced to compete on price and quality. They can no longer assume that customers will come to them no matter what they charge, or that their customers do not know how good a job they do. And suddenly the employees can actually keep their costs down by being smart shoppers and keeping themselves healthier. They are at risk for their choices, and they have the tools to make smart decisions.

---

* "5th Annual CIGNA Choice Fund Experience Study," October 19, 2010. Accessed at: http://newsroom.cigna.com/images/56/839403_choicefundexecsummary_v8hr.pdf

But there might be another part of the formula: getting more involved in the medical care itself.

The Boeing Experience

In the spring of 2010, Boeing announced the results of a very innovative 30-month trial of what they called their Outpatient Intensive Care Program. It was a new initiative in which 750 employees with multiple chronic conditions were given intensive personal attention. Multidisciplinary clinical teams actively reached out to them and followed their progress in order to help them manage their conditions.

Why was Boeing willing to pour so much money and effort into the personal care of their employees? Because Boeing has a lot of high-value employees, especially hard-to-replace aircraft engineers. The company is concerned not only with medical costs, but with turnover, disability, productivity, and absenteeism. Boeing is self-insured (with the plan managed by Regence Blue Shield), so any improvements in cost would drop straight to the bottom line. It was a risk worth taking.

Designed with help from Arnold Milstein, MD, MPH, of the Pacific Business Group on Health, the experiment was a collaboration between Boeing, Regence Blue Cross, and three major healthcare providers in the Seattle area—Everett Clinic, Virginia Mason Medical Center, and Valley Medical. Boeing paid the clinical teams extra to take a long-term approach and really get to know the patients.

Boeing had tried before, with a program that required employees to switch to a new doctor. That didn't work. Jeremy Smerd highlighted the differences in this approach in a BusinessInsurance.com article:

> The program was voluntary for doctors and patients alike, so the clinics that got involved had the "right mind-set," said Pranav Kothari, co-founder of Renaissance Health Inc., a medical consulting firm in Cambridge, Mass., and one of the consultants on the project. ...
>
> "We're asking them to do motivational interviewing, compassionate listening, help patients change their behavior, and change the caregiver relationship to one of care partnership that works with a patient's social support system," Mr. Kothari said. "They're not really taught this in medical school." ...
>
> Sherry Stoll, a nurse administrator at Virginia Mason, says doctors "talk about 'Boy, you need to lose weight' or, 'You are not managing your insulin.' They have those conversations. What's different about this program is asking the patient why.... What the nurse does is explain why this is important." ...

> "In the normal way health care works, patients like that woman are labeled noncompliant, difficult, recalcitrant," [Everett Clinic nurse Joleen] Rodgers said. "That's a label without getting into why they may be that way."[*]

The program acknowledged that people have a lot of psychological barriers getting in the way of taking better care of themselves, and helped them surmount those barriers.

A good test has a control group, a set of subjects not in the experimental program who are sufficiently like those who are in the program to be used as a comparison group. This test had a control group of 750 people who had similar health profiles and Boeing employees' usual access to healthcare, and who voluntarily declined to participate in the project. The results were spectacular: comparing the test group to the control group over the course of the test, counting the extra cost of the clinician teams, the intensive effort saved 20% of the healthcare costs of those in the test program, and dropped their absenteeism by 56%.

Twenty percent cost reduction on patients with multiple conditions is a big result. Notice that this is not another insurance program. No insurance company is on the hook for the costs or the savings. It is a business model, in which Boeing is paying the healthcare providers in a different, packaged way, with performance guarantees built in.

Boeing is now expanding the program with its employees in Puget Sound, Chicago, St. Louis, and San Diego.[†] Each of the providers involved with Boeing is now offering the concept as an extra service for all of the employers in the area. A success like Boeing's—dropping costs by improving the health of the people who need it most—does not go unnoticed. As experiences and results like Boeing's and others become better known among large employers, we will see many more examples like this.

On-Site Clinics

Some employers are getting even more involved in medical care itself, by installing clinics right in the workplace. These next-generation on-site clinics are "not your grandfather's company doctor," as the website of clinic company WeCare TLC puts it.

---

[*] Smerd, J., "Boeing Pilot Program Focuses on Medical Home: Initial Results Show Program Saved 20% in Health Care Costs," BusinessInsurance.com, August 8, 2010, accessed July 26, 2011, at http://www.businessinsurance.com/article/20100808/ISSUE01/308089981.

[†] Personal communications with officials of Boeing and Blue Cross/Blue Shield of Illinois, August 2011.

Clinics built on an advanced model designed to drive patient health are popping up in companies across the country, especially large ones that fund their own healthcare. Many of these are full-service clinics, with x-ray machines and labs, as well as dentists, dermatologists, and psychiatrists.

By 2009, according to the employee benefits company Mercer, 11% of U.S. companies with more than 500 employees had one of these new-model clinics. By 2010, that had grown to 15%. The percentage was even higher among really big companies with more than 20,000 employees, such as Qualcomm, Walt Disney, and American Express.*

WeCare TLC is one of about 30 firms that will simply pop a clinic into your worksite and run it. The chain ran 13 on-site clinics in five states at the beginning of 2011. Comprehensive Health Services in Reston, Virginia, has seen its business double to 100 clinics in 23 states in just the last three years. The largest vendor, Walgreen's subsidiary Take Care Health Systems of San Diego, employs 2,500 doctors, nurses, and other healthcare workers in 360 centers across the country, including a 15,000-square-foot giant clinic at Disney's Epcot Center in Orlando.

Advanced on-site clinics use nurse health coaches, evidence-based medicine, full digitization, registries, and an array of other tools to become "fully-realized medical homes and integrated full-continuum medical management machines located in the front end of the care delivery system," according to Brian Klepper, WeCare TLC's chief development officer.

Do these clinics actually save medical costs? Companies typically do not release such internal data. Most of these clinics are fairly new, and detailed studies have not yet been published. But those in the industry claim that it does save medical costs. Klepper, for instance, claims that, depending on the local situation, clients who install a WeCare TLC clinic can expect a rapid 25% to 35% reduction in their overall healthcare costs. Without giving numbers, Qualcomm claims that its Take Care clinics save on medical claims, ER visits, and hospitalizations.

The business model is simple: the client pays the up-front costs to install the clinic. One WeCare TLC client, for instance, is the union for the civilian laborers at a submarine base in Georgia. The capital cost of installing the clinic was less than one month's healthcare costs for the union. Once the clinic is up and running, WeCare TLC bills the client for the actual itemized cost of running the clinic, from salaries to drugs, plus a management fee. There is no insurance involved. For a self-funded employer, much of the employees' regular utilization of outside doctors goes away, because the clinic is so much more convenient.

---

* Helfand, D., "More Employers Are Offering On-Site Medical Clinics," *Los Angeles Times*, July 3, 2011, accessed July 3, 2011, at http://articles.latimes.com/2011/jul/03/business/la-fi-company-clinics-20110703.

The model offers something for everyone. The employees still have their usual array of choices. They can use their insurance to go to whatever doctor they want. But if they go to the on-site clinic, not only is it far more convenient, but there is no copay, and no payment for pharmaceuticals. Experience shows that employees with such a clinic are much more likely to stay on track with their chronic syndromes. The employer gets not only a lower and better-controlled healthcare bill, but employees take less time off for doctor visits, and are less likely to be absent for problems that were not adequately taken care of up front. The doctors involved typically make more money at the clinic than in a regular practice, especially since they waste no time arguing with insurance companies or filling out forms. All they do is treat patients. This is the combination we are looking for across healthcare: better health for less money.

The rule of thumb in the past has been that an on-site clinic only makes sense when the employer has a minimum of 750 to 1,000 employees at a single site. With aggressive medical management and scalable hours, WeCare TLC has made it work economically at sites with as few as 62 employees.

On-Site Clinics without Employers?

Could this model, a clinic, fully paid for by the client entity, structured as an integrated full-continuum medical management machine, work for Medicare patients, Medicaid patients, people in convalescent homes, or as a different type of federally qualified health center? There is no reason why it could not work for any population as long as the population is close enough to the clinic to get there easily and some entity is at risk for their healthcare costs. Even insurance companies are likely to warm to it as part of their offering, as it is a way that they can offer better healthcare for less money to employers and employees.

Medicaid-Based Business Models

One more example: If you were to look around, as an entrepreneur, for a way to make money by helping some population be healthier, what populations would seem to be the "low-hanging fruit"? Would you think, "Ah, yes! Frail, elderly people on Medicaid in state-supported convalescent homes! And kids on Medicaid with disabilities!" Probably not. And yet that is exactly what happened in Illinois. McKesson's disease management subsidiary contracted with the state to provide its Your Healthcare Plus services to just such populations. Teams of doctors, nurses, and case managers, many of them on-site across the state, working with the patients' existing providers, measurably improved the health of these patients. Counting the costs and fees for running the program, McKesson saved the state of Illinois $569 million over the four years of the program, and dropped the inflation rate of medical care for these populations from more than 7% to less than 3%—all by giving people more services of the right kind of care and attention, not less.[*]

Disease Management Programs That Fail

In January of 2012, headlines announced: "Government study shows disease management not worth it." Much of this book argues for the extraordinary value of helping people manage their health early, with as many resources as necessary. You might think that one report knocked all of my arguments in the nearest ash can.

As with many articles, the headline was misleading. The Congressional Budget Office report did not show that disease management programs were not worth it. The CBO had looked at the results of experimental disease management, care coordination, and value-based purchasing programs that the Centers for Medicare and Medicaid Services (CMS) had authorized. It turns out that the experiments had a wide variety of results. Most, counting the hefty fees paid the providers, actually cost CMS more than if the disease managers had just left those patients alone. Some saved money, but on average, the ones that saved money did not save enough to make up for their fees.

If all the programs were the same, there would be nothing to learn here, except: Don't try to help patients manage their health, because 90% of the time, those programs fail to save any money. But the programs were not the same. Some in fact did save far more than the fees they charged, and they differed on a noticeable pattern, a pattern that made sense.

All of the programs that cost more stinted on contact. The patients, the patients' family caregivers, and the patients' doctors never met the disease manager/care coordinator face to face. They were just voices on the phone, just strangers trying to butt in. In the programs that saved more, the outsider went to the patients' homes, convalescent homes, bedsides, or living rooms. They got to know the patients, the caregivers, the doctors. Sometimes they rounded with the doctors, working directly with the doctor in the patients' presence.[†]

All good medical care, all good health management, is built on trusted relationships. There is no substitute. Without real human relationships built on trust, no amount of information, measurement, guidelines, or incentives will

---

[*] Berkey, A. (McKesson VP), "McKesson and Your Healthcare Plus (YHP)," personal communication to author, May 12, 2011.

[†] Nelson L., et al., "Lessons From Medicare's Demonstration Projects on Disease Management, Care Coordination, and Value-Based Payment," Congressional Budget Office Issue Brief, January 2012. Available at http://www.cbo.gov

get people healthier, bring them more appropriate care, or care that costs less. "Care" is not a euphemism.

Disease Management Programs That Work

We can tell whether a disease management programs is likely to work ahead of time by looking at its design. To do this, ask four principal questions. Is the program:

Targeted—Does it focus on the most vulnerable populations, where the leverage for improvement is greatest? Or does it attempt to blanket enroll whole populations?

Personal—Do the disease managers/care coordinators work from actual personal relationships with the patients and their caregivers? Do they get to know people and gain their trust? Or do they depend on robo-calls and strangers working from scripts?

Voluntary—Are the patients auto-enrolled? Or do they or their family caregivers have to make some personal commitment to engage in the process? This is not always possible, but programs do better when the patients or their caregivers say, "Yes, please help us out here."

Incentivized—Were the disease managers simply paid per person per month? Or did some or much of their compensation depend on their success in lowering overall costs and improving health status? If they are paid per person per month, obviously their incentive is to enroll as many people as possible, regardless of their ability to help them. If their pay depends upon their success, they will focus on the cases in which they can do a lot of good.

This is the same incentive problem, as we have seen, that underlies most of the problems in healthcare: People do exactly what you pay them to do—and we are mostly not paying people for what we actually want.

The CBO report itself acknowledged that the central problem is the fee-for-service system itself: "Demonstrations aimed at reducing spending and increasing quality of care face significant challenges in overcoming the incentives inherent in Medicare's fee-for-service payment system....The results of those Medicare demonstrations suggest that substantial changes to payment and delivery systems will probably be necessary for programs involving disease management and care coordination or value-based payment to significantly reduce spending and either maintain or improve the quality of care provided to patients."*

---

* Ibid.

In other words: Route around the fee-for-service system, and get close, really close, to the patients. Here's another way to do just that.

Direct Primary Care

If you don't happen to work for one of these massive, self-funded corporations with on-site clinics, you may need some other business model that gets around the fee-for-service, insurance-supported trap. One way to do it is to split off primary care (everyday doctoring, checkups, coughs and colds, and the "Do I need to worry about this bump?" visit) from catastrophic care, by signing up for direct primary care with a low-cost doctor.

Some primary care doctors are opting out of the fee-for-service system in their own way. Many are heading for the high end of the market, turning their practices into what they call concierge services: pay a hefty annual fee, and you get full access to preventive and maintenance services and consultations, full patient tracking, and a roster of other services with set prices.

Increasingly we are seeing primary care doctors head for the low end of the market, offering their services packaged in a way that almost anyone can afford them. MedLion, in California's Silicon Valley and Monterey areas, offers a complete primary care package for $49 per month and $10 per visit.[*] In Utah, After Hours Medical offers a similar plan: as an individual member, you pay $49 per month and $5 per visit for all primary care. Companies can sign up their employees for $30 per month per person and $5 per visit.[†] The Direct Primary Care Coalition lists 77 similar practices across the country on its website (http://www.dpcare.org/),[‡] with monthly fees from $49 to $129. Combine a direct primary care membership with a high-deductible catastrophic health insurance plan (far less expensive than comprehensive insurance), and you've got coverage for the big stuff and continual attention for the small stuff.

How can doctors offer care at these low prices? Largely, it's because the cost of insurance is dropped right out of the equation—not only the cost of insurance company profits, plus insurance company infrastructure, plus brokers' fees and commissions, but the enormous cost to the medical office of documenting and coding every action, filing claims, and fighting claim denials. According

---

[*] Chase, D. "The Most Important Organization in Silicon Valley That No One Has Heard About," TechCrunch, June 19, 2011, accessed June 19, 2011, at http://techcrunch.com/2011/06/19/the-most-important-organization-in-silicon-valley-that-no-one-has-heard-about/.

[†] AfterHoursMedical.com, accessed August 10, 2011.

[‡] Accessed August 10, 2011.

to estimates by the Direct Primary Care Coalition, as much as 40% of the cost of primary care is simply the cost of insurance, not the cost of medicine itself. Remember the $27.6 billion mentioned earlier that is wasted in the U.S. system just wrestling with insurance forms and appeals and authorizations in physician offices? This amounts to over $80,000 per physician each year. For a small physician practice, that's a lot.*

Like the doctors working in on-site clinics, doctors in direct primary care practices love not having to fill their hours wrangling with insurance companies. They would much rather spend their time being doctors and serving their patients.

Direct Primary Care—Online

Add this into the mix: just as dating, hanging out, shopping, news, and nearly everything else has migrated online, so has medical practice. From its foundation in the early 1990s, one of the largest, most important ways people used the newly public Internet and the World Wide Web was to find health information. When you are feeling sick, compromised, and vulnerable, finding an answer is paramount. People will use any means at their disposal to help themselves, their parents, their children, or their spouse feel better and stay safe.

But information is one thing. In recent years we have seen the flowering of actual medical care online: not just reading a Wikipedia page or a PatientsLikeMe. com forum, but talking to a real live board-certified doctor, now, on your computer, tablet, or smart phone. Got a problem? Don't wait until next week, when you can see your doctor. Don't take half a day off and go to the emergency room or the urgent care clinic in the mall. Just fire up the laptop and go to MDLiveCare. com, Teladoc.com, EasyHealthMD.com, or InteractiveMD.com. You can call, email, or do live chat. Got a webcam? Show the doctor the rash, the cut, the color of your tongue. Get a doctor who can tell you, "Don't worry about it, it's just a bump," or "Here's a prescription for that," or "You need to see a neurologist. Here are several in your area," or "Dial 911 now!" Feeling depressed, anxious, lost? Some have licensed mental health professionals waiting to talk to you.

Costs vary, but they are low. Online doctor services are still working through their business models, and they all offer a variety of packages for individuals, companies, and health plans. Some have monthly, annual, or sign-up fees, others don't. Per-visit costs run from $25 to $50, far below a typical $100 cost for visiting a primary care physician's office, $150 for an urgent care visit, or $750 for an ER visit.

---

* Yahoo News and Agence France-Presse, "Simplifying US Health Care Could Save Billions," August 4, 2011, accessed August 4, 2011, at http://news.yahoo.com/simplifying-us-health-care-could-save-billions-study-042711819.html.

Such 24/7/365 online services are no substitute for a regular, face-to-face, trusted relationship with a doctor who knows you and tracks you over time. But they definitely fill a need: at that moment when you need a doctor, you don't need a doctor next week or next month or across town, you need a doctor right here, right now. The insurance-supported fee-for-service system has not fostered the kind of competition in healthcare that would encourage physicians to change their habits to meet your needs. Find ways around the insurance-supported fee-for-service system, and suddenly inventive new business models pop up, eager for your business, eager to give you what you want and need: better health and healthcare, as conveniently as possible, as low cost as possible.

Think of any other business like consumer electronics or autos or fishing boats or vacation packages, businesses that are constantly innovating to meet customers' needs, finding new ways to package and finance their products and services, testing the market, listening to its feedback, hitting a variety of price points. This kind of market research and outreach is common in every other business, but in healthcare it is surprising, strange, and clarifying. What a concept: a healthcare system that is truly built around all my needs for the product or service along with convenient access to it.

Structure Matters

These solutions are structural. The ordinary structures of healthcare, with doctors, clinics, and hospitals in strict fee-for-service relationships with payers, have great difficulty acting as if the patient is a customer, not just part of a revenue stream.

If we are to get out of this mess, we need to tweak those old structures and build new ones. That's why we are seeing fascinating, weird experimental structures arising across healthcare—extended medical home physician-hospital organizations (PHOs) and virtual accountable care organizations. Almost all of these are new forms of partnerships, ad hoc contractual relationships that cut across the traditional structural lines to deal with the health of particular populations. The contracts set up incentive relationships that guarantee that someone makes a profit specifically by tending to the total needs of the patient, not just by providing services to the patient. Innovative structures are popping up all over the place now, taking different shapes to fill niches in the vast ecology of healthcare.

Hospitals and health systems can form these OWAs (a technical healthcare economists term meaning "other weird arrangements") in all kinds of shapes, from at-risk contracts with insurers or Medicare, to shared-risk medical home arrangements with PHOs, to disease management contracts with government agencies. We are seeing these OWAs increasingly because in the new healthcare environment the overburden of high cost and low capacity is killing us. We simply must find more efficient and effective ways of serving our customers.

What all these structures have in common: they pay healthcare providers directly to work in teams to save healthcare dollars by improving the health of specific target populations.

Structure matters. The old attitude toward business models was that there was only one: fee-for-service. The emerging attitude is that there are many business models, both simple and complex, working with different customers who have different objectives. With the right structure, you make money by saving money. Help the customers meet their objectives, and you get paid for it.

Share the Risk

Risks and rewards drive behavior. If players in any system are not doing what we think they should be doing to make the system work well, chances are they are not getting rewarded, or put at knowing risk, in a way that matches their effect on the system.

In economics, risk does not mean uncertainty. Uncertainty means that things may be different in the future in ways that you can't know and can't do anything about. You are uncertain what your healthcare premiums might be next year, but typically you have no way to affect those premiums. On the other hand, you are at risk for things that you can do something about. If you have a business, you put money at risk when you invest it in the business because if you can manage the business well, you can make a profit.

Risks in a traditionally insurance-supported fee-for-service system are wildly ill-distributed. The insured patient has all the personal risk of getting sick or dying, but none of the financial risk, because the healthcare is all paid for up front. The patient who overuses the system (whether a patient with first-dollar coverage or a homeless person with no coverage ending up in the emergency room) has no financial risk in using the system.

The doctor or clinic, on the other hand, has almost all of the knowledge and resources, but very little of the financial risk. The only financial risk for the doctor or clinic is how much activity the business generates—how many office visits, tests, and procedures patients bring in.

The health plan or the government has almost all of the financial risk, with limited abilities to control that risk. However, what is at risk for the payer is not the actual cost of healthcare, but only the spread between that cost and the funds it receives in the form of premiums or taxes. As long as the payer can take in more money than it pays out for care, the payer is financially healthy.

Here's the key point: no one in the system is at financial risk for producing the best outcome at the lowest cost. Unlike other businesses, in traditional insurance-supported fee-for-service healthcare, no one makes their living by providing me, the customer, with what I need. There is no feedback loop serving to drive costs down and waste out of the system.

Is it possible to rebalance risk in healthcare to make it work better and cheaper for everyone? Yes, at the personal level and the system level.

A Brief History of Risk in Healthcare

Thirty years ago, insurance paid the full price demanded by doctors and hospitals, and Medicare rates were based on whatever was "usual and customary" in a given market. There was no attempt at all to cap prices, much less to measure the quality of what was delivered.

In the absence of any market pressure prices tended to rise. But until 1980, just about the time that the federal government (and then the private payers) began to try to control healthcare cost by capping prices, overall healthcare costs in the United States closely resembled costs in other countries in percentage of gross domestic product (GDP) or in dollars per person. Starting in the early 1980s, U.S. healthcare costs took off on their own trajectory, growing monstrously out of relationship with those of other countries. It would seem that those cost-controlling efforts got it wrong, somehow. In wrongly distributing financial risk, these cost-control efforts actually drove costs steadily higher over the decades since.

In the early 1980s, to combat rising costs, the federal government instituted diagnostic-related groupings (DRGs) to establish fixed prices for a cardiac artery bypass graft, setting a broken bone, or prescribing an antibiotic for an ear infection. Private insurers soon came up with their own lists of payments, based on the government's DRG payments. This transferred some risk to the providers. But it was a small risk. If they could keep their overall costs below their overall reimbursements with a lot of shifting of costs from one payer to another, they were good to go. And there was no rating of quality, or outcomes, or appropriateness. As long as the provider had a medical justification for a procedure, and the right code, they could charge for it.

In the 1990s, as the Clinton healthcare initiative failed, a new fad arose in the battle to control costs. Insurers looked at Kaiser and other staff model HMOs (health maintenance organizations with salaried doctors on staff) that combined the insurance function with the clinical delivery. The organization took in one premium payment from the individual (or the individual's employer) and provided whatever the individual needed, from a flu shot to brain surgery. In this capitated model, the HMO took on the financial risk of delivering the promised healthcare for the price of the premium. "Ah!" said insurance companies, "Perfect! HMOs! That's what we'll do! We'll call it 'managed care' and do it a little differently. Since we have all the risk anyway, we'll be like Kaiser and control the clinical side as well, and drive down costs. Bingo!"

This was actually a good idea—but it is not what they did. Managed care turned out to be quite a different animal. The HMOs that the insurance companies built in the 1980s were not real, staff model HMOs. The doctors did not actually work for the HMO. There was no clinical integration, there were no teams, there was no tracking of quality or outcomes. What there was instead was cost control by contract, with primary care physicians installed as gatekeepers to specialists and all services beyond the primary care office, and all physicians working at discount rates. Primary care physicians were paid bonuses to deny treatment by other physicians. It was called managed care, but there was no real care management, only cost management. It was just a variation on the same business model insurance companies had always had: avoiding risk by avoiding treatment whenever possible. Patients hated it, doctors hated it. It was, in fact, exactly the kind of interference with clinical medicine by Soviet-style functionaries that the insurance companies had told the public that healthcare reform would bring. We had a Soviet-style system, it was just outsourced to the private sector. Once consumers and employers experienced this form of discount healthcare, the rush to managed care slowed, and the hunt continued for a true, systemic way to find value in healthcare.

Only in the last 10 years have we seen the slow growth of more subtle and flexible ways of truly spreading risk appropriately among patients, providers, and payers.

Putting the Customer at Financial Risk

In other businesses, such as retail, the seller only takes the risk that there is something wrong with the product. The customer takes all the financial risk of making a wrong decision, of buying something that is wasteful or unnecessary.

Why don't we just do that in healthcare? That may seem like an odd question, but I have been asked this very question in public forums, and it lurks as an assumption behind many of the public debates about healthcare financing. If we just let people pay for the healthcare they need when they need it, the questioner argues, they certainly would not overuse the system. There are five reasons why that wouldn't work:

■ Though most healthcare, most of the time, is not all that expensive, *when you really need it, it's crushingly expensive*—and most of us really need it sooner or later. If we couldn't find a way to fund that risk over time, almost all of us would sooner or later go bankrupt, and the healthcare system would wither in the face of all those unpaid bills.

■ *Your risk of needing healthcare varies wildly* over your lifetime, in predictable ways (more risk as you age, for instance, when you take up smoking, or when you participate in a dangerous hobby like skiing or a job like fishing or mining), in unpredictable ways (lightning, terrorist attack, or cancer could strike anyone at any time), and in usually invisible ways (you may have a gene that predisposes you to some disease and not know it).

■ *You share some of your risk* with the people next to you on the plane, people in your industry, or people who live in your area: environmental risks and communicable diseases hit populations, not just individuals.

■ *People are terrible at evaluating their own real risk* for needing healthcare any time soon. They are even worse at prudent financial planning over decades of their lives. There is little chance that most people could realistically match their ability to finance healthcare at any given moment with their need for it. If we want most people to be able to afford healthcare, we have to spread their financial risk across their lifetimes, whether they need it at that particular moment or not. If we want the healthcare system to be there for us when we need it, we need to find some way that people can afford to use it.

■ *People's risk of needing healthcare varies significantly* across the population in ways that have little to do with their ability to pay for it. In fact, the heaviest users of the system are often those with the least ability to pay, such as the working poor and the frail elderly. If we don't want such people to just suffer and die without help, we need to spread the financial risk across classes and ages.

This wild mismatch of risk, people's ability to assess risk, and people's ability to pay for healthcare at any given moment in their lives shows a clear logic: we all should pay for healthcare, in one way or another, since over our lives and across the population, our risk averages out, while our ability to assess it and pay for it swings wildly. Single-payer architectures simply spread the risk across the whole society through taxes. For the part of our population over 65, we do that in the United States in exactly the same way—through taxes assessed on people under 65 who are still working. For those still working, this is the argument for an individual mandate to buy healthcare insurance; not buying healthcare insurance is, in effect, a bet that you will have no health problems in the foreseeable future, and you are willing to let somebody else pay for it if you do. At the same time, any individual mandate must be subsidized: while people's actual risk of needing healthcare averages out across the population, their ability to pay for insurance does not.

So why don't we just *capitate* all healthcare (the industry term that means "pay for all of it in one big lump sum, whether through a single-payer system or through insurance") and let the provider take the financial risk? I get this question too in public forums. This is the argument for a truly socialized system like Canada's. The answer is easy to see: anything that is completely free of cost to the user becomes overused. Canada's provinces have struggled for 50 years with this. They have no way of holding down demand, so they have to hold down supply—which results in the horrendous wait times, and the difficulty of getting high-end services, that Canadians often complain about.

The answer that has emerged over the last two decades is to get the end customer to take on some risk, a carefully titrated amount of risk for using the system, through deductibles and copays and specialized health savings accounts. Intelligently designed high-deductible health plans matched with health savings accounts and the right set of incentives are proving to be a workable way for the consumer to accept some financial risk.

Even fully capitated systems like Kaiser have introduced deductibles and copays on most plans. As a patient, deciding to go to the doctor will cost you some money.

But it shouldn't cost you too much money, or you'll skip going at all, and end up with a worse problem.

On the other hand, Kaiser does not make its living on those copays. It makes its living by delivering all the customers' healthcare for less than the customers pay in. So a visit to a Kaiser primary care doctor can be highly efficient. When I recently asked my doctor to look at a tiny bump on my hand, I also ended up with a full physical, prescription renewals, and three vaccinations, all in about 40 minutes. Neither the doctor nor the system would benefit from making me come back for separate appointments for all these different elements.

"But Capitation Doesn't Work"

The most common reaction to this discussion is that capitation does not work, that it flips the incentives so completely that it drives providers to avoid treating at all whenever possible.

Here's a rule of thumb: any idea will fail if it is stupidly implemented. Capitation and managed care were stupidly implemented in most cases when they became a fad in the 1990s, implemented in ways that drove people away from their healthcare providers. Most managed care schemes simply got doctors to agree to discount their services, and then gave bonus payments to primary care docs to refuse to refer patients on to specialists. It directly put a clear conflict of interest into the center of the primary care practice. This not only drove both doctors and patients crazy, but seriously damaged the trust between them.

What is advocated here is what seems to work in a number of different examples across healthcare: the financial risk taken on by the customer must be carefully designed for his or her financial situation, and to affect decisions that he or she actually control. There is no point in penalizing the customer for going to the emergency department when her child has a fever if there is no late-night primary care available. There is no point in trying to charge homeless people $50 a visit. Some things need to be free to the customer in any system design. Some things are impossible to overuse (How many people get recreational vaccinations?). Many preventive services are so much cheaper than what they prevent that worrying about overuse is absurdly beside the point.

The devil is in the details. Designing a risk and incentive program that actually works for different types of customers is key to getting good results—but it absolutely can be done.

Putting the Provider At Risk

So putting the customers at some level of financial risk for their choices helps them make sensible choices about how to use healthcare. But what about the providers?

There are many ways, large and small, for providers to take on appropriate risk. For instance, bundling an entire replaced hip, or a mitral valve replacement, into a single complete package with published prices, is a way to take on risk. The system is saying, "We are willing to take the risk that we can deliver, say, an uncomplicated birth as one package for this price." Warranties are another way. The system is saying, "We are willing to take the risk that we can deliver quality on demand." A "mini-cap" is capitation-style prepaid care for some specific part of your needs, such as a diabetes care subscription. This is another way of transferring some risk to a health system. The system is saying, "We are willing to take the risk that we can deliver all the services you need for a set price—because if we do it right, we can actually drive down the cost of those services and make money on the deal."

To make money at coordinating care, or through avoiding solution costs and system costs, you have to be at risk for the cost of that size of solution. To make money at bundled payments, you have to be able to control the costs of all parts of the bundle. To make money through cutting solution and system costs, you have to be at risk for the entire solution. In a fee-for-service universe, if you help a patient avoid a foot amputation by aggressively treating the foot abscesses, or by avoiding abscesses altogether, your bottom line just took a huge hit because you missed the high-ticket item, the amputation surgery. In a universe in which you are at risk for the health of that patient because you have a capitated contract for their diabetes care or for their overall care, your bottom line looks better for every cost you can avoid.

Providers At Risk Behave Differently

Providers who are held at some kind of business risk for the cost and quality of their product at differently. Here's a small, focused example: A few years ago, executives of Aetna in the Seattle area had a meeting with the executives of Virginia Mason Medical Center. The dialogue went something like this:

Aetna:	We're establishing a new premium network of the highest quality healthcare providers in the area.
VM:	Great! We are very high quality, and can prove it.
Aetna:	But you're not going to be on the list, because you cost too much. For many things you cost twice as much as other high-quality providers.
VM:	Whoah, hold on, let's talk about this. Show us the problems.

Aetna, analyzing its claims data, actually had a clearer picture of the cost per episode of different diseases and problems than their healthcare providers did. Virginia Mason actually had no idea until then how their overall costs stacked up against other providers. But Virginia Mason already had a strong grip on its practices, and employed all its doctors in a strong team environment. So it set out to discover why it cost so much, and rectify the situation. It asked Aetna's medical director, Dr. Don Storey, to present Aetna's findings to all of Virginia Mason's 26 department heads. Then Virginia Mason's chief of medicine, Dr. Robert Mecklenburg, set out to talk directly to the employers.

For instance, one of the big employers in the area that Aetna worked with was Starbucks. What do you imagine is one of the main health problems of Starbucks baristas (besides insomnia)? Back problems. They work standing up all day. Virginia Mason operates a major back clinic. Dr. Mecklenburg sat down with the benefits director at Starbucks, Annette King, to talk about the problem—which in itself surprised King. She later told a reporter, "I couldn't believe a doctor was making an appointment with me and asking what I wanted." She ran through Virginia Mason's process along these lines: Look, when we refer a Starbucks employee to you for back trouble, the first thing you do is pop them in an MRI. Then they have to come back sometimes weeks later for an interpretation of the scan. But most of those MRIs don't tell you anything you didn't already know. It turns out that 85 percent don't need anything more than physical therapy and painkillers—surgery or other invasive procedures are actually not the best thing for them. What would it hurt if you were to do a quick triage when they walked in the door to determine whether they had an obvious, serious, problem, give all of them some painkillers and a referral to physical therapy right there, and then see them again only if they don't improve? That's what the medical literature says, anyway. That would be faster and less inconvenient for the employee, and far cheaper for us.

In traditional healthcare, no medical director would ever have asked an HR director of an employer for any ideas about clinical processes. It was a sign that we are turning the corner into a new era when the medical director said, "Let me talk to our back docs about that." He did talk to them, and they redesigned their processes the way the HR director had suggested—and found they had the capacity to deal with five times as many patients.

But there was another step: Because of the sunk costs of the imaging center, Virginia Mason now found that they were losing money on every case on which they did not do an MRI. Virginia Mason went back to Aetna and Starbucks for a slight upward adjustment of the amount they were paid per office visit and per physical therapy visit. This put them back in the black, even at far lower charges per episode.

Now driving not only for quality but for cost-effectiveness, Virginia Mason made similar process adjustments in a number of other areas demanded by Aetna and the employers.[*]

Putting Providers Systemically At Risk

Let's look at one example of a serious attempt to put healthcare providers—doctors and hospitals—at risk for providing the lowest cost, most effective care and keeping their patients healthier: the Alternative Quality Contract program from Blue Cross/Blue Shield of Massachusetts.

Massachusetts passed its state version of healthcare reform in 2006. That got a lot more people covered by insurance, but it didn't do much to cut costs. Massachusetts is a major state, with world-class medical institutions and high costs. The largest commercial insurer, Blue Cross Blue Shield of Massachusetts (BCBSMA), decided to get down in the weeds to figure out the details of a plan that would really work, over time, to bring healthcare inflation down.

Here's how Alternative Quality Contracts work:[†] First, it's based on primary care. Organizations that sign up for it have to have primary care docs caring for at least 5,000 patients. It's a five-year contract, so the organizations have time to adjust. Instead of paying the contracting organization for each action they per-

---

[*] "A Novel Plan Helps Hospital Wean Itself Off Pricey Tests," Wall Street Journal, January 12, 2007.

[†] Blue Cross/Blue Shield of Massachusetts web site: http://www.bluecrossma.com. Chernew et al. "Private-Payer Innovation In Massachusetts: The 'Alternative Quality Contract'" Health Affairs, 30, no. 1 (2011):51–61 1/20/11. Available online at: http://content.healthaffairs.org/content/30/1/51.full.html. Personal interviews by the author with BCBSMA executives.

form ("fee-for-service"), the AQC pays them a set amount per person per month, then adds in bonuses for meeting a set of quality standards (such as seeing that all diabetes patients have foot exams). They've set up a system of incentives for giving good care while meeting the needs of the organization for predictable cash flow.

BCBSMA negotiates with each organization. The starting point is the total amount BCBSMA paid in the previous year for all services for the patients for which the organization provided primary care. That is: "Here are these 10,000 patients that get their primary care from you. Last year, counting all there are, even surgery and complex care they received in other hospitals and systems, we paid out this amount. That is your starting budget for all of their care." Each year a small increment is allowed to keep step with general inflation (not the much higher medical inflation), plus the quality bonuses. The healthcare providers who sign up are responsible for the total amount spent on their patients, even if it is spent somewhere else. For example, if the organization is an independent physicians organization (IPO) that owns no hospitals, and one of its patients ends up in the hospital, that cost comes out of the IPO's contract.

Throughout the year, the organization continues to bill BCBSMA as in a fee-for-service system. But at the end of the year they settle up: If the organization's billings came in under the budget, it gets the difference back from BCBSMA. If it came in over the budget, it has to pay BCBSMA the difference.

As the year goes on, BCBSMA uses sophisticated tracking databases to let the organizations know exactly how things are going for them. For instance, if one of their patients is admitted to another hospital or shows up in an ER, BCBS alerts them immediately. The alerts can get really detailed. For example, the drug costs for managing high blood pressure can vary all over the map among different doctors. The biggest difference is which class of drugs the doctors prescribe: angiotensin-converting enzyme (ACE) inhibitors or angiotensin II receptor blockers (ARBs). ARBs cost a lot more than ACE inhibitors. Medical evidence suggests that only 10% to 15% of patients actually need the expensive ARBs, but 30% of patients get them—a big unnecessary cost. BCBSMA drills down into the claims data and gives provider groups physician-specific numbers on who is prescribing a lot more ARBs than seems called for. The provider groups can encourage those doctors to take a look at what they are prescribing, and have good conversations with their patients regarding the costs and benefits of each class of drugs. If the drugs cost less, patients are more likely to actually take them, keep their blood pressure down, and avoid heart attacks and strokes.[*]

---

[*] Greene, R., Beckman, H., and Mahoney, T., "Beyond the Efficiency Index: Finding a Better Way to Reduce Overuse and Increase Efficiency in Physician Care," *Health Affairs*, Vol. 27, No. 4, 2008, pp. w250–59.

This illustrates an important principal of risk-sharing: Lodge some financial risk with those who can affect the outcome, at the operational level. If those who are making clinical decisions do better financially, both if the patient does better and if the treatment costs less, we will see quick improvements in both cost and quality. The potential cost savings are large enough and the bonuses for the right quality are big enough that an organization may well make more money under an alternative quality contract than under the traditional fee-for-service, at least in the early years. So far, in the first years of the contracts, all the contracted organizations have met the quality targets, gotten the bonuses, and come in under budget, capturing the rebate.

Does this save money? Not immediately. But over time, BCBSMA expects that the organizations will get strong control of their processes and will make enough money on systemic cost savings that BCBSMA will be able to ratchet the budgets downward. The bonuses and incentives will push the providers to make strong structural changes and deploy their resources differently to become low-cost/high-quality providers. Because these changes are structural—strengthening your primary care group and the coordination with specialists and hospitals, forming proper patient disease registries, and investing in strong patient-tracking IT, for instance—the provider can't make these changes for just the BCBSMA patients. The provider has to make the changes for the whole system, serving all patients. They will become organizations focused on providing the best care for the least money, rather than focused on doing more actions that they can bill for.

Once they have done that, they will have learned how to handle risk-based contracting and make money at it. But they will be in a pickle: they will be making money on the risk contracts (like alternative quality contracts) and losing money on the fee-for-service contracts. Now that they know how to make money on risk contracts, the providers will push other payers (other commercial payers, and Medicare and Medicaid) to give them risk contracts for their patients too—and the system will begin to ratchet its costs downward, while giving patients better attention.

From the customers' point of view, the better attention tends to just show up, without any announcement or fanfare or special sign-up procedure. Suddenly, rather than the patient begging for an appointment, the doctor's office is calling them to check on their situation, eager to get them in to keep all the preventive scores up, because the doctor has new incentives. Some patients have called it "concierge care without the concierge fees."

Shopping

If there is one thing we Americans pride ourselves on, it's our skill at shopping. But we are terrible at it in healthcare, because we often lack the information, the ability to choose, and the incentive to choose wisely. People often protest vehemently, "How do you expect a regular person to choose something as complicated as medical care? That's ridiculous!" But we seem to do pretty well choosing complex things like places to live, retirement plans, and computers—with the help of experts who evaluate these things for us and offer alternatives.

If you put the customer at financial risk, you have to give them the opportunity to express their shopping gene. For instance, customers of BCBSMA on the Blue Options plan can find providers near them ranked in tiers based on a combination of cost and quality. The plan steers people to the highest-quality/lowest-cost providers. They can go to any provider that accepts BCBS; they pay more out of pocket depending on how their choice of provider rates on the measure of cost versus quality.*

If you have the Hospital Choice Cost Sharing feature in your plan, you can choose to use a higher-cost facility or a lower-cost facility for the same work, but you will bear a big share of the extra cost if you choose the more expensive one. For instance, suppose you need an MRI. One nearby facility charges $1,250, the other $750, though both have the highest quality ratings. Use the more expensive one, and you will foot a $450 copay. Use the less expensive one, and you pay nothing.

This is a powerful incentive to go for the lowest-cost of the high-quality providers—and a powerful incentive for the providers to get their costs down.

Virtuous Deflationary Spiral

If many of these attempts to corral costs seem anemic in their results, if they are a far cry from "healthcare at half the cost," consider this: all of these reductions are happening in an environment in which every supplier has been keyed to "more, more, more"—a far cry from the ethos of, for instance, consumer electronics, where the way to compete is to provide more in next year's model, but with a lower price tag.

A few examples: Some specialties are far more lucrative than others, including some that practice the inappropriate therapies we looked at earlier. Spine surgery, for instance, is a lucrative specialty in a market in which spine surgeons are reimbursed for thousands of unnecessary and unhelpful complex back fusions for simple back pain every year. Similarly, total knee replacement is a lucrative practice, though not always the best value approach to a problem knee. Kaiser, as a fully capitated system, manages to steer many of its patients with bad backs and knees into lower-cost, lower-risk alternatives with equal or better outcomes, including exercise, weight loss, steroids, and nonsteroidal anti-inflammatories.

---

* Accessed August 18, 20100, on the BCBSMA website: http://www.bluecrossma.com/plan-education/medical/blue-options/index.html.

But Kaiser still does some spine surgeries and total knee replacements. It has to recruit those surgeons in the general market, where being a spine or knee surgeon is a highly lucrative specialty, and has to pay competitive salaries. So despite taking the sensible, lower-cost route with many of its back and knee patients, Kaiser has to pay the market price for its surgeons. If the market stops rewarding inappropriate therapies, the value of back and knee surgeons will fall.

Similarly, a patient in the traditional insurance-supported fee-for-service system getting, say, a cardiac artery bypass graft, would have little incentive to shop around for the best value, or to seek out lower-cost alternatives. But patients on high-deductible plans increasingly will discover that the cost of an airline ticket to Southeast Asia, plus the surgery in a highly rated medical center like Bangkok's Bumrungrad International Hospital, plus hotel stay, can be significantly less than their deductibles and copays stateside. Suddenly all alternatives are being evaluated not against something that costs 5% or 10% less but 70% or 80% less for the same value.

One could pick a similar example from any part of healthcare. These are the same competitive cost pressures that every other industry faces all the time. Until now, the traditional fee-for-service system has sheltered healthcare and its suppliers from them.

When the expectation of a significant part of the market shifts to "we will do this better for less money," we will see a rapid and significant shift in all parts of the market. Companies that have been competing to provide what they claim to be the best solution for as much money as they can get away with, will now compete to provide the provably better solution for less, just as in any other industry.

Do we need another set of laws to restrain us and make us do the right thing? Mostly, the answer is no. What we need, and what we are getting, is far more vigorous and demanding customers, and something approaching real transparency. If we don't create a competitive, risk-accepting provider market ourselves, our customers will find ways to create it for us.

Yes, we all care about the health of the people we serve. We are all in this together, serving the public. Let's all hold hands and sing one more chorus of "Kumbaya" around the campfire. Then let's get back to work to create organizations that are not just not for profit, but "not for comfort," organizations willing and able to take on real risk, to actually compete for customers on the basis of real results and real prices.

Redesigning Markets

The Patient Protection and Affordable Care Act (PPACA) reform law calls for building accountable care organizations (ACOs). These work a lot like the alternative quality contracts we just discussed: they reward large organizations for the total care of a population of patients, while putting those organizations at risk for the quality of the healthcare. When an ACO saves Medicare money through its efficiencies, Medicare kicks back a percentage of the savings to the organization as a reward.

But we don't need to just build ACOs and ACO-like ad hoc arrangements and patient-centered medical homes across healthcare. We need to redesign regional healthcare markets to create real competition for particular types of care.

> The goal: Real competition within each region for measurable price and quality goals at the level at which buyers make choices.

Let's unpack this:

Competition. Real competition exists in a given market when the buyers:
- Have the ability to make choices (they are not locked in by law, contract, or some other constraint)
- Have suppliers of comparable goods and services they can choose among
- Have real information about the costs and benefits of the choices

Buyers. Buyers are those who choose a product and pay for it. The buyers in healthcare are health plans, employers, and government, as well as patients and their families who (together with doctors) drive individual utilization decisions. In a more transparent, consumer-directed world, we can expect the health plans and employers, especially, to get very aggressive in shopping for the best healthcare at the lowest cost.

Region. The definition of *region* (or buyer catchment area) varies with the nature of the service. People will travel for laser eye services or hip replacements if there is a much better provider elsewhere. Birthing? You'd better be able to get there after the contractions start.

Measurement. There is no competition if you can't tell the buyers how much it will actually cost them and show them how good it is.

Level of choice. For the most part, when people go to the doctor or to a clinic, they are not trying to buy healthcare. They are trying to buy solutions to their health problems. Despite all the industry's efforts at branding, patients usually do not make choices based on their perception of which is the best system. Instead, they ask, "What's the best place to deal with my particular problem?"

It's the employer and health plan that must ask the larger questions: "In a consumer-directed system, how do we make the right choices available for the treatment of an aching back, a diabetes diagnosis, a metabolic syndrome, or a pregnancy?" The consumer asks, "What's the best solution?" Employers and health plans increasingly must act at the system level of organization as proxies for their employees and members in order to create the options needed.

If you don't have each of these elements, you don't have a truly competitive market. Increasingly, if medical systems do not create real competition in their area, employers and health plans will find ways to create or find real competition, especially against the medical systems' most profitable service lines.

In the face of these marketplace pressures, we will see a proliferation of ways of working in healthcare. What we need, and what we can bet will arise, are disruptive ideas, disruptive technologies, disruptive business models, and entire disruptive value chains. They'll be disruptive to the extent that they provide solutions to the disjunctures and fissures of the current healthcare marketplace and shoulder aside our current business models.

Explode the Business Model

That's the start: Break the pattern. Kick the fee-for-service habit. Find ways to move at least some portion of medical care outside of the traditional commodified insurance-supported fee-for-service model, which just rewards medical activity, and get it into models that reward results. If you get what you pay for, make sure you're paying for what you want.

As soon as you explode the business model, it becomes really obvious that you have to turn healthcare upside down. The system that is built on the relationship between hospitals and expensive specialists, but with family practitioners and other primary providers only as an afterthought, as mere providers of a "patient stream" for expensive procedures, has to be rebuilt, from the bottom up. It has to be rebuilt on a foundation of strong, smart, dedicated, focused primary care.

Chapter 7

2. Build on Smart Primary Care

Every healthcare system worldwide that delivers healthcare better and cheaper than the U.S. system has a stronger primary care sector. This is by design. Specifics in the policies of other governments support the primary physician.

Our primary physicians have been left to languish.[*] The difference in income between primary care physicians (PCPs) and specialists is huge: The average primary care physician earns 55% of what the average specialist earns, and a mere 30% of what, for instance, an orthopedic surgeon does.[†] Only 27% of primary care physicians describe their practice as "robust" and satisfactory.[‡] Primary care physicians are flocking to sign on with hospitals; hospital employment is rapidly becoming the norm. This year it is expected that an estimated 40% of active primary care physicians will be on hospital payrolls.[§]

Every year the medical schools produce fewer doctors who elect to go into primary care, at the very time when demographic shifts and the reform act mean we are facing a massive shortage of primary care docs. But the money, relatively

---

[*] Otherwise uncredited data about primary care practices on the first two pages of this chapter are from "Blueprint for the Medical Home: Transforming Primary Care to Improve Practice Economics, Care Coordination, and Patient Engagement," Innovations Center, Advisory Board, 2010.

[†] Data include family practice (without OB), internal medicine, and pediatrics/adolescent medicine. "Physician Compensation and Production Survey 2008," based on 2007 data, Medical Group Management Association.

[‡] "2008 Survey of Primary Care Physicians," Merritt Hawkins & Associates, 2008.

[§] Health Care Advisory Board 2008 Survey on Physician Employment Trends.

poor as it is, is not actually the main thing burning docs out of primary care. It's the burden of the work.

Medicine is becoming increasingly complex. The average Medicare beneficiary sees seven physicians across four practices in a year, which means the average PCP is trying to coordinate care with 229 other physicians across 117 practices.*

As health planner Andrea McKillop recently put it to me, "The primary care physicians I know are seriously bent out of shape, but it's less about the money than about the burden of work. Scheduling patients in 10-minute increments does not allow them to give the kind of care they want to. They're upset that some specialists don't appear to give a whit whether they ever get back to them about their patients; they're upset that they don't have good places to refer people for things like inpatient rehab; they're upset that they have to fight insurers to get their patients appropriate, timely, and reasonable medications, treatment, and secondary and tertiary care."†

And on and on. These are, indeed, the complaints I hear across healthcare, all over the country at conferences I'm addressing and over dinner conversations. The job of primary care physicians has become not only not very remunerative, but nearly impossible to perform. All of the changes that would make healthcare work better, faster, and cheaper begin with making the job of the primary care physician easier, more streamlined, and better connected both to the patient and to the rest of the healthcare world.

The Medical Home

The medical home rubric does the job—if it is done right. The experience of different systems across the country shows that it can seriously improve clinical quality, improve the economics of primary care, and make both physicians and their patients happier.

The phrase means far more than just "be a good doc." The goals of the medical home model are pretty clear: Give each patient a real, personal relationship with a physician leading the team responsible for that patient's care—all their care, whether acute, chronic, preventive, or even end of life. Coordinate their care with specialists, hospitals, long-term care centers, however they get care. Track their care (especially their chronic problems) using disease registries and comprehensive medical records. Use information technology to support evidence-based medicine. Involve the patients and their families in decision making. Have open scheduling and expanded hours and other ways of making it more convenient for the patient to get care. And pay for all this by a combination of enhanced fees for

---

* Pham, H., et al., "Primary Care Physicians' Links to Other Physicians through Medicare Patients: The Scope of Care Coordination," *Annals of Internal Medicine*, Vol. 150, 2009, pp. 236–42.

† The Well (http://www.Well.com), private communication, October 12, 2010.

visits, special per-person per-month payments, pay-for-performance incentives, and gain-sharing payments from payers who save money.*

See the following table to compare the ideals of the medical home model to what is too often the regular experience of primary care doctors and their patients:

Medical Home	Common Traditional Experience
Patient centered	Not sharply focused on what the patient wants and needs
Team based, using other team members "at the top of their license"	Doctor often does all the care
Tracked	Chronic patients often lost in the shuffle
Coordinated	Communication with other parts of the system difficult, slow, incomplete, and sometimes nonexistent
Information dense	Information sparse; patient often feels uncertain what test results or diagnoses mean; physician often lacks information from test results, specialists, or hospital encounters
Evidence based	Based on physician's previous training, habits, and memory
Transparent	Opaque to the patient and family
Convenient	Convenient only for the physician

It seems like a tall order. Yet various pilot programs have shown that it can be done: all this can be given to the patient, while the physician makes a better income. It takes organizing it and understanding it. A great deal of information about how to build a medical home, the economics of medical homes, and the requirements for rating medical homes is now easily available.†

---

* http://www.medicalhomeinfo.org/about/medical_home/index.aspx.
† The American Academy of Pediatrics provides an excellent set of guides and a "Building Your Medical Home" toolkit at http://www.medicalhomeinfo.org.
   The American Academy of Family Physicians (http://www.aafp.org/online/en/home.html) has its own helpful, clear guides and toolkit.
   The Advisory Board has put out a thoughtful, comprehensive guide: "Blueprint for the Medical Home: Transforming Primary Care to Improve Practice Economics, Care Coordination, and Patient Engagement," Innovations Center, Advisory Board, 2010.
   The National Center for Quality Assurance (NCQA) has published program standards: "Standards and Guidelines for Physician Practice Connections—Patient-Centered Medical Home," available at http://www.ncqa.org/tabid/631/Default.aspx.

Medical homes have been built in many different parts of healthcare, structured in many different ways. Hospitals can help establish them with physicians in their employ, physicians in physician-hospital organizations (PHOs), or they can help independent physicians to understand and implement the necessary changes in their practices. Medicaid programs have sponsored medical home projects in some states; employers have sponsored them. Some have been designed for specific medical populations, such as people with diabetes, or "frequent fliers" in emergency departments, the small part of the population who keep coming back over and over again.

How a Medical Home Actually Works

The experience of practices that have implemented medical home models shows that the size of the investment can vary enormously. For example, the Capital District Health Plan in Albany, New York, founded and run by physicians, decided to pilot the medical home idea in three practices, based on a risk-adjusted capitated payment model—that is, they got paid a set amount per patient, per month, adjusted to the level of risk that each patient represented. To make the transition, the physicians invested in an electronic medical records (EMR) system, and hired an extra nurse practitioner, another RN, a data manager for the electronic records and registries, a half-time nutritionist, and a half-time social worker. It was a big investment.

Integrated Health Partners of Battle Creek, Michigan, took the opposite tack. A 180-physician physician-hospital organization (PHO) jointly owned by the Calhoun County Physicians and Battle Creek Health System, it moved to a medical home model (specifically the Wagner's Chronic Care Model) by leveraging existing staff and using an open source disease registry (which keeps track of all the patients with a given chronic condition, such as diabetes or cardiovascular problems).[*]

The Health Care Advisory Board has estimated the added annual costs of converting a practice to a full medical home model at $10,500 to $52,100 for a sole practitioner leveraging existing staff, and $126,00 to $346,500 for a five-physician practice hiring two RN health coaches.[†]

---

[*] Porter, S., "N.Y. Initiative Couples Payment Reform and Practice Reform," *AAFP News Now*, American Academy of Family Physicians, June 6, 2008.

Goroll, A., et al., "Fundamental Payment Reform for Adult Primary Care," *Journal of General Internal Medicine*, Vol. 22, pp. 410–15.

[†] "Blueprint for the Medical Home: Transforming Primary Care to Improve Practice Economics, Care Coordination, and Patient Engagement," Innovations Center, Advisory Board, 2010.

Doctors can convert to a medical home model on the cheap. On the other hand, in the experience of most practices trying it, investing in it up front is faster, and gets them more quickly to the increased revenue that it will bring in.

Making More Money by Being a Better Doctor

In a well-structured medical home, the costs are more than offset by additional revenue. Consider Mercy Clinics, a 150-physician group (70% primary), employed by Mercy Medical Center in Des Moines, Iowa. They estimated a four-to-one return on investment from hiring RN health coaches. The coaches got chronic care patients more compliant on treatment, which meant more office visits and tests, better documentation, and upcoding of office visits to greater complexity (doctors get paid more for office visits that take care of more complex problems). The Health Care Advisory Board's example analysis of one of the Mercy Clinics (a 10-physician practice) showed increased annual revenue of $122,000 from increased diabetes care and testing, $114,000 from pay-for-performance bonuses, and $15,000 from saved nurse and physician time, against costs of $73,000 for health coach staffing, $10,000 for a more expensive microalbumin test, and $5,000 for a more expensive HbA1c test, for a total bottom-line contribution of $163,000. The basic "business case" for the medical home includes increased office visit revenue, increased lab revenue, shared medical appointments, capturing pay-for-performance incentive fees, and increased clinician productivity (by having all clinicians operating "at the top of their license," that is, spending most of their time at their highest and best use).[*]

Taking on Risk

Once again, notice how the medical home rubric ties into the other parts of the framework. The model shares risk with primary care physicians, pays them for taking on that risk, and rewards them for actions that result in better outcomes. A medical home is a strong method of integrating clinically and economically with other parts of the healthcare system, even if the doctors remain independent. The idea proposes new business models and arrangements that will support the medical home to make healthcare better and cheaper at the same time.

---

[*] "Mercy Clinics: The Medical Home," *Group Practice Journal*, April 2008.
Swieskowski, D., "Improving Chronic Care: Health Coaches and the Business Case", available at http://www.idph.state.ia.us/hcr_committees/common/pdf/prevention_chronic_care_mgmt/improvingchronic_care_presentation.pdf.
"Blueprint for the Medical Home."

The Massachusetts Blues' Alternative Quality Contract is one example of how that works in detail.

Integration: It's Not Just "Kumbaya"

If you're thoughtful, if you're thinking about how healthcare in the United States actually works, if you've been following the bouncing ball here about why it costs so much for such mediocre results, if you've been thinking about all the partnerships in the examples in the previous section, you're thinking: integrate. Get the docs and the hospitals playing on the same team. Align the incentives.

If you've ever tried any version of this patchwork, Rube-Goldberg-style, bee-corralling exercise, you're thinking, *Good luck with that.*

Acres of print in *Health Affairs*; the entire suite of studies from Dartmouth's Institute for Health Policy and Clinical Practice; the books I have mentioned by Porter and Teisberg, and Christensen, Grossman, and Hwang; "The Cost Conundrum," Atul Gawande's justly famous article in the June 1, 2009, *New Yorker*; the writings of Regina Herzlinger, Elliot Fisher, Don Berwick, Jack Wennberg, Karen Davis, and a host of other thoughtful analysts—all have somewhat differing prescriptions for fixing the mess we are in.

But all these sources, my examination of systems across the country, and countless discussions with healthcare executives and economists, make it abundantly clear that the answer (or answers) lies in the direction of some kind of integration. The organizations in U.S. healthcare that seem to work best, that provide the highest-quality healthcare at the most reasonable cost—the organizations that continually pop up as examples of healthcare done better all operate at some greater than average level of integration. There's Pennsylvania's Geisinger Health System, which studied its processes to be able to offer the first warranties for surgeries. In Temple, Texas, there is Scott and White, a large integrated multispecialty practice that dominates its region and has brought healthcare costs significantly below the rest of Texas. Salt Lake-based Intermountain Health is famous for pushing the frontiers on patient safety and quality. There are Kaiser Permanente, the oldest and largest of the staff model HMOs; the Bozeman [Montana] Clinic; the Mayo Clinic; and the Cleveland Clinic—all work from some form of integration.

In many markets across the country, healthcare institutions are hiring physicians by the boatload because many physicians are desperate to find a way to make a living, and many healthcare institutions are desperate to rationalize their patient flow. But a hired physician is not an integrated physician.

And a hired physician is often not a productive physician. More than one healthcare CEO I have talked to has used the phrase "dead men walking" to describe hired physicians, usually older physicians with long-established work habits, suddenly released from decades of having to grind patients through the mill in order to make a living, now "retired on the job." Truly integrated care runs much deeper than a paycheck. It's a philosophy and a way of life, and not every physician is ready for it.

At the same time, physicians who have sold their practices to a health system and taken salaries often end up regretting it. The litany of complaints is long and brutal, and most of them speak to how tone-deaf hospital managers can be. Doctors complain that they are not paid fairly. They often are surprised to see that they no longer get income from in-house imaging, and they may discover that the fine print says that they are on the hook for all their old receivables; that is, the money that insurers or customers owed them when they sold has now become money that they owe the hospital. They are surprised to be told that their practice is a money loser in need of subsidy, though it was profitable when they owned it, because the hospital's overhead is causing all the red ink. Doctors may find their practice shifted across town, away from their patient base, and then find themselves blamed for not bringing in enough patients. Their hours may be shifted, their patient caseload increased, or their longtime assistants taken away, all without consulting them. And once they regret it, they may find that they can't get out of the agreement without moving out of town, because they signed a noncompete agreement as part of the sale.

But it is no news that if you do something badly it doesn't work—and there are a thousand ways to integrate with physicians.

The old image of partnering between physicians and hospitals was that there was only one model. It was simple, loose, and voluntary. The emerging image of partnerships is that there are many models, simple and complex, and they are contractual, built to the purpose of an overarching business model with specific goals and incentives.

None of these partnerships can work without clarity on what it is that the whole partnership is trying to produce: evidence-based health.

From Evidence-Based Medicine to Evidence-Based Health

Over the last decade, it has become common for hospitals and physicians to brag that they practice evidence-based medicine, that is, standardized medicine based on industry-wide clinical guidelines backed up by the best data that medical science can provide. That seems obvious to an outsider. Which of us would tell our doctor or surgeon, "Evidence-based medicine? Nah, give me the other stuff, the kind with no evidence." Yet the adoption of standardized, evidence-based medicine has been a long, slow slog in healthcare; it is still not industry-wide, and it is still not as widespread as the bragging about it is.

At the same time, it has become evident that evidence-based medicine is not enough, that it is only part of a more comprehensive goal: evidence-based health.*

Evidence-based medicine looks at a patient coming into the ER in diabetic shock and asks: "What are the proven, standardized best methods for stabilizing this patient, getting him out of shock and back to a condition in which his blood sugar is balanced and he is ready to go home?"

Evidence-based health asks a broader question: "How did this patient end up here with this preventable condition? What will it take to help her so that she doesn't end up back here with the same condition next week?"

Evidence-based health is a backbone-brilliant concept that actually produces better healthcare, and better health, for significantly less money—and a concept that America may be too politically hypnotized to ever put into wide practice. "Evidence-based" means it's about what really works—"health," because that's the goal.

Medicine is not itself the goal, it's a tool. Evidence-based medicine doesn't get you there. Evidence-based health hooks up advanced medical home primary practices with community health, behavioral health, and other staff right in their office, to help patients do what they need to do to get healthier. Most interventions in chronic disease fail for reasons that have nothing to do with medicine. To make them work, you have to get out there in the community and deal with what gets in the way of health.

Good solid evidence-based health primary care saves large amounts of money while making people healthier.

Explode the Business Model and Build on Smart Primary Care

So the first two points: Find ways to move at least some portion of medical care outside of the traditional insurance-supported fee-for-service model that rewards medical activity and instead get it into models that reward results. If you get what you pay for, make sure you're paying for what you want.

And build the whole structure on a foundation of strong, smart, primary care.

It turns out, though, that you can't do either of these working with individuals. You have to work with teams.

---

* Moskowitz, D., and Bodenheime, T., "Moving from Evidence-Based Medicine to Evidence-Based Health," *Journal of General Internal Medicine*, January 4, 2011, doi: 10.1007/s11606-010-1606-47, accessed August 19, 2011, at http:// www.ncbi.nlm.nih.gov/pubmed/21203858.

Chapter 8

3. Put a Crew on It

There's a conundrum at the heart of healthcare.

Medicine has always been a solo affair: one doctor, one patient. The doctor uses his or her own training and judgment. On a particularly tough case, the doctor might consult with a colleague. More often, the doctor will refer the patient to a specialist, who also works alone. Even doctors in large, multispecialty practices do not work as part of a team. They have staff, of course: clerical staff, people to process claims, a receptionist, a nurse to help out. But there is little truly collegial about most of medicine. Traditional medicine is solo work, not teamwork.

There's the conundrum: Survey the literature about the cost, quality, and effectiveness of medicine, visit hundreds of hospitals and clinics, talk to doctors and administrators, looking for what really works, and you won't really see a deep divide between for-profit or not-for-profit medicine, between church based or government based, between doctors that are in their own group practices and those that take a salary from a system like Kaiser or the VA. The one deep divide that you will find is this: all effective and efficient healthcare is team based. In one way or another, groups of people bringing their diverse talents and training to bear to deliver better medicine, more evidence-based health, more efficiently, than doctors working alone.

This is one of the key advantages of groups like Mayo, the Cleveland Clinic, Geisinger, the Bozeman Clinic, Texas' Scott and White, and Kaiser. Mayo is the oldest and still the largest multispecialty practice. The Cleveland Clinic, Geisinger, Scott and White, and the Bozeman Clinic are nearly as old and organized along similar lines. The doctors at 70-year-old Kaiser are organized as the Permanente Medical Group. The details of their structure and payment systems are not identical. But in one way or another, these doctors' incomes do not depend on how many medical actions they personally can bill for. Rather, they depend on the collective reputation of the group as a whole. For that, they depend on one another. Their payment structure, with all of them on salary to a group that makes its living on its reputation, aligns directly with the reality of the best medicine: delivering it through tight teamwork is what works most consistently at the lowest cost. But several things are at least as important for these groups as their structure: they tend to work physically close to one another. They see each other all the time in the course of a normal day's work, outside of formal referrals and consultations. All of these groups have deeply collegial traditions. You won't make it as a Mayo doc or Kaiser doc if you try to just do things your own way. All of these groups have a team-based culture that brings people other than the doctors themselves into direct patient care.

We also see this pattern in many of the high-end, specialized "solution shops" we mentioned before, such as Texas's M.D. Anderson Cancer Center; National Jewish Health in Denver for pulmonary disease, particularly asthma; or the Texas Heart Institute: tight, specialized teams who can work together to learn from their experience.

A Team Care Example: Diabetes

In a traditional physician encounter with a patient with diabetes, the doctor might simply counsel the patient to watch his or her diet and sugar intake, give him or her a prescription, and give him or her whatever other advice could be sandwiched into a few minutes in the exam room—that is, if the patient even came in for an examination in the first place.

In contrast, an evidence-based diabetes team, set up to work with a population of people with diabetes (say, all the diabetes patients of a multispecialty practice) might include as many as 11 people in one capacity or another. For instance, it might include:

- The primary care physician on each case
- An endocrinologist
- A nephrologist (kidney specialist)
- A dentist, a podiatrist, an ophthalmologist (because people with diabetes get into serious problems with their teeth, feet, and eyes)
- A pharmacist
- A psychologist or other behavioral specialist (to help the patients deal with the family and personal problems that are preventing them from taking good care of themselves)

- A data nurse to keep the patient registry and mine the data for patterns and outliers, and to maintain strong communications with the patients
- A nutrition education specialist (since people don't necessarily know how to watch their diet and sugar intake without some help)
- A community health specialist (to help them find what they need, from better places to shop for food, less expensive diabetes supplies, and better insurance access, to a more convenient bus route or jitney to get them in for appointments)

Such a team can bring highly efficient but customized and detailed care to a surprising number of patients, lowering their costs by improving their health.

Teamwork at All Levels

The need for tight coordination goes far beyond clinical teams. Healthcare has long been characterized by loose affiliations of professionals and institutions, and what we might call loading dock relationships between institutions and their suppliers and affiliates, in which the institution is just a customer, not a partner. Health plans have traditionally had only an adversarial relationship with institutions, clinics, and doctors. Employers, among the largest payers for healthcare, have for the most part had no relationship at all with the institutions and organizations that actually supply what they are paying for. The contrast between typical healthcare relationships and the tight relationships between, say, Toyota and General Motors and their suppliers, or between Boeing and its suppliers and customers, is striking.

For instance, far from seeking out the best, most innovative, and least expensive solutions to clinical problems in the supply chain, healthcare institutions in recent years have increasingly set up structures specifically designed to make it difficult for innovative vendors to even get a hearing within the institution's walls. If you design a new walker, for instance, that reduces the staff necessary to help a patient stroll down the hallway, you often have to pay an outside vendor certification firm a large fee just to be admitted to make your case to a hospital's materials manager. And the materials manager is often given incentives to keep new products out, or to evaluate products solely on unit costs rather than system costs. If your walker that reduces staff costs has a slightly higher price tag than the traditional one, you have no hope of having it accepted. You certainly have no hope of talking to the hospital's chief financial officer, who would be able to see the systemic advantages of your innovation. And every time you want to talk to another hospital, even one in the same chain, you have to get recertified and pay another huge fee to the vendor certification firm.

This is one tiny example of the thousands of ways that parts of the healthcare system are not at all on the same team. Institutional barriers have arisen that discourage working toward the common goal of serving the customer better for less.

Getting on the Same Team with the Docs

How should physicians and hospitals and other parts of healthcare get on the same team? Every which way. That's the real, pragmatic answer: every way that might work with the resources in their area, the payers in that market, and the other physicians in the area. There is no law of gravity that says that physicians must be on the same paycheck as everybody else. But they must find ways to work more tightly with the rest of healthcare—and healthcare must find ways to work more tightly with its suppliers, payers, and customers.

The Vermont Blueprint is a good example. This project places community health teams in primary care offices. Led by nurses, these teams are charged with tracking chronic patients and offering whatever help they need to manage their situation, as well as coordinating the physicians' offices with community prevention efforts. The cost, which is borne jointly by private and government payers, comes to roughly $350,000 per team per year. Each team can cover about 20,000 people. Do the arithmetic: $17 per patient per year. Result: better health, 22% lower cost in inpatient admissions, 36% lower cost in emergency visits, and 11.6% lower costs overall.[*] That's big—and this was for a population, including working people, uninsured, children, and Medicare-age people.

Clinical teamwork can make a huge difference in outcomes for patients. For instance, Kaiser of Northern California set out 10 years ago to lower the rate of heart attacks (acute myocardial infarctions (AMIs)) among its members. They put a crew on it, clinical teams who worked together toward that single goal. Over 10 years they were able to lower the rate of AMIs by 24%, and serious AMIs requiring hospitalization and surgery by 68%.[†] That's good work.

Geisinger in northeastern Pennsylvania is an integrated system, working mostly with its own salaried physicians. But its insurance company, Geisinger Choice, insures many patients of independent doctors in the area. Geisinger went to these independent primary care physicians with a deal: We will pay

---

[*] Bielaszka-DuVernay, C., "Vermont's Blueprint for Medical Homes, Community Health Teams, and Better Health at Lower Cost," *Health Affairs*, Vol. 30, No. 3, 2011, pp. 383–86, available at http://content.healthaffairs.org/content/30/3/383.full.html.

[†] Yeh, R., et al., "Population Trends in the Incidence and Outcomes of Acute Myocardial Infarction," *New England Journal of Medicine*, Vol. 362, No. 23, 2010, accessed August 19, 2011, at http://www.nejm.org.

for an extra nurse to work in your office. Her sole job will be to track your chronic patients. We believe we will save money by doing this. We will share the savings with you 50/50, if you promise to spread that rebate out across your whole staff. The result of this simple intervention? An 18% reduction in hospital admissions for those tracked patients—and a 7% reduction in their overall healthcare costs.*

North Shore/LIJ Health System has been offering a deal to independent doctors in its area: You're computerizing your office? We'll pay half. If you do it in a way that allows us to share your data, so we can track what works and what doesn't in dealing with chronic disease, we'll pay 85%. Put that together with incentives in the HITECH Act (part of the 2009 ARRA "stimulus" legislation), and doctors in the North Shore/LIJ area can actually make a profit computerizing their offices.

These are all examples of ways to knit doctors more tightly with each other, and with the hospitals and other providers in their area.

Increasingly we are seeing a different kind of team in healthcare: teams actually built around the patient. One of the best examples has risen out of a chronically underfunded and underserviced population: Native Americans, particularly the Alaska Natives.

Alaska Native Healthcare

In a 2008 paper† describing their health system in *Family Practice Management*, Katherine Gottlieb, Ileen Sylvester, and Dr. Douglas Eby commented:

> There's a lot of talk in health care today about being "patient centered." Unfortunately, what that usually means is that the patient is put in the middle and then all the "really smart, professional people" stand around and try to decide what's best for that person.

The Alaska Natives healthcare story is really quite different, unexpected, perhaps unexpectable, yet it illustrates a working model of much of what we are talking about here.

---

* Abelson, R., "A Health Insurer Pays More to Save," *New York Times*, June 21, 2010.
† Gottlieb, K., et al., "Transforming Your Practice: What Matters Most—When Customers Drive the System, It Changes Everything—for the Better," *Family Practice Management*, Vol. 15, No. 1, 2008, pp. 32–38, available at http://www.aafp.org/fpm/2008/0100/p32.html.

The healthcare of Native Alaskans for generations came under the Indian Health Service (IHS). In 1975, Congress recognized that it would be better if Native Americans could be in charge of their own healthcare, and set up a mechanism to hand over the management of healthcare to tribal governments that could take it on. In the 1980s, under the tribal authority of the Cook Inlet Region, Inc., the Southcentral Foundation (SCF) began the process, contracting from the IHS for specific services. By 1999, they were ready for the new Alaska Native Health Corporation to take over all the health services for Native Alaskans in 150,000 square miles of Alaska from the Kenai Peninsula to the Bering Straits, and from the Aleutian Islands to Anchorage. With the Alaska Tribal Health Consortium, the SCF owns and manages the Alaska Native Medical Center, which includes a 150-bed hospital in Anchorage, along with an array of clinics and other services.

Rather than simply duplicate the traditional, straight fee-for-service, doctor-centered service, the SCF set out to build a service entirely on what the Native Alaskans saw as their tribal values. They asked the people they were serving: What would medical care look like if it started from the patient out—the patient, the family, the tribe—rather from the doctor and the payer?

The first instance is obvious to any outsider: when a Native Alaskan shows up at a Native Alaskan health facility, the people behind the counter look familiar, because most of them are Native Alaskans, as well. So are most of the clinicians and other people they might encounter in the exam room or lab.

But the differences are far more pervasive and subtle. Tribal culture tends to be more family and group oriented. So the exam rooms are large enough to include the family in the discussion, when the patient would like the support.

Similarly, the doctors have no private offices. There are private "talking rooms" available for confidential discussions, but the doctors' desks are in group carrels especially designed as a base for the entire core clinical team: one or two primary care providers (doctors, nurse practitioners, or physician assistants), their medical assistants, the nurse case manager and the case management assistants, and the behavioral specialist.

This team together manages the health of a panel of patients that typically might number 1,200 or so. The patients can pick their own team to be attached to. But as much as possible, those patients see only that team and the team sees only the patients for whose health they are responsible.

And responsible they are, for the core of the system is this: the doctors and other clinicians are on salary. How much money they make does not depend on how many patients they see in a day, or how many procedures or tests they order and bill for. Their bonuses, salary increases, and promotion depend not on their own individual success, but on the team's success in caring for that panel of patients.

So the service has exploded the fee-for-service business model at the primary level, and built teams that can make more money not by doing more procedures, but by improving the health and healthcare of a set group of patients.

So how's that working for them? Direct cost comparisons don't work so well, since the revamped service is substantially different from the old service, incorporating more services, more revenue streams, and more payers (such as Medicare, Medicaid, and private insurance). But tracking the data of their patients from the time of the tribal takeover to the present, the Southcentral Foundation reports that their population has shown a 50% drop in emergency and urgent care, a 40% drop in hospital admissions, a 60% drop in the use of specialists, a 70% drop in pediatric asthma admissions, and even a 20% drop in primary care visits, since many problems are now taken care of over the phone or through email. At the same time, their quality scores (using the industry-standard Healthcare Effectiveness Data and Information Set (HEDIS) tool) have risen into a consistent 75 to 90 percentile range. And satisfaction surveys of both staff and customers have risen from the 20% range to be consistently over 90%.*

What Makes a Team? A Scoreboard

Pay a clinical organization by its results—better process markers, better measurable outcomes—and it turns into a team really fast. Its members become a team, focused on the scoreboard. Or they go out of business. Just like anyone else in any other business. Figure out what the customers need and give it to them. Or go home.

Remember our two cardinal rules of economics from the first section?

People do what you pay them to do.
People do *exactly* what you pay them to do.

Find the measurable markers that serve as reliable proxies for what you really want, and pay for those markers, and you'll get what you want. That's what we are seeing in the Alaska Natives example, the BCBSMA Alternative Quality Contracts example, and other examples popping up around healthcare: physicians and provider organizations are being paid for better health and better healthcare, rather than doing tests, procedures, and visits.

There is art and science to getting the markers right. There are process markers and outcome markers. A process marker for a diabetes patient might be whether

---

* Eby, D., MD, MPH, "The SCF/NUKA Model: Customer-Owned, Customer-Driven Healthcare—Facility Design: Primary Care," PowerPoint presentation, February 7, 2011.

that patient's A1c score (his or her average blood glucose level) was known within the last 60 days. An outcome marker would be whether the A1c score was within the acceptable range—something much harder to achieve, as it requires much more cooperation from the patient, and much more engagement from the provider. In scoring providers for their quality bonuses, BCBSMA gives outcome measures three times the weight of process measures.

The best markers are measurable outcomes that are directly linked to major chronic diseases, especially the kinds of diseases that we can do something about and that patients can easily ignore until something catastrophic and irreversible happens, like diabetes and hypertension. Working with customers (patients, members) to make those markers improve is something that both payers and customers will gladly pay for, especially because it is amazingly cheaper than trying to clean up the results of untreated chronic disease.

Explode the Business Model, Build on Smart Primary Care, and Put a Crew on It

So now we have three strategies working together: Kick out the walls of the traditional insurance-supported fee-for-service business model. Get away from rewarding mere medical activity. Start rewarding results.

Build the whole structure on a foundation of strong, smart primary care.

Reward teams for providing not just evidence-based medicine, but evidence-based health.

New business models. Strong primary care. Teams. But to make these three work, we need another element: we've got to give the customer some serious help.

Chapter 9

4. Swarm the Customer

Give the customer more help, not less, in becoming and staying healthy. Do it in every way that works, in language and modes the customer wants and will work with. Give special help to those who cost the system the most.

In Washington and the state capitals, every policy discussion about how to save money in healthcare is focused on how to provide less: less medical care, less help of all kinds. No example we can find of actually reducing the real costs of the whole system did it by cutting back, by rationing, by throttling supply. Every example that works does it by providing more help, but smarter help, earlier, closer to the customers, in their faces, in their ears, in their pockets.

Some people will call this an extension of the "nanny state," a further intrusion of the government, or your employer, or some massive health plan, into our private lives and our private choices. But none of these programs are coercive. Truly coercive programs don't work. You can't order anyone to lose weight or stop smoking, and if you try you'll just make it less likely that they will give it a try themselves. People have to want to be healthier.

On the other hand, your individual choice to not try to make yourself healthier is putting a burden on the whole system and costing the rest of us a lot of money. So it's not unreasonable to say that you should pay a bit more for making that choice. Call it a disincentive.

The Magic of Mr. Moon

In the late 1990s Darrell Moon quit being a hospital executive. He had worked at a number of institutions, he had risen to the CEO level, he was good at it, he understood how the system worked.

That's why he quit. He had real clarity on how the system worked and he could see why the costs were rising, he could see why people were not getting what they needed. And he thought he could see how to change that.

Mr. Moon is a Mormon in Salt Lake City with a passel of kids. He's a slim, reserved man with close-trimmed gray hair and a quiet ferocity about what he is doing.

In 2011, his small company had a bit of a coming out. It changed its name to Orriant. It built a new website. And after more than a dozen years, it released its first quantified results: the costs and outcomes of its four largest clients over the previous four years. To someone used to looking at cost graphs in health-care, the graphs tucked away on the company's website can be rather startling. Most of them compare the cost trend of the clients' employees who signed up for Orriant's wellness plans with those who did not sign up. The trend lines of those who did not sign up mimic the trend lines of the rest of the country, high and rising steeply in every category: doctor's office claims, emergency claims, inpatient and outpatient hospital claims, pharmaceutical claims, total claims. The trend lines of those in Orriant's wellness programs are dramatically lower. Total claims end up at about a third of those of the nonparticipants. Hospital claims, ER claims, and doctor's office claims are actually lower for the partici-pants at the end of the period than at the beginning.

The fine print explains that the data leave out outliers, people with claims greater than $30,000 in a given year. This seems fair, for two reasons: people of working age who, for instance, contract something like metastatic pancreatic cancer are in most cases the least likely to have been helped by a wellness pro-gram. And for small and medium-sized companies, a single outlier can easily obscure the underlying trend, the great difference in costs between those who participate in wellness programs and those who do not.

One typical client is a chain of auto dealerships. Over a five-year period, total healthcare costs for the dealerships' 1,400 employees dropped 7%, over a period in which the country as a whole experienced a 44% rise. By the end of the period, the average premium cost for the dealerships' employees was $3,574 less than the Utah average, and $4,293 less than the national average. Over those five years, the company saved $6 million.

The employees in the program were healthier, showing marked year-over-year improvements in such markers as body mass index, cholesterol, blood glucose, blood pressure, and triglycerides. And the employees were happy with the program: 66% rated it "very good" or "excellent." Another 26% rated it "good," while only 8% called it "fair" or "poor."

What's Mr. Moon's magic? How does his wellness program get so much better results?

It seems to be a mixture of three elements.

First, the wellness program is carefully structured based on evidence of what works and what doesn't, culled from what is now several decades of pilots and experiments across the country in a variety of settings.

Second, behavioral health is not an afterthought. The wellness program leads with behavioral assessments and goals. This is for a very simple reason: studies of the risk factors present in high healthcare spenders show with remarkable consistency that the top factors, by a large margin, are not physical. They are psychological. The two biggest predictors of high use of healthcare resources are depression and stress.* Help people deal with depression, stress, and anxiety, and you help them change their life, which includes changing their health.

The most important reason that people don't change the habits that hurt their health is because they don't believe they can. Darrell Moon has found that people don't actually believe that they have much control over their own decisions: what they eat, how much alcohol or drugs they consume, how much they exercise.

So the health counselor working with the employee gets him or her to set some goals. They don't have to be big goals. They don't even have to be health goals. An initial goal would not be "stop smoking." It might be just "count your cigarettes in writing." The early goals are designed to be so simple that the employee is almost guaranteed to meet them. This is simply to train them to the thought that they can decide to do something differently, and do it. For many people, this by itself is a life-changing revelation.

The third magic element is incentives. People who do not sign up for the program pay a little more in premiums, and those who do sign up a little less. The difference in premium between those who opt in and those who opt out varies with each employer, but it might amount to $100 or $200 per month. The amounts are another carefully studied design element, as they are in the CIGNA Choice Fund and similar programs. They must be large enough to make a real difference to the employees, but not so large as to seem punitive or impossible. These incentives encourage people to sign on to the program, to set goals, and to meet them on a consistent basis, so that they have that extra $100 or $200 in their pocket every month.

Part of the magic in Mr. Moon's programs from the employers' point of view is that typically some 20% to 30% of the employees elect not to sign up, but

---

* Goetzel, A., Whitmer, R.W., et al., "Association between Health Risks and Medical Expenditures," *Journal of Occupational and Environmental Medicine*, Vol. 40, No. 10, 1998, pp. 1–12.

choose simply to pay the higher premiums—and those higher premiums pay for the whole wellness program for those who do sign up. The extra cost is borne entirely by those who choose not to try to improve their health.*

A medium-sized business dropping healthcare costs by 7% in a period when the rest of us are getting hit with a rise of 44%, while the employees get healthier—that's not bad. Not bad at all.

But there is still one thing missing. Bill Antonello, a regional segment marketing officer for CIGNA (and heavily involved in CIGNA's Choice Fund rollout), put it most succinctly to me: "The only people who we get into wellness programs are those who don't need it." The people who choose to pay an extra premium to not sit down with a health counselor and set a few easy goals correlate pretty well with those who have the most health problems, who are most likely to be overweight, depressed, anxious, smokers, or have problems with substance abuse.

Almost every discussion of how to fix healthcare comes, at some point, to the subject of these people, the outliers who for one reason or another can't or won't take care of themselves and who suck up an inordinate amount of the healthcare dollar.

What do we do about them? It turns out that the easiest, simplest, least expensive, most effective strategy is not to give them less help, but more help. Way more.

The Pareto Principle in Healthcare

In 1906 an Italian gardener named Vilfredo Pareto was harvesting his peas, when something interesting struck him. Pareto was an amateur gardener, but a professional economist, so the things that struck him as interesting in his garden might be different from what the rest of us might notice. He noticed that some pods held far more peas than other pods. He began to track the high-volume pods and the low-volume pods, and discovered that 20% of the pods delivered 80% of the peas. Pareto had been studying land ownership, so he dug into his data and, sure enough, he found that 80% of the land in Italy was owned by 20% of the people. He wrote his findings for economic journals, and went on to find similar patterns elsewhere. Joseph Juran, the late twentieth-century business consultant and champion of quality management, named this the Pareto principle. Others call it the 80/20 rule, though there is nothing sacred about the exact ratio. It has become a common rule of thumb in business, such as "80% of your sales come from 20% of your customers," or "80% of your defects come from 20% of your processes." The implication, usually, is "pay more attention to the 20% than to the other 80%."

---

* Interviews with Moon, D., material from Orriant.com. Case studies sent by D. Moon.

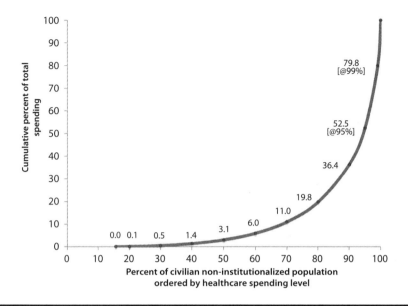

Figure 9.1   Percent of population using percent of healthcare dollar.

The Pareto principle is vividly present in healthcare. In any given year 80% of the costs are generated by 20% of the people.

That makes sense, of course: most people are healthy at any given time.

But as you slice the statistics differently, it becomes even more vivid: half of the costs are generated by just 5% of the people. In fact, a full 20% of the costs are generated by 1% of the people.

Take a look at Figure 9.1.* It's pretty thought provoking when you study it. It shows how much each percentage of the population spends on healthcare in a given year. Find the 50% mark: half the population spends only 3% of the money. Most of us have a physical, maybe, go to the doctor with the flu, maybe, get a vaccination, maybe, but not much else.

Find the 80% mark: it fits Pareto's 80/20 rule almost exactly. Eighty percent of the population spends 19.8% of the healthcare resources, the other 20% spend 80.2%. At the 95% level, we finally break the halfway mark in expenditures: that top 5% of the population uses 47.5% of the healthcare dollar (that is, 100 minus 52.5). The top 1%? They use 20.2% (100 minus 79.8).

---

* National Institute for Health Care Management Foundation, analysis of data from the 2008 Medical Expenditure Panel Survey, available at http://www.meps.ahrq.gov/data_stats/meps_query.jsp. Published in "Understanding U.S. Health Care Spending." NIHCM Foundation Data Brief, July 2011.

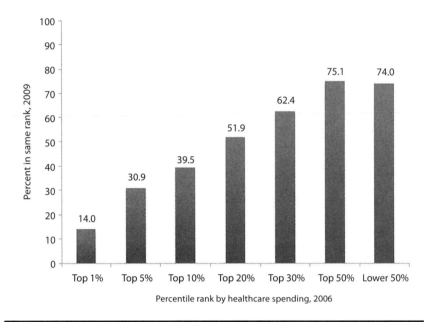

Figure 9.2 Percent of the population in the same healthcare spending rank two years later.

That's a big chunk.

But it gets more interesting when you ask, "Who are these people? Why do they cost so much?" Some of them, of course, just got hit by a bus or contracted pancreatic cancer. Some of them are premature newborns spending months in the neonatal intensive care unit. Such people are getting intensive care now, but by next year they probably won't be, one way or another. More interesting, because their costs are more manageable, are those who are in the same high-spending category year after year.

Of the highest-spending 1%, most quickly died or got better, but 14% were still in that category the next year (Figure 9.2). Of the top 5%, the ones who use half of all the resources, nearly 31% were still there the next year. Of the top 20%, who use 80% of all the resources, more than half were there the next year.[*]

Who are these people who, year after year, spend more than 80% of the healthcare dollar? The great majority are people with multiple poorly managed

---

[*] Center for Financing, Access, and Cost Trends, Agency for Healthcare Research and Quality, Household Component of the Medical Expenditure Panel Survey, HC-114 (Panel 11, 2006–2007). Cited in Cohen, S., and Yu, W., "The Concentration and Persistence in the Level of Health Expenditures over Time: Estimates for the U.S. Population, 2006–2007," Medical Expenditure Panel Survey, Statistical Brief 278, AHRQ, March 2010.

chronic problems, such as diabetes, congestive heart failure (CHF), or chronic obstructive pulmonary disorder (COPD). Many of them are frail elderly people who are in and out of the hospital repeatedly. Others are the outliers of the healthcare world, often morbidly obese, or with compromised immune systems, or with addictions or psychological problems that land them repeatedly in the ER and the hospital.

By and large, we don't treat these people's chronic conditions, only their acute crises. We don't help them manage their condition. We don't help them plot a return to health. We don't help them deal with the underlying problems that cause them to be sick.

What would it look like if we did? What if we aggressively went after the top 1%, the top 5%, with help, resources, advice, and attention?

We don't have to wonder, because some people have done it.

Hotspotting

About 10 years ago a doctor in Camden, New Jersey, got appointed to a police reform commission. As reported in *The New Yorker* magazine by writer/surgeon Atul Gawande, Dr. Jeffrey Brenner, a local family physician, saw a presentation about hotspotting. Police in recent decades have used simple geographic information systems (GIS) to make strategy decisions. Imagine a map of the city, with a dot for every arrest. Imagine a time series of such maps showing arrests at different times of day. Police in a number of cities have run such map series and experimented with concentrating police presence at particular intersections, on-ramps, parks, or housing projects at particular parts of the day, and succeeded in bringing down street crime. The Camden police would have none of this new-fangled idea, though. Brenner thought he could replicate the work without police cooperation by mapping ambulance calls for serious trauma instead.

The reform commission was stymied, and eventually gave up, but Brenner kept playing with the data on his computer. He found that his maps showed extraordinary clusterings of particular types of injuries and acute health crises. One apartment building, for instance, had an extraordinary number of falls. But another bit of data emerged from his talks with the emergency crews, one that any ER doctor could tell you: Some of these people were the same people, in the ER over and over again with the same problem.

But he needed better data: Where exactly were the huge costs of care coming from? How could they make it work better, on the ground, in this very poor and dysfunctional city? Brenner was in the process of building a working group of local docs called the Camden Coalition of Healthcare Providers.* They began

---

* http://www.camdenhealth.org.

talking to the three local hospitals and other agencies, and eventually pried their databases loose from them to set up a comprehensive database of local health and healthcare. What they found was a more extreme version of the Pareto principle we looked at above. Half the people in Camden had been in an emergency department at least once in the past year, mostly for nonemergencies like colds and sore throats. One citizen had shown up in the ED 113 times, an average of about once every three days.

In Camden, 80% of the costs were spent on 13% of the patients, and 90% of the costs were spent on 20% of the patients. The total cost for hospital and ED care in Camden over five years was $650 million, mostly public funds.

Brenner massaged his data. He was not particularly focused on cost. He was focused on care. Clearly what he was finding here were people who were not well served by healthcare. As he told Gawande: "Emergency room visits and hospital admissions should be considered failures of the healthcare system until proven otherwise"—failures of prevention and timely, effective care. So Brenner wanted to know who these people were, and where they were coming from. He mapped the data, block by block. Of the two most expensive blocks, one had a low-income housing tower, the other a huge nursing home. According to Gawande, Brenner found that the inhabitants of these two buildings alone had racked up enormous medical bills. Over a span of six years,

> some nine hundred people in the two buildings accounted for more than four thousand hospital visits and about two hundred million dollars in healthcare bills. One patient had three hundred and twenty-four hospital admissions in five years. The most expensive patient cost insurers $3.5 million.[*]

What Brenner did next was extraordinary. He decided to focus on treating those repeat ambulance riders. Due to the HIPAA privacy restrictions, he could not simply paw through the patient records looking for them. Since he was a doctor in local family practice, he simply went to the other doctors in town and said, "Send me your worst cases." They were happy to refer the intractable repeaters to him.

The first patient referred to him weighed 560 pounds. He had everything in the book: congestive heart failure, a hypothyroid condition, uncontrolled diabetes, asthma, and gout. He smoked and had a history of alcohol and cocaine abuse. Brenner met him in intensive care, where he was in septic shock from a gallbladder infection. Brenner got to know him, began guiding his treatment, and spent an inordinate amount of time at his bedside.

---

[*] Gawande, A., "The Hot Spotters: Can We Lower Medical Costs by Giving the Neediest Patients Better Care?" *The New Yorker*, January 24, 2011, pp. 41–51.

Brenner gradually assembled a team to help him with such extreme patients, helping them not only medically but with their lives, finding them better places to live, getting them on disability if necessary, finding ways to pay for their care, helping them stabilize their lives and leave their addictions behind, helping them find hope.

After three years, this original patient had lost 220 pounds, gotten his congestive heart failure and diabetes under control, and gotten out of his addictions to nicotine, alcohol, and cocaine.

Over time, Brenner and his team began treating dozens, then eventually hundreds, of such "permanent patients" in Camden with the same intensive, hands-on, full-attention care. In May 2009 he closed his regular practice to focus completely on the permanent patients. He and his few nurse assistants had no budget for a clinic. They worked in borrowed office space, on the phone, in ERs and intensive care units, and in the homes of the patients. As Brenner puts it, the tables have to be turned so that the system serves the patients, rather than the healthcare industry. "The magic pill," he says, "is relationships."*

You could read such a story and think, "What a hero! What a great man, caring for the poor, the ones least able to care for themselves!" And you would be absolutely right. Jeff Brenner is a hero of healthcare.

But that's not the deepest takeaway here. The deepest takeaway is: Why does it take a hero? Why has Brenner found it so difficult to find funding? He and his team can take in the meager Medicaid rates for the specifically medical things they do for these patients, but not for anything else—the home visits, the sitting with people to get to know them, tracking them down in ERs, finding ways to get them into AA groups, or to get a disability check or into a homeless housing program. In a study of the first 36 such patients, Brenner showed that within the first year, he had cut their hospitalization costs by 56%, from $1.2 million per month to $500,000 per month. On just those three dozen people, he and his team were saving the state over $8 million per year. Clearly, with an eventual roster of 300 patients he and his team were saving the state tens of millions of dollars per year. You would think that the state would bankroll a clinic and more staff, so that he could save even more. If he is saving so much money by making people better, why isn't what he is doing normal?

Roughly, it's because no one is set up to make money at it, or to spend money for it, whether it saves the system money or not. The system he saved the money for (state Medicaid mostly) was not the system giving these people care (local hospitals, mostly). No institution in charge of care for these permanent patients was able to see how they could directly benefit financially from giving them this kind

---

* Darragh, T., "'Dr. Hotspot' Coming to Allentown," *Morning Call* (Allentown, Pennsylvania), September 25, 2011.

of intensive attention. The actual clinicians who dealt with them (in the ERs, for instance) were just doing the job they were paid to do, patching the patients up and sending them on their way. They could not do otherwise, as no one was paying them to, or giving the time and resources to do what really needs to be done.

Equally important, no one believed that such intensive attention would be medically beneficial, let alone save money, because they had never seen it happen.

Finally in 2011, Governor Chris Christie signed a bill that would allow Brenner special fees for a pilot program. The state would not pay Brenner's team anything directly. If he could show that they had saved the state money, they could get a small portion of the savings kicked back to them.

Brenner's Camden Coalition of Healthcare Providers focuses on the outliers, the permanent patients, the 1% who drive 20% or more of the costs. Typically, these people were so sidelined by health and behavioral problems that they were out of the workforce. But the same principle, which we could call Pareto-driven targeting, works when applied to a broader group within the workforce—the 5% who drive half of all healthcare costs.

The 5% That Does the 50%

Think back to the Boeing experiment mentioned earlier. It is a targeted program, offered specifically to those in the workforce with multiple chronic problems. Think of CIGNA's Choice Fund. It applies to the whole workforce, and is voluntary—but also has ways to identify particular employees as being in greater need of help. CIGNA has exclusive licensing rights to a University of Michigan health trends system that CIGNA executives call "health risk assessment on steroids," which they claim can predict individuals' level of risk over the next three years with 82% accuracy.[*]

Similarly, the Archimedes Model, developed by population health pioneer David Eddy, MD, PhD, can help predict the effect and return on investment of specific interventions with specific groups, such as employees with asthma, or smokers, or people with metabolic syndrome.[†] Organizations such as Verisk can drill down through millions of health claims records to identify people in need of special intervention as a way of reducing costs.[‡] Tools like these could cut down enormously on healthcare expenditures while improving health.

---

[*] Author's discussions with CIGNA executives.

[†] Author's discussions with Dr. Eddy. Also http://archimedesmodel.com.

[‡] Verisk Analytics: Healthcare Analytics and Predictive Modeling at http://www.verisk.com/Landing-Pages/Landing-Pages/Verisk-Health-Healthcare-Analytics-and-Predictive-Modeling.html.

Some programs take a simpler approach, either (as Boeing did) targeting people by clusters of chronic problems, or simply targeting the top 5% of healthcare users. That was the method chosen by one of the most successful Pareto-driven targeting programs, the Special Care Center in Atlantic City, New Jersey.

This clinic was organized by Dr. Rushika Fernandopulle, a young Sri Lanka-born internist trained at Harvard. It offers special attention, team-based care, and walk-in immediacy to the top 5% of healthcare spenders among two groups of employees: the employees of the Atlantic City casinos and the employees of the AtlantiCare Medical System. These are insured employees, but the extra attention is offered for no copay, no deductibles, and even the drugs are free. The clinic is located close to the casinos and the AtlantiCare Medical Center. Dr. Fernandopulle's group does not passively wait for the patients to show up. Following the model of the Vermont Blueprint, the Alaska Natives, and other groups, they engage them directly, call them up, get them in for care, find translators when necessary. The whole group meets every morning and goes over their panel of patients—who's in the hospital, who is scheduled to come in for a test, what's happening with the person that we have not seen in a while.

A study comparing this top-spending 5% to a carefully matched group of casino employees and healthcare workers in Las Vegas shows that the Special Care Center effected a 40% drop in its patients' ER and hospital costs, and a 25% drop in overall costs for the people under its care, even counting the costs of the clinic.* Is this big? Yes. The population does not include the permanent patients that Brenner treats, the top 1% of the whole population, since those folks are mostly out of the workforce. But in any population, the top 5% drives 50% of that population's costs—so working with the top 5% alone, Dr. Fernandopulle's group is likely lowering the overall healthcare costs of the whole population (casino and healthcare employees) by 12.5%.

Recall that the $100 billion per year thought necessary to provide coverage to all Americans without health insurance comes to 4% of the nation's total health spend. If a result like saving 12.5% of a population's total health spend by focusing on its heaviest users holds up for the whole U.S. population, we would be talking about three times as much as it would cost to cover all uninsured Americans. That is, indeed, big.

More Help, Smarter, Earlier

The pattern repeats in every example we see that works to bring down healthcare costs: rationing and cutbacks don't really save money. What saves money is more

---

* Gawande.

care and attention, delivered earlier, smarter, closer to the customer, in more trusted ways. Give more help to everyone, but especially to those who need the most help, and you'll cut costs and help people be healthier at the same time.

So, *explode the business model*, moving at least some substantial portion of the great mass of healthcare transactions out of the dominant fee-for-service model into bundled care, prepaid care, and other kinds of contracts that spread risk intelligently to the providers and, in measured ways, to the customer. *Build your system on smart primary care. Put a crew on it*: reshape every aspect of healthcare away from the siloed, uncommunicative, wasteful, repetitive model we have now to true team care at every level. And *swarm the customer* with help, information, advice, resources, hand-holding, early, often, and as close as possible.

One more aspect is missing: we can't execute any of this with the old systems of healthcare, sloppy Dickensian data-free systems built entirely on custom, on the convenience of the doctors and hospitals, and the profit of suppliers. If we are going to make healthcare better and cheaper for everyone, healthcare has to get smart the way other industries have, has to drive intelligence, data, and operational wisdom through the system at every level. It has to rebuild every process constantly.

Chapter 10

5. Rebuild Every Process

While new payment schemes, price transparencies, and increasing competition are driving many healthcare organizations to hack and trim in desperate efforts to survive, the executives at increasing numbers of organizations are taking a different tack. Facing a risk-based world in which the end customers increasingly are making informed choices about where to get their healthcare needs taken care of, these organizations are attempting to build healthcare centers with the customer-friendliness of Nordstrom, the reliability of FedEx, and the transactional accuracy and simplicity of American Express. They believe that making medical encounters more pleasant will pump up market share and revenues, boost the quality of clinical care, create less stress for the staff, and generally turn their business around. They are remaking themselves to better serve the wants and needs of the consumer.

The Tough Business of Caring

Visibly, vividly, most of today's medical environments do not work for the customer. Rik Elswit, the legendary guitarist for the cult rock band Dr. Hook, struggled with cancer for years. Ask him about the treatment and cure, and he lights up, burbling with praise for the miracles of modern medicine and the skill of its practitioners. Ask about his experiences as a patient, though, and his face changes completely. "I don't see why, just because I was sick," he says, "they had to treat me like a prisoner."

Most physicians and health professionals agree that Elswit's experience is typical: sick people are treated like prisoners. But some parts of the healthcare industry are responding to this situation as a call to arms. They see it as little short of shameful that hospitals, doctor's offices, and clinics should add to the pain and trauma of being sick or injured.

There's no shortage of low-cost opportunities to build a better patient relationship. Some patient-centered innovations are clinical, such as doctors and nurses washing their hands between treatments, proper ventilation, and someone actually responding to the call button. (In a 2004 study of hospital accidents, the Center for Health Design found that a major cause of accidents was patients struggling out of bed alone to go to the bathroom because no one showed up to help them.) Others provide simple dignity: giving patients hospital gowns with Velcro closure tabs or straps, for modesty; training staff to answer telephones by the third ring, to knock before entering a patient's room, and to introduce themselves and explain what they're there to do.

But most hospital executives have traditionally paid little attention to the details of customer care—since most didn't even think of their patients as customers. The customers of hospitals, traditionally, were the payers, and the doctors who brought in the patients.

In such a system, clinical quality and the patient experience are consistently undervalued. Doctors and hospitals hide their mistakes, and patients and payers take it for granted that they are getting the "best care." For the most part, the patient's experience figures nowhere in the equation.

Time to Get Fierce

Putting the provider at risk, measuring quality, giving the patient the power of a consumer: all these taken together change the landscape completely. It's time for healthcare to get fierce about efficiency and effectiveness, about clinical quality, and about the patient experience. Driving down the process cost of everything you do is a good thing no matter how you make your money. And the improvements in quality that come out of such efficiency efforts will help with pay-for-performance bonuses, with ACO-type kickbacks, with every type of value-based purchasing.

To get fierce about efficiency and processes, you have to be able to see into them. This not only means wall-to-wall computerization and automation, but also means designing the system so that you can continually mine the data it produces, continually query the system for answers to questions you never thought of before, for patterns, outliers, and anomalies. The first level of information efficiency allows clinicians to quickly gather and understand all the data and images they need; to quickly and easily record their actions, observations, and orders; and to extract reimbursement codes directly from the record with minimal work.

The deeper level of information efficiency allows a director of nursing, for instance, to notice that a particular nurse tends to override the "soft bumpers" on drug perfusion pumps to give patients higher than prescribed dosages, allows a director of security to notice when a patient or family member has wandered into an off-limits area, or allows a chief medical officer and chief financial officer to determine that an unusual percentage of expensive, uninsured ER admit cases come from a particular neighborhood, and strategize whether locating a clinic in that neighborhood might cut costs while serving the patients better.

If you are in the hotel business, not having control of your processes results in lost reservations and slow room turnover. If you are in the cement business, it means air pockets and rusting rebar. In healthcare, it means dead patients, disrupted lives, families driven into poverty. Repeated studies over the last dozen years have shown this vividly. The federal Institute of Medicine's justly famous 1999 study *To Err Is Human* put the number of premature deaths from medical misadventure in the scores of thousands to over a hundred thousand per year—all preventable. A later Kaiser Family Fund study put the number even higher. A 2006 IOM study, *Preventing Medication Errors*, estimated that, on average, there is one medication error per patient per day in U.S. hospitals.* Jack Wennberg, the founder of the Dartmouth Institute for Health Policy and Clinical Practice and its annual *Dartmouth Atlas of Healthcare*, has for decades now, with his colleagues, repeatedly shown variations for no reason across healthcare—doctors in one town doing six times as many Caesarean sections as doctors in the next town, or back surgeries, or mastectomies, or CT scans, or doing wildly different diagnoses and order sets from the same presenting symptoms or images, all with little or no difference in outcomes. These "Wennberg variations" have been disputed in various ways. Some studies show some reasons for some of the variations: Though everyone insists that their patients are sicker, some areas actually do have more of a disease burden. Some areas have extra costs because of more undocumented aliens, or more medical education. And costs are somewhat different in the private market than in the over-65 Medicare market. But even after backing out all of these differences, the seemingly random variations remain. Any student of quality control knows that variation for no reason is automatically a sign of a quality problem.

Perfecting Clinical Processes

When the idea of evidence-based medicine began to take hold during the 1990s it became obvious that much of medicine had little evidence going for it. New drugs are subjected to rigorous testing by the FDA. And if someone comes up with a new procedure or surgical technique, he or she may do some studies and

---

* Institute of Medicine studies, available at http://www.iom.edu/Global/News%20 Announcements/Crossing-the-Quality-Chasm-The-IOM-Health-Care-Quality-Initiative.aspx.

publish the results. But few of those studies of techniques meet the gold standard of double-blind comparative studies on large, controlled groups. And many specific procedures had never been studied at all—or the studies had been ignored. There has been no mechanism by which proven best practices become standard practice.

In the unmeasured, unstandardized world of traditional healthcare, many people who run institutions actually have no idea whether their institutions are fighting the good fight on quality or not. For a 2009 *Health Affairs* article, physicians Ashish Jha and Arnold Epstein surveyed the chairmen of 700 hospitals, and discovered that, in the opinion of their chairmen, their institutions were like the children in Garrison Keillor's Lake Wobegon—they were all above average. Among the hospitals that Medicare data suggested were among the worst in the country, 58% thought their hospital was above average. Not one thought his hospital was below average. These chairmen, who are supposed to guide policy at their institutions, and hire and fire top executives, had no clue, though the data were obvious, simple, and easily obtained. Few of them rated "clinical quality" as among their top concerns as chairmen.*

Evidence or Intuition?

There is a battle going on in medicine between intuition and data—and these days the data side is beginning to win the battle.

The last few decades have seen a proliferation of drugs and tests and therapies that have been proven to work in at least some situations. In the absence of clear evidence about which is best for a given situation, the fee-for-service system encourages doctors and patients to use more of them, and to use the more expensive ones in the mistaken belief that cost is a marker for real medical value—while less well-compensated therapies and tests are often neglected.

Human bodies are complex systems, and any condition that affects multiple organs and systems at once can have surprising results, and respond differently to a range of different treatments. This is where the doctor's long experience and intuition come to the fore. The traditional view of doctors' autonomy allowed doctors to make their own independent decisions about every single thing they did.

But in much, probably most, of medicine, there is a provably right way to do something, and many wrong ways. Walk through a few obvious examples with me: There are not wild variations on what to do about a compound fracture: you set it and cast it. Telling a simple sore throat from a strep infection, or differentiating an ocular migraine from a stroke, is not a matter of opinion and intuition; there are simple, measurable markers that can be followed up with more complex tests.

---

* Cited in Leonhardt, D., "Making Health Care Better," *New York Times*, November 8, 2009, available at http://www.nytimes.com/2009/11/08/magazine/08Healthcare-t.html.

There are many variations of diabetes, and many ways that diabetics respond to treatment. But there is little doubt that knowing their A1c scores, getting their feet and eyes checked regularly, and getting regular education and help in managing their condition are good for patients. There is no good medical argument for not doing these things, yet they are often neglected.

Intubating a patient (doing a tracheotomy to insert a breathing tube into the throat) is not some kind of free-form jazz. There is one right way to do it (with a few variations depending on what kind of assistive device is used), and one right way to monitor it (again with a few variations). In traditional, unstructured medicine, a shocking 8% of tracheotomies ended up not in the trachea, the airway, but in the esophagus, the passage to the stomach. Patients still die every day because the tube ends up in the esophagus instead of the airway, and no one checked to make sure it worked.

Similarly, virtually every patient going into surgery should be given an antibiotic to guard against infections. Every patient should be dosed with this perioperative antibiotic unless there is some specific reason not to, such as when the patient has an allergy to the antibiotic, or a shortage of white blood cells, because it reduces the chance of infection by two orders of magnitude. Yet a shockingly high number of patients do not get the antibiotic, not because they don't meet the criteria, but simply because the doctor forgot to order it, or had a different, unsupported opinion about the effectiveness and necessity of the drug.

Labor should not be induced before the 39th week of pregnancy just for the convenience of the doctor or the family, or to reduce the anxiety of the mother, because it is hard to know when the 39th week is, and you risk bringing out a child that is really only 36 weeks along, with incompletely formed lungs. Yet early induced labor without a medical reason is still too common.

These, and many others of the thousands of different medical situations in a doctor's everyday experience, are not subject to intuition. The variation for no reason is often not due to a clinician's intuition that something about this patient is different, but to more mundane factors, such as simple habit, convenience, ignorance of the data, or plain negligence.

Varying from best practices should be a matter of considered opinion and consultation with other physicians. And not all variants are mere improvisations: there are often best practices for choosing a variant in unusual circumstances.

We want to believe that the doctor is always right. As President Obama expressed it in an interview with the *New York Times Sunday Magazine*, "I'm a pretty well educated layperson when it comes to medical care; I know how to ask good questions of my doctor. But ultimately, he's the guy with the medical degree."

But the doctor cannot always be right when different doctors come up with different diagnoses and therapies for the same condition. Either someone is wrong, or it's an area that we don't know enough about yet to say for sure who is right, and there are multiple acceptable paths to try.

That's the fuzzy, gray area that Brent James is trying to narrow—James and, increasingly, his followers, students, and colleagues throughout medicine.

Measure It—and Get It Right

Brent James is the chief quality officer of Intermountain Health, a large system based in Salt Lake City, with 23 hospitals and dozens of clinics throughout Utah and Idaho. For years, as head of the Institute for Health Care Delivery Research at Intermountain, he has been attacking one clinical problem after another. Over and over, he urges the doctors at Intermountain to stop arguing about the right way to do a particular procedure and just pick one. He tells the Intermountain doctors, "Guys, it's more important that you do it the same way than what you think is the right way." If they do it the same way, they can measure the results, tweak what they are doing, and measure again, until they arrive at a provably better result.

Intermountain started this study in the 1980s by looking at acute respiratory distress syndrome (ARDS), a kind of infection acquired by people on ventilators. A national study had shown that, once people acquired this infection, only 10% survived. Intermountain pulmonologist Alan Morris got his colleagues to write a protocol for the ventilator settings in an attempt to figure out what works best to prevent infections, and to help people survive the infections they got. Even at their first pass, with protocols that they quickly realized needed improvement, the survival rate shot up to 40%.

In the past two decades, Intermountain teams have studied more than 50 conditions in the same way: standardize, measure, tweak, remeasure. They have drastically reduced preterm deliveries and the number of babies that need neonatal intensive care. They have cut adverse drug events (wrong drug, wrong dose, wrong time, wrong patient) in half, cut the mortality rate for cardiac artery bypass surgery in half, and cut the mortality rate of one major type of pneumonia by 40%. The interventions of James's teams have saved thousands of lives over the years at Intermountain alone. One single, seemingly minuscule intervention, standardizing the discharge process of heart bypass patients, has resulted in 450 saved lives every year. These results are the root of James's passionate belief in evidence-based medicine. As described by David Leonhardt in the *New York Times Sunday Magazine*:

> It must be done right ... and James acknowledges it isn't always done right. He is not defending protocols per se. He is defending measurement. "Don't argue philosophy," he told me. "Show me your mortality rates, and then I'll believe you."*

---

* Leonhardt.

At his institute, James runs an advanced training program, a four-month course teaching people from across healthcare how to use statistical analysis and quality management techniques to find out what works and what doesn't in healthcare. Over the last decade, his students have opened their own institutes and courses at 35 major teaching hospitals across the country, spreading a gospel of applying scientific techniques to examining the actual processes of medicine.

Check It Out, Dude!

About a decade ago, Dr. Peter Pronovost of Johns Hopkins University Medical Center in Baltimore got a kind of fixation on central line infections. When you come into an ER in rough condition, one common thing the doctors are likely to do is to insert a thin plastic tube into a vein that has a fairly direct line to your heart, and thus the rest of your circulatory system. They do this in case they need to get a lot of some drug into you fast as they battle whatever trauma you came in with. Setting a central line venous catheter is a common procedure, and it can be dangerous: nationally, about 10% of central line placements resulted in infections that could be deadly. In the early 2000s, some 80,000 people per year were getting infections from these central lines—and the infections were killing 30,000 of them. That's a lot.

Pronovost was convinced that none of those patients needed to have died. He scoured the literature and asked his fellow clinicians at Johns Hopkins what would lower the infection rate. He came up with a consensus list of five things that would make a difference. These were not the complex, difficult instructions for how to place a central line. These were simple things that most people might have come up with if they thought about the problem, things like "cover the patient completely," and "scrub up, mask up, glove up," and "avoid putting the line in the groin, if possible—infection is more likely there." He found that, though pretty much everyone knew all these things would help, for various reasons, even at Johns Hopkins, a world-renowned institution decorated with Nobel laureates, clinicians only hit all five points about 30% of the time—and Johns Hopkins' infection rate was near the national average at 11%.

So he did something very simple: He put the five points on a simple checklist, like pilots use before takeoff. He printed copies of the checklist, posted them everywhere that central lines were put in. He asked the staff, as a test, to check off each point each time they put in a central line, then write their name on the bottom and sign it.

In 90 days, the number of infections dropped to zero. None.

Armed with this impressive result, he looked for a state to try out the idea. The Michigan Hospital Association took up the challenge. In the 2004–2005 Keystone Initiative, he got 108 institutions to try the same experiment. Some institutions had to make some changes to make it work. Some, for instance, did not stock full-length drapes where the central lines were being put in; others did not have the sterilizing solutions ready to hand at that spot. The results across all 108 institutions were equally impressive. As the study says, "Within three months after implementation, the median rate of infection was zero, a rate sustained throughout the remaining 15 months of follow-up."[*]

Zero is a good rate for infections. The project saved an estimated 1,500 lives over the 18 months. In a later study, Pronovost and his colleagues showed that the direct savings from dropping the infection rate came to over $1 million per hospital per year, something over $100 million per year for Michigan, which has 1/30 of the population of the United States. The arithmetic works out like this: 1,500 lives over 18 months equals 1,000 lives per year in 1/30 of the U.S. population. Multiply times 30 (if we imagine that these averages hold for the whole country), and we are talking about a potential savings across the country of 30,000 lives and $3 billion per year. Not bad work for a low-tech five-point paper checklist.

The checklist has not been universally adopted. But in the last five years, Pronovost has propagated this simple idea to hospitals in all 50 states and a number of foreign countries. As a result of this and other efforts, the Centers for Disease Control recently reported that central line infections dropped by 58% in the United States from 2001 to 2009.[†]

Another team used checklists to improve surgery. The World Health Organization had done a large-scale study to determine how we could kill fewer people on the operating table. The study cited 19 factors. The Safe Surgery Saves Lives Study Group decided to test these 19 factors as a surgical checklist. Again, the items on the list were not instructions on how to be a surgeon. They were simple procedural matters, such as: Determine, out loud, who is in the room under all those caps and masks, and what their roles are. Before you put patients under, ask them who they are and what they are there for. Identify the patient's condition, and the anticipated procedure. Identify who is in charge of counting the sponges and forceps, so that none are left in the patient. Basic stuff.

For their test, the Pronovost team managed to assemble hospitals that spanned the globe, and worked in a wide variety of conditions, from Toronto to New Delhi to Manila. Their test covered nearly 8,000 operations, half of them controls that did not use the checklist.

---

[*] Pronovost, P., et al., "An Intervention to Decrease Catheter-Related Bloodstream Infections in the ICU," *New England Journal of Medicine*, Vol. 355, December 28, 2006, pp. 2725–32. Available at: http://www.nejm.org/doi/full/10.1056/NEJMoa061115.

[†] Johns Hopkins press release, "Program Reduces Infections, Saves Lives and Money" 08/22/2011 Available at: http://www.hopkinsmedicine.org/news/media/releases/program_reduces_infections_saves_lives_and_money

They cut the mortality rate in half. They cut the complication rate by 40%. With a simple 19-point checklist.*

Other Industries: "Quality Is Job One"

Over the last several decades, most industries have learned how to steadily improve themselves to create better, more reliable products more efficiently. They have computerized and automated their operations. They have used a variety of new management techniques, such as total quality management, Six Sigma quality control, Lean manufacturing, benchmarking, and the theory of constraints, to overhaul their processes, identify useless activities and bottlenecks, eliminate needless opportunities for mistakes, waste, and reworking, and steadily increase the productivity of the American worker. They have streamlined the value chain of suppliers, eliminating extra steps and unnecessary inventory. A new car, home appliance, or television bought today is orders of magnitude more reliable, durable, safe, capable, and efficient than one from the 1970s. The processes of manufacturing, of transportation, of agriculture, of many other industries are far more productive and less wasteful today than they were a generation ago.

There is nothing automatic about this effort. It is the product of constant grueling work to look at every aspect of every process and make it better.

Healthcare has done very little of this kind of work. Only in this century has all this effort started to leak into healthcare, and only in this decade has it begun to be applied broadly across the industry.

The actual systems by which most of healthcare works day to day are still antiquated and sclerotic. Even today, much of the everyday work in a surprising fraction of the clinical environment would still seem familiar to Charles Dickens: clinical orders scrawled on sheets of paper and hand-carried to labs and pharmacies, barely legible and incomplete medical records clamped to clipboards.

Healthcare is a vast, complex industry made up of billions of transactions every day: handoffs, industrial processes large and small, reporting and documenting processes, multilayered and largely opaque payment systems, as well as vastly complicated electrical, computing, imaging, plumbing, and chemical systems, all built into unbelievably intricate physical plants. Traditionally, healthcare has not really managed its systems at all. Different parts of the system tend to have a "loading dock" relationship: I deliver a product to you, I send

---

* Haynes, A.B., et al., "A Surgical Safety Checklist to Reduce Morbidity and Mortality in a Global Population," New England Journal of Medicine, 360;5 January 29, 2009. Available at: http://www.nejm.org/doi/full/10.1056/NEJMsa0810119.

an invoice, and that's all our relationship consists of. What I deliver might be a patient, a tissue sample, a CT scan, a pharmaceutical dose, or a moment's attention to the patient record, any one of thousands of different units of supply and production. But in traditional healthcare it's a transaction, not a relationship. In traditional healthcare, no one was looking at the overall system and managing the systemic interactions.

Using new management techniques can lead to major productivity improvements over short timeframes. Applying basic new management techniques to healthcare can also greatly improve clinical quality, that is, save lives and decrease suffering.

Take just three small examples:

■ Seattle's Virginia Mason famously devised its own version of the Toyota Production System (TPS), dubbed the Virginia Mason Production System. Over just a few years it drove inventory down by half, lead time by 53%, while driving productivity up 44% (the equivalent of hiring 77 new full-time employees), and saving some $12 million to $15 million per year in capital costs.

■ Seattle Children's in-patient psych ward cut the length of stay in half (from 20 days to 10), and increased the number of kids it could help from 400 to 650 per year, without adding new beds, all while patient satisfaction rose. The hospital as a whole cut per-patient costs by 3.7%. It estimated its savings in 2009 at $23 million—while serving 38,000 patients, a 41% increase since 2004, with no new beds.

■ St. Joseph's, a medium-sized community hospital in Parkersburg, West Virginia, put a task force to work on freeing up nurses' time from inefficient tasks. In four weeks of meetings and other part-time work mixed with their other duties, the task force freed up 10,139 nurse hours per year—mostly by instituting better systems for making sure that supplies were where the nurses need them, so they don't have to go foraging. The return on the investment of staff time: 1,016%. Any way you want to measure it, as productivity, reduced costs, lead time, or waiting time, the Toyota Production System in healthcare tends to show improvements of 50% or more wherever it is applied vigorously.

The Institute for Healthcare Improvement

In 1991 a Boston pediatrician set out with some colleagues to improve the quality of medical practice. Appalled by what they saw around them every day in the medical world, Dr. Don Berwick and his friends founded the Institute for

Healthcare Improvement (IHI). They set out not to just write policy papers, or to do studies, but to inspire projects in actual working healthcare institutions to make measurable changes.

There are a lot of organizations dedicated to improving patient safety, but over the past two decades, IHI has become the most effective and influential across the industry.

Berwick's speaking and advocacy across the industry became legendary. He spoke repeatedly at industry functions, arguing for higher-quality standards and practices. On December 4, 2003, at IHI's annual meeting, he delivered the talk that would become a classic, "My Right Knee." Knowing that his knee would have to be replaced soon, he laid out five requirements he would demand of any medical institution that would do his surgery:

1. Don't kill me (no needless deaths).
2. Do help me, and don't hurt me (no needless pain).
3. Don't make me feel helpless.
4. Don't keep me waiting.
5. Don't waste resources, mine or anyone else's.

Berwick felt that every patient should be able to make exactly such a demand. But given what he knew of the medical establishment, he was not at all sure that he could find any institution in the United States that could deliver on those five promises.

> Generating the energy, insight, and courage we need to get to "total quality" may require those of us who work in health care to get much better at seeing images of ourselves in the people we help. As Gandhi said, "You must be the change you wish to see in the world."[*]

This is striking, coming from a doctor who was probably as intimately aware of how healthcare institutions work as anyone alive: "Given my requirements, it is not clear that any health care institution in the United States will want to take me on as a patient."

Over time, IHI launched the 100,000 Lives Campaign, which challenged institutions across the country to come up with specific projects that would improve their practices and cut down on the 100,000 or more lives that the federal Institute of Medicine and Kaiser Family Fund studies showed are cut short every year through "medical misadventure." The campaign enlisted 3,000 hospitals

---

[*] Berwick D "My Right Knee," *Annals of Internal Medicine*, January 18, 2005 vol. 142 no. 2 121–125. Abstract available at: ttp://www.annals.org/content/142/2/121.

and inspired real changes in the system. After that, IHI launched the 5 Million Lives Campaign, a further challenge to prevent 5 million incidents of medical harm—and this time 4,000 hospitals signed up.*

In recent years, IHI has broadened its focus from the individual experience of medical care to include two other related aims: the health of the population, and the per capita cost of providing medical care. As we have seen here, these three elements of the IHI's Triple Aim are actually tightly related: the only way to do healthcare for less is truly to do it better—and to do it earlier across the whole population. The three not only can work together, but they must work together.

Comparative Effectiveness Research

Some 13,000 clinical studies start up every year. At this writing, about 118,000 are running.† They ask essentially two questions: Is the drug or procedure safe? And is it effective? That is, is it any more likely to kill or harm you than whatever disease you are fighting? And does it have some effect?

They do not ask the big question that we really want to know: Is it safer or more effective than other treatments for the same condition? Is patented Nexium (the "purple pill") any better at controlling chronic heartburn than the far cheaper, nearly identical (but off-patent) Prilosec (omeprazole)? Is vertebroplasty any better at solving back pain than the far cheaper medical management, or acupuncture? Who knows? Answering those kinds of questions is the job of comparative effectiveness research (CER), which almost no one does. In the last year for which we have good data, 2008, of the 112,000 studies then running, only 689 could be called CER.‡ That is, only 0.6% of trials asked the real question: In a given medical situation, what do we know about which treatment might work better?

Why is this research so slighted? Go back to incentives: lots of people get paid to know of something that might work, but almost no one really gets paid to know what works best. If vertebroplasty works just about as often as ibuprofen and yoga, but costs as much as $14,000 more, who will benefit financially from choosing the "i + y" medical management routine? Not the doctor, who will get paid either way but paid more to do the more elaborate procedure. Not the health plan, which gets a percentage of all medical payments. Not Medicare. Not the patient, unless the patient is at risk for some part of it. Flip the incentives,

* IHI history available at: http://www.ihi.org/about/Pages/History.aspx.
† http://www.clinicaltrials.gov/.
‡ Holve, E. and Pittman, P. "A First Look at the Volume and Cost of Comparative Effectiveness Research in the United States," AcademyHealth, June 2009. Accessed online at: http://www.academyhealth. org/files/FileDownloads/AH_Monograph_09FINAL7.pdf

though, and suddenly CER is very interesting indeed. A medical organization that is paid a bundled fee to manage the back pain of 1,000 warehouse workers, and is paid based on outcome, that is, how much do their backs actually hurt and how many days of work do they miss, will be intensely interested in what works best, fastest, for the least money.

Like anything that threatens to make healthcare actually more effective and efficient, comparative effectiveness research draws its share of attackers. We have already seen how the Newt Gingrich-controlled Republican House went out of its way to throttle such studies in the 1990s. A study recently published by the Pacific Research Institute found that, because of comparative effectiveness research, "under conservative assumptions, R&D investment in new and improved pharmaceuticals and devices and equipment would be reduced by about $10 billion per year over the period 2014 through 2025, or about 10–12 percent." This massive slowdown in the rapid onrush of new medical technologies "would impose an expected loss of about 5 million life-years annually, with a conservative economic value of $500 billion, an amount substantially greater than the entire U.S. market for pharmaceuticals and devices and equipment."*

I haven't read the study. I don't need to, since it is so obviously true, if we just make certain assumptions, such as:

- Every dime spent on research and development for drugs and devices is wisely spent, on advances that will save and improve lives.
- Every dime spent on finding out whether those drugs and devices actually work as advertised, and don't actually kill people, and do it better or cheaper than other drugs and devices, is a dime wasted. Comparative effectiveness research just slows down legitimate, helpful research.
- Experience does not show us any examples of wasteful or unnecessary drugs or devices. Those multiple peer-reviewed research papers showing that we waste hundreds of billions of dollars every year on useless complex back surgeries, the 22% of implanted defibrillators that are unnecessary, tens of millions of unnecessary scans, coronary stents put in people with stable heart disease and no heart pain, the heartburn surgeries that work no better than over-the-counter drugs—those studies are all false, wrong, some kind of mumbo-jumbo that we can safely ignore.

If we just make those few simple assumptions, the study has a valid point. If we don't accept those assumptions, we have to wonder about people who would cook up such "studies."

---

* Available online at: http://www.pacificresearch.org/docLib/20110715_Zycher_CER_F.pdf.

The Obama administration has greatly increased the money going to find out what actually works. The 2009 stimulus package included $1.1 billion for comparative effectiveness research. The 2010 PPACA reform bill established the Patient-Centered Outcomes Research Institute (PCORI) with a steady funding source that should grow to over $500 million per year. PCORI is forbidden by law from taking cost into account, or from directly recommending whether or not the government or private payers should cover a given treatment. But it should have enormous influence anyway. If it finds that treatment X is marginally better (or no better) than treatment Y, and anyone can easily find out that it costs 30 times as much (as is often the case), it will be harder and harder for treatment X to find funding.* Over time, in an atmosphere of flipped incentives and real competition to provide the best care for less, comparative effectiveness research will become of profound importance in healthcare.

Evidence-Based Design

Do clinicians wash their hands more frequently if the hand washing station is in the hallway or in the patient room?

It's nice to have art on the walls, and a view of nature from the hospital bed, and people say it helps the patients get better faster. Does it really? Is a poster or painting just as good as a window?

What are the best ways to clean a room so that pathogens are not transferred from one patient to another? Are some surfaces and shapes harder to clean than others?

Do hospitals have to be such noisy places? Does the noise actually hinder patients' recovery?

There are literally thousands of such questions confronting anyone designing a clinical space—a hospital, a clinic, a physician's office, a new building, a conversion, even an interior decorating project. And there are thousands of good, solidly researched answers. Yes, people do recover more quickly if they can see out a window. Draperies gather up pathogens from patients' and staff's hands and pass them on. Premature babies do better in neonatal intensive care if they experience a natural circadian rhythm of dark and light. Smart bed design can reduce patient falls. Sight lines between the nurses' normal workstation and

---

* Brown, D. "Comparative effectiveness research tackles medicines unanswered questions," Washington Post, Aug. 15, 2011. Accessed online at: http://www.washingtonpost.com/national/healthscience/comparative-effectiveness-research-tackles-medicines-unanswered-questions/2011/08/01/gIQA7RJSHJ_story.html

the intensive care unit beds matter. The level of noise matters. The colors on the walls matter. The size of the bathroom doorway matters.

Yet most of our healthcare facilities have been designed and built in ignorance of these answers, even in the building boom of the last 10 years. And hospitals and other healthcare facilities remain very dangerous places for both patients and staff alike, with hospital-caused (nosocomial) infections, accidents, and other problems among the nation's leading causes of death.

The Center for Health Design (CHD) was formed in 1993 to advance a single idea—that design could be used to improve patient outcomes in healthcare environments. It seemed a radical idea at the time, yet even then evidence was accumulating in multiple studies that the lighting, the surfaces, the doorknobs, the sound levels, the workflow, the placement of elevators, indeed every detail from site planning to cleaning solvents, could promote or impede the patients' healing, and the efficiency and work effectiveness of the staff. But these studies mostly had no effect on the actual design of real facilities. Most architects, planners, and interior designers of healthcare facilities were generalists, with no special training in healthcare environments. There were no special certifications in the field, and few healthcare conferences paid attention to it.

The Center for Health Design set out to change that. Over time its journal (*Healthcare Design*) and annual conference became robust centers of activity that pull together suppliers, architects, interior designers, researchers, and healthcare professionals and executives. It sponsors research and has completed a series of landmark meta-studies that surveyed the growing field and presented the findings of hundreds of studies in neat packages with their rationales: Make the bathroom door this wide, and here's why. Solve the nurses' supply problem in these five ways; here are the findings.

The first of these came out in 2004. CHD launched the Designing the 21st Century Hospital Project with backing from the Robert Wood Johnson Foundation. Researchers Roger Ulrich and Craig Zimring (both members of the CHD board) and their teams gathered thousands of studies, vetted them for sound research methods and good data, combed the resulting 600, and published "The Role of the Physical Environment in the Hospital of the 21st Century: A Once-in-a-Lifetime Opportunity."* It was a packed 69-page document: 26 pages of results and recommendations, followed by 47/42 pages of references to the original 600 studies. Ulrich and Zimring updated their findings

---

* Available online at: http://www.healthdesign.org/chd/research/role-physical-environment-hospital-21st-century.

in an even more comprehensive paper, "A Review of the Research Literature on Evidence-Based Healthcare Design," in 2008.*

As part of the same project another team of researchers and architects affiliated with CHD built the Fable Hospital. This analysis of an imaginary hospital project had a somewhat different goal: demonstrating that there is a solid business case for evidence-based design.

Here we see the same theme: Better healthcare is cheaper. Smart healthcare is Leaner and less expensive than stupid healthcare.

Evidence-based design is more expensive on the front end. For instance, it calls for single patient rooms, and larger ones; far better ventilation than usual; and a host of other refinements. But the results in fewer accidents, shorter patient stays, fewer infections, and other outcome improvements actually pay for the refinements over a relatively short period of time. When the team updated the Fable Hospital Report in 2011, the refined figures, based on another seven years of experience and experiment, came to this: on a $350 million hospital project, the evidence-based refinements would cost about $29 million extra. Evidence showed that the savings engendered by these refinements would come to about $10 million per year. They would pay for themselves in just three years.†

Some of the new information comes from actual new hospitals built to principles of evidence-based design. They are called the CHD's Pebble Projects, as in pebbles tossed into a pond creating waves that change the whole pond. Healthcare organizations with construction projects sign up with the CHD for guidance, and at the same time agree to conduct specific new research on the facility after it opens, comparing accident rates or infection rates to the facility it replaced, or another facility of different design, or in different parts of the same new facility. Some three dozen facilities have participated since the program's founding in 2000.

In 2008, the CHD began training and certifying architects, planners, and interior designers in the principles and data, in a new Evidence-Based Design Accreditation and Certification (EDAC) program, which quickly expanded to hundreds of professionals.

This is heroic work. It is boring to all except those who are doing it. Most of it is invisible to most of the people it affects. But all this research, education, and turning the data into actual buildings—all of it is hard, detailed, tough-minded, relentless labor that ultimately saves lives, reduces suffering, and makes healthcare more available to all by reducing costs.

---

* Available online at http://www.healthdesign.org/chd/research/reviewresearch-literature-evidence-based-healthcare-design.

† Sadler, B., et al. "Fable Hospital 2.0: The Business Case for Building Better Health Care Facilities," Hastings Center Report, January-February 2011. This report and a wide array of other research available online at: http://www.healthdesign.org/chd/research.

The Lean Medical Practice

The second of our core strategies is to build on smart primary care. To do that we need more primary care doctors. How can we quickly create more? The quickest and simplest way? Make better use of the ones we have. Here again, it's efficiency and effectiveness: "better" is the quickest path to "costs less." Yet primary care doctors have come to question whether it is even possible to make a living as a doctor, especially in solo or small practice.

In the late 1990s, a physician in Rochester, New York, L. Gordon Moore, MD, started a little revolt in healthcare by taking that question seriously: What would it take, in these times, to make a living just being a doc, by himself? He set out to discover just how inexpensively and efficiently he could run a primary care practice—and he believed that it was possible. And not just any primary care, but care that was available 24/7, in which patient could see his or her own doctor that day, in which the doctor and the patient have a real relationship, in which the doctor provides the bulk of the patient's care and guides the rest of his or her care in the healthcare system. To make this happen, the practice had to be high-tech, low overhead, constantly measured and improved. And it had to be proactive in taking care of the patients' chronic problems.

Could he do it? He could. In 2002 he published the results in a pair of articles in *Family Practice Management* as "Going Solo: Making the Leap" and "Going Solo: One Doc, One Room, One Year Later."*

His ideas got some fans, and the fans set out to try them out themselves. The results for a dozen doctors, complete with actual figures for rent, tech, and salaries, were published in a series of articles in *Family Practice Management* in 2007 and 2008, under the rubric, ideal medical practice (IMP).† By actually establishing a number of practices across the country, Moore and his coauthors showed that it is possible to use basic, freely available, even low-cost software and hardware to reduce staff, increase the doctor's time with patients, and increase the quality of the patient's experience, all at once. The model even includes micro-IMPs—solo doctors going "bareback" with no staff at all, or a

---

* Moore, L.G. "Going Solo: Making The Leap, Family Practice Management, February 2002. Fam Pract Manag. 2002 Feb;9(2):29-32. Available at: http://www.aafp.org/fpm/2002/0200/p29.html.
  Moore, L.G. "One Doc, One Room, One Year Later," Family Practice Management, March 2002. Fam Pract Manag. 2002 Mar;9(3):25-29. Available at: http://www.aafp.org/fpm/2002/0300/p25.html.
† Moore, L.G. and Wasson, J. "The Ideal Medical Practice Model: Improving Efficiency, Quality and the Doctor-Patient Relationship" Family Practice Management, September 2007. Fam Pract Manag. 2007 Sep;14(8):20-24. Available at: http://www.aafp.org/fpm/2007/0900/p20.html#fpm20070900p20-bt1.

single outsourced, very part-time person working on billing and bookkeeping. They are buying computers off the shelf at Costco or Office Depot, downloading free software or signing up for low-cost online services, and outsourcing billing.

Doing It Cheaper

Part of this vision is the cheap software. A doctor's office needs a lot of computing: administration, billing, patient registries, access to medical databases, ability to view complex medical images and lab results, electronic medical records, and computerized order entry.

Doctors have been sold the idea that this computing requires such highly specialized hardware, software, and customization that they must spend as much as $50,000 per physician, plus thousands of dollars in subscriptions per month, to install, maintain, and run the system.

This is false.

As the Ideal Medical Practice movement showed, doctors can buy their computers the same places anyone else does, and stock them with cheap or free software customized to their needs.

The most glaring example: The Veterans Administration began to take its healthcare system digital over 25 years ago. The VistA system that it developed has been continually expanded, refined, and ported to various operating systems—and it is in the public domain, available for free on the VA website, modified for nongovernmental use as OpenVista. A number of companies have made it their business to customize it and install it for private use in everything from solo doctors' offices to multihospital systems. An OpenVista installation at even a major multihospital system can cost as little as 10% of what a rival commercial system might cost. Consider this: A couple of years ago the West Virginia University Hospital System spent about $90 million to install commercial healthcare enterprise software from a major brand name vendor in seven hospitals. At just about the same time the West Virginia Health and Human Resources Department installed OpenVista in eight hospitals. The installation and customization by a private vendor across all eight hospitals cost $9 million.* There is absolutely no reason to assume that the university system got 10 times the value out of its installation than the health department did from its installation.

The Resource and Patient Management System (RPMS), a version of VistA designed for doctors' offices and clinics, is used throughout the Indian Health Service, as well as hundreds of other offices and clinics across the country. All VistA software is open-source software, much like Linux. As programmers

---

* Brewin, B. "VA's health record system cited as a model for national network," March 27, 2009. Available at: ww.nextgov.com/nextgov/ng_20090327_6548.php.

inside or outside of the government make improvements on it or add modules, those can be shared with anyone else using the software.

Other companies are offering free or cheap software for doctors. Practice Fusion (practicefusion.com) is an entire suite of doctors' office software, available free as a web-based service, supported by unobtrusive ads at the bottom of each page. If the ads bother you, pony up $100 per clinician per month and away they go. Some services, like billing, are extra-cost add-ons. The company claims a five-minute installation and over 100,000 users. Patient Fusion (patientfusion. com) is a companion free web service with which the patient can view his or her medical records, make appointments, and message privately with the doctor.

Doctations (docpatient.com), designed by groups of doctors, with input from patients, provides comprehensive services, including billing and order entry, and access to medical databases, for $499 per provider per month—or $36,000 for a lifetime contract.

Like nearly every idea for making healthcare better and cheaper, the movement toward Lean, inexpensive ideal medical practice-style primary care is threatening to traditional healthcare. Why? Because under the fee-for-service business model, healthcare institutions traditionally get paid for their inefficiencies. IMP founder L. Gordon Moore, MD, recounts a conversation that is unfortunately fairly typical of the point of view of traditional big medicine:

> The first time I heard a hospital CFO tell me that improved access in the hospital's primary care practices was a problem for him I was shocked.
> "I'm not sure I get the problem here," said naive me.

The arithmetic that the CFO ran for him was fairly simple: his system could bill and recoup an average of $450 for each ED visit, but only $50 for a primary care visit. So why make the primary care more accessible and convenient?

> "But ..." (picture me turning a bit red and breaking a sweat here) "but ... when people see their primary care doc they get better care. I mean of course the Emergency Department is great, but there are really great studies ..."
> He's glazing over. He doesn't want to hear about studies.

Moore argued what the studies show anyway: good, personalized, nuanced primary care, tailored to the individual, leads to better outcomes, a happier patient, and lower costs, all in one.

> "But that's just my point," says the CFO. "Costs are lower because you're taking money out of my pocket. This is a business. It's my job to make it work. What you're doing is unacceptable, and it needs to stop."

Moore reports this conversation not because it was so freakish but because it was so common:

> This is the norm, not the exception. Of course there are exceptions and there are great health systems that figure out how to make ends meet while practicing ethically. The problem is that so much of insurance payment policy is lined up against the ethical practice of medicine.*

We can't build better healthcare without rebuilding primary care practices to be Lean, smart, data-heavy, transparent, low-overhead operations—whether they are independent, or part of large health systems.

Lean, smart primary care does not work just for the boutique market. In fact, like cell phones and other modern advances that started out at the top of the market but have made the biggest difference in the lives of people at the low end, so will smart primary care.

Raise a Glass to Carlos

You drink beer? Next time you pop a cold one, raise a toast to Carlos Olivares.

Why? Beer is made from hops. That's about all I know about hops, except for one more thing: three-quarters of all the hops in the United States come from the thousand square miles of the Yakima Valley in eastern Washington state. You can't have beer without hops. You can't have hops without farm workers to plant them, irrigate them, harvest them, and load them into trucks bound for the breweries. The growers know that you can't have farm workers if somebody doesn't patch them up when they are injured and dose them when they are sick.

That's Carlos and the doctors and nurses he employs. The small, soft-spoken, energetic man from Bolivia has run the Yakima Valley Farm Workers Community Clinic for 25 years. He does things that are simple, basic, and smart, things that go right to the point, like this: he convinced local doctors to open after-hours clinics so that the farm workers don't have to drive all the way to the hospital in Spokane and show up in the emergency room when all they have is the flu or an infected cut. Farm workers don't have much money, and most of them don't have health insurance, so doctors weren't interested in serving them better. The docs have practices to run and bills to pay. So Carlos did the math, put together a PowerPoint, called a little meeting, and showed the doctors that they could actually make a good bit of money at it, all by saving money for the poor farm workers, and making it easier for them to stay healthy at the same time.

The doctors who took part nearly doubled their income. The farm workers were healthier. The agricultural giants who grow the hops got better, more

---

* http://www.idealmedicalpractice.com/info.html.

productive workers—and they weren't even paying for health insurance for these employees. Would it be smart of the agribusiness companies to subsidize the clinics to keep the workers even healthier? Yes. But it was even smarter of Olivares to build a Lean, smart, well-run clinic that could help the docs make a living doing what they do best—for the poor farm workers.

In the hop fields of the Yakima Valley or the barrios of Southern California or the baking suburbs of Phoenix, healthcare costs less when you do it right, when you do it smart, close to the customer, ethical, with heart and brain, not just by the book.

The brain of healthcare—the brain of the system itself—needs awakening.

Big Data

Here's Carol McCall, chief actuary of Health Analytics Innovations: "We are running huge experiments every day in healthcare, but until now we have forgotten to capture the data. Besides having a terrible business model, healthcare has a huge learning disability. What we need is a new kind of analytics that will allow us to learn from our everyday experiments."*

Here's what we mean by *big data*: Every day millions of Americans work in the U.S. healthcare system, are treated in it, manage to stay out of it, exercise or don't, take their medicines or don't, are operated on, inspected, tested, scanned, get better, get worse, muddle through, die. In every encounter with the healthcare system, huge amounts of data are generated. But from the point of view of the system, almost all of that data is lost. It never becomes available to answer the big questions. If we could mine that data on a vast scale, we could learn so much. That's the promise of big data.

We can do controlled scientific studies, as the FDA demands, for drug approval. These are important, but they are limited to situations in which you can control as many of the variables as possible—and the results sometimes fail in the real world. Many things are not subject to study in a double-blind controlled study. Some studies would be unethical to do, such as comparing a treatment with people who got no treatment at all. Others are impossible to do, because it is hard to gather a large number of people with exactly the right constellation of symptoms all in one facility at one time, for instance. But we have a huge treasure trove of data generated every day that would tell us vastly more than we have ever known about what works and what doesn't—if we can only mine the data.

In 1993, in one of the earliest issues of the then-trail-blazing *Wired* magazine, I painted a "wired," data-intensive future for healthcare. In one section of the article, I pictured a doctor trying to deal with a difficult case, and able to query

---

the massive cloud of medical data generated by hundreds of millions of cases every year. Standing at the bedside, using a handheld computer, the doctor could reach out into the nationwide data cloud to find the tens of thousands of cases that match this patient's age, gender, presenting condition, complicating conditions, weight range, and pharmaceuticals being used—and compare the outcomes of those on medicine X vs. medicine Y, or compare both with those using a different therapy altogether. In effect, in a few minutes the doctor could conduct her own real-world, retrospective clinical study using the anonymized medical data of thousands of real patients matched to her patient, to discover what is most likely to work, not in the abstract, but in this patient, here, now, in this bed.

That was just a vision in 1993, a futuristic fantasy. There was no cloud, there were no real, workable, wireless tablet computers. Very few medical records were digitized, and there were no data standards that would make the data recognizable outside of its home system. The public Internet was just opening, high-speed and wireless Internet connections were nonexistent, and there were few electronic connections between medical systems.

Now all of that has changed, in ways that make this and many other new ways of using information in healthcare not only possible, but inexpensive, standardizable, linkable. In the early 1990s, these things were fantastic hopes. In the 2010s they are rapidly becoming the workaday reality of healthcare.

Finally, healthcare is computerizing, digitizing, automating. Finally, healthcare is investing in enterprise systems that can link together clinical data with operations data and administrative data such as billing, costs, and investments.

At the same moment, the techniques of data mining are blossoming and maturing. Health plans and medical systems can drill down into the data to find the 5%, find the 1%, and find ways to treat them more effectively. And the drilling into the data is itself becoming automated to an amazing degree.

As Colin Hill of GNS Healthcare put it recently, "Causality has been industrialized. Cause and effect can be extracted from the Big Data stream. Machines increasingly are able to sample all kinds of hypotheses, and even generate the hypotheses, and then we need humans to evaluate the results." Hill mentioned a still-proprietary study in which GNS Healthcare computers "combed through 45 quadrillion drug/drug interactions, and found 250 that could be responsible for the problem we were researching."

Analytics for the Country

Put yourself in the shoes of the Centers for Disease Control and Prevention for a moment. To help the country protect its health, you need to know what is coming, and what is here, as quickly as possible. The CDC practices what they call "sentinel surveillance," with listening posts around the world through affiliations with healthcare institutions. In the United States, there are elaborate reporting networks gathering information from local health departments and emergency departments (EDs). But think about this: when some new disease hits and begins to peak, there is something that happens, a visible behavior, that arises well before the ED is swamped with cases. What is one of the very first things, say, a parent does when a child wakes up with a sore throat and a fever?

They Google it. They start searching for symptoms, medicines, disease names, advice. Every time the flu hits, there is a wave of searches that matches its symptoms.

Google has a tool called Google Correlate. If you have a database that has a time series of any kind, you can upload years of data into Google Correlate. The program will analyze the data and its waveforms, and search the vast database of Google searches for keywords that match those waveforms most exactly. If you have data for, say, sales of snow skis, Google would show you what else people were looking for at the peak times, such as mittens or goggles. It can also show you where they are doing most of the buying. Mostly the correlations are not surprising, but sometimes the tool can show you something very interesting.

The CDC's intelligence operation is called BioSense. One of its tools is BioSense Correlate. By combining its data on past disease outbreaks, the tool finds what searches are the leading indicators of particular disease outbreaks. Researchers can use millions of ordinary Google searches to catch disease trends early, or even predict them. Taha Kass-Hout, the deputy division director of Information Science at CDC, says, "We can put our fingers on the pulse of the nation's health."*

This is just one example of the growing field called infodemiology, in which researchers mine the search engine flows, and Twitter feeds, and pictures on Facebook, and other publicly available personal online information to gain insight into emerging epidemics or other public health problems. A University of Iowa team used tweets to study the outbreak of the H1N1 epidemic. Researchers at Johns Hopkins modeled the regular flu epidemic using tweets.

Such researches cannot be as sensitive as the researchers might like, since they are records not of actual pathogens, but of people's self-reported symptoms. But combined with other sources of data, they can make the picture more accurate, richer, and deeper—and can alert researchers to some emerging phenomenon before they hear about it in official reports.

The Healthmap Project, for instance, pulls in data streams from online news, eyewitness reports, expert discussions, and official reports, to "achieve a unified and comprehensive view of the current global state of infectious diseases" and displays the information on maps. As quoted in a recent *Time* magazine article,

---

* Panel at Health 2.0 2011, San Francisco, California, September 27, 2011.

one of its creators likened it to "taking the local-weather forecast idea and making it applicable to disease.'"

The amount of data being thrown up in the web every day is vast, deep, and growing. We are rapidly becoming more sophisticated in being able to mine it for meaning about public health.

Analytics for Systems

People have been talking for decades about decentralizing much of healthcare away from massive Big Brick Memorial Hospital—for lots of good, sound reasons revolving around the efficacy of convenient primary care and home care, and the improvement in communications. It hasn't happened much because these are all "should" reasons, not "have you by the throat" (HYBTT) reasons.

The HYBTT reason is arriving: in the approaching rapid changes and instabilities of healthcare, provider organizations (today's institutions or others that will arise to compete with them) increasingly will be identifying particular populations in their service area whose primary care (or chronic conditions) they can manage under risk contracts. See my hotspotting screed in Chapter 9.

These medical providers will be doing this so that they can give these people earlier, smarter, resource-rich care, and profit from driving the cost of care down and the effectiveness up. To serve these populations, providers will locate wherever is most convenient to that population, because especially in chronic and primary care, convenience is critical. It makes a big difference if the people you are serving can get care downstairs, down the hall, or down the block, instead of across town, down the freeway, at the end of three bus transfers. So, as we saw in Chapter 9, we will see a lot of forward-stationed clinics in workplaces, union halls, schools, convalescent homes, neighborhoods, wherever the risk-contracted population hangs out.

This drives the second strategic observation: geographic data mining. Providers are not doing this yet very much, but when they come to be at risk for the health costs of populations they will be all over it like your favorite metaphor.

There are already companies that are selling this kind of geographic information system (GIS) capability. Software like the healthcare analytics from Stratasan (stratasan.com) "geocodes" right down to the level of the individual address where customers are coming from (but in a suitably anonymous, HIPAA-compliant form, as dots on a map)—and can break out those addresses by cost, by disease, even by profitability from any set of records. It can lay that

---

* Walsh B. "Outbreak.com: Using the Web to Track Deadly Diseases in Real Time," Time Magazine, Aug. 16, 2011. Available at: http://www.time.com/time/health/article/0,8599,2088868,00.html.

data over consumption patterns by city block. Armed with this information, for instance, you might obviously decide to site some forward-stationed facilities in places that are more convenient to your well-insured, higher-paying customers. But what about the other end? You might also decide to lower your costs for the money-losing populations by forward-stationing free clinics in their neighborhoods, where you will at least lose less money treating them than you would in your ER. More aggressively, you might find ways to take on risk contracts for the money-losing populations, give them better, earlier, smarter care, thereby turning their care and costs around, and creating new positive revenue streams.

You can't drive any of the business models we have discussed here without big data and big analytics to set benchmarks, reward quality, find outliers, and build appropriate relationships between organizations managing the healthcare of hundreds of thousands to millions of people. The Cleveland Clinic, for instance, uses the Population Explorer from Explorys to analyze thousands of clinical concepts across billions of data points to detect underlying patterns and associations of disease processes. Explorys's EPM Measure brings together clinical, operational, and financial data at the level of the whole enterprise, the facility, the department, the individual clinician, or the individual patient. This kind of software can help manage specific populations, look at specific process measures, track outcomes, or compare an institution to its peers. You can use it to drill down to individual patients, and even run future trends on risk factors over time, all to continually ask and answer the fundamental questions: What works? What doesn't? What's waste? What makes it easier? What gets in the way? In an economic environment in which providers are increasingly at risk for the health and health costs of populations, this information will drive a lot of strategic decisions.

Analytics for You

We want healthcare to be better and cheaper. We can only get there if the buyers of healthcare—individuals and employers—can "shop" for healthcare. But you can't shop without knowing what you are shopping for, having some idea what your options are, and having some incentive to make a good choice.

Employers are increasingly pushing some of the cost of healthcare onto their employees in the form of high-deductible health plans, health savings accounts, and copays. That should drive people to shop around more—and employers should be shopping more themselves. But most people do not know the two most basic facts about the economics of healthcare, that prices vary wildly, and that price is not a marker for quality. Prices are all over the map. In San Francisco, for instance, you can pay $11 for a cholesterol test, or $150. You can pay the $11,000 list price for a cardiovascular stress test in Bakersfield,

California, or $1,950 list price at Henry Ford Hospital in Detroit, or get the discounted $500 version a friend of mine paid for in Ukiah, California. A branded drug might cost 20 times as much as its generic equivalent.

In most industries, price is at least a general marker for quality. A Mercedes is a better-made car than a Kia, and the $100 acoustic dreadnought guitar in a cardboard box that you can buy at Target is no match for a $3,000 Taylor. In healthcare, that basic rule of thumb does not hold—correlations of charges and quality look like random spatter graphs. The differing prices do not derive from differing quality, but out of such internal business concerns as what kind of deal the institution is able to strike with which insurance company.

At the same time, people commonly say, "How can I be expected to choose medical care? I'm not a doctor. It's too complex." In reality, people shop for complex things all the time—cars, vacations, houses—without being experts in those fields. They turn to experts, counselors, agents, and rating websites to make better choices.

So how do you turn yourself (or your company) into a smart healthcare shopper? Where do you get solid information about what is available, how much it costs, and how good it is—something better, more firmly based than random anonymous reviews on Yelp?

A number of insurance companies, including Aetna, CIGNA, and United Health, are trying to arm their customers with that kind of information—cost and quality ratings. After all, they have the data right there in their claims databases. Interestingly, the CEO of Aetna, Mark Bertolini, has declared that Aetna is first a healthcare information technology company, and only secondly an insurance company.* But health plans have some constraints. Contracts with healthcare providers often forbid them from disclosing the actual price paid for tests and procedures. They are less likely to have accurate information on providers that are not in their network. And people have trust issues with insurance companies. They have difficulty trusting that they are getting the real, unbiased information from such a strongly interested source.

In this mix, where there is such a powerful need for specialized, localized, solid information, we can expect independent sources to arise—and in fact they already are arising. One emerging independent source, for instance, is Castlight (castlighthealth.com). Founded by Giovanni Colella with Todd Park, who is now chief technology officer of the U.S. Department of Health and Human Services in the Obama administration, Castlight is "dedicated to helping people actually figure out what their healthcare is going to cost them personally," according to Colella. "Some providers, like Aetna, are dedicated to price transparency. Others

---

* Panel at Health 2.0 2011, San Francisco, California, September 27, 2011.

are dedicated against it. We're bringing you information that is dedicated to you, to your plan, and your employer's situation."

Castlight gives ratings and reviews of providers, along with actual payment amounts to help you make your choice. "We want to make it the Kayak.com of healthcare," says Colella. "We want to make it as much a pleasure to use as that travel site. We're going to give you a really good seat to a really bad movie."*

With the Doctor

So suppose you use Castlight or some other support tool to find the right doctor and the right healthcare organization. There you are with the doctor. How do you make good decisions in the clinical moment? Remember Dr. David Eddy's Archimedes software mentioned in Chapter 9? Archimedes has an app for the individual patient working with the doctor in the encounter moment. The app is called IndiGO. It pulls together information from the patient's electronic health record (with the identifying information redacted), from data warehouses, and disease registries to calculate the patient's risks of different diseases. Then it gives scores for both the risks and the likely benefits of different combinations of interventions. It displays this information graphically so that the clinician and patient can compare the effects of the different choices he or she might make. Getting the patient involved in seeing all the risks and benefits not only helps him or her make good choices, but he or she is much more likely to follow out the choices, take the medicine, do the tests, create the lifestyle changes.

Taking It Home

But there you are, after the clinical encounter for yourself, or your mom, or your kid. How do you manage your health and the health of those you love? Most people do poorly at managing their own health; it helps to do it in connection with other people. The most typical pattern is that women tend to manage the health of their mates, their children, and their parents. So why not give this family care manager (male or female) a tool? Dossia (dossia.org) is one such tool: it's a personal health manager, but it can connect together different profiles. So there's Dad (with his permission), husband, kids, all on one dashboard, where you can follow their progress and talk about it. You can put in personal challenges for you as a group to take on, such as an exercise goal or a change in eating habits. It even has a game interface, turning the challenge into a video game. You can extend these challenges to any group you want to

---

* Panel at Health 2.0 2011, San Francisco, California, September 27, 2011.

involve—friends, coworkers, members of your book club—even if they don't use Dossia themselves. The program can offer up crowd-sourced comments on drugs and therapies from across the country.

Like most of the technologies we are talking about, Dossia is a for-profit enterprise. But its development was funded by 10 employers for use by their 5 million employees and dependents of employees. Smart employers are coming to understand that giving employees the tools they need to stay healthy has a strong return on investment.

There are, in fact, numerous such start-ups and software suites emerging to help patients/customers navigate the healthcare system, take care of themselves and their families, and make smart choices about it all.

Apps

If we want to imagine the true power of all these different patient interfaces, we have to look further, beyond today's Internet browser-driven information world to the new platforms arising right now: the smart phone and tablet computers—that is, the generic categories pioneered by the iPhone and the iPad.

When Steve Jobs died in the fall of 2011, quickly followed by the publication of Walter Isaacson's biography of Jobs, the Internet and the media were flooded with encomiums to his genius (as well as anecdotes showing Jobs as not such a nice guy). But the media storm missed what exactly is revolutionary about these iOS devices, the one aspect that cannot be patented. The iPhone, or the iPad, is not just an object, a product, a thing. It is a platform. The core of the idea is not the device itself, it is the combination of cheap or free apps on a relatively open platform for which anyone can design.

By opening the iPhone App Store to all comers rather than just selling apps built by Apple, Jobs guaranteed that there would be a lot of apps. By making developers come through the App Store and meet Apple's standards, Jobs made consumers feel safe downloading apps—at least they would not infect your iPhone, or bombard you with spam. Most important, by getting the developers to set "free" as the most common price, with many apps priced at just a few dollars, and almost all under $10, Jobs set the expectations that apps would be cheap, that customers would use a lot of them, try different ones, and buy a more expensive version when they wanted something more. This, in turn, made the iPhone far more valuable. You can use the one instrument for almost anything you could imagine, and for a lot of things you couldn't imagine until you saw it. The result: by summer of 2011, the 200 million iOS users worldwide could browse nearly half a million available apps, and had downloaded 15 billion of them—an average of 75 for every user. And even while $30, $50, and higher-priced apps have shown up, the average price of an app has actually fallen over time.

At the same time, Android and other operating systems for smart phones and tablets have collectively overtaken iOS devices in the speed of their growth.

All of these smart phones and tablets are relatively expensive devices, but prices will fall and cheaper imitations will arise. The experience with netbooks and cell phones provide the model. Since their inception, the retail price of laptop computers had been set at around $1,000 and above. Responding to a challenge by One Laptop Per Child Foundation and the United Nations Development Program at the 2006 World Economic Forum in Davos, Switzerland, Taiwanese computer manufacturers set out to design tiny, rugged, low-power, lightweight laptops that could access the web for a target retail price of $100. No one had attempted anything so cheap until this challenge arose. But as they succeeded in producing these "netbooks" in the below-$200 range, the manufacturers discovered that not only could they build something that cheaply, but that there was a retail market for them far larger than the developing world educational market. Five years down the road, you can order a new netbook off the web for little more than $200.

Similarly, both cell phones and cell phone accounts were rather expensive when they first began to penetrate the consumer market in the early 1990s. As late as 1997, only 18% of the population of developed countries had cell phones. Today, more than 90% of the world's people live in an area with cell phone coverage, and there are approximately 6 billion cell phone accounts—in a world with 7 billion people. And this is an important point: the majority of those accounts connect not to rich or middle-class people, but to poor people. In India and China, at the start of 2011, the penetration rates were 70% and 64%, respectively.* Clearly most of those people are not members of the much smaller emerging middle classes of these countries. They are poor people.

Why are poor people so eager to get a cell phone and an account? Because while a cell phone, with its access to education, information, and connection, is a great convenience for someone in the middle class, it is a life transformer for a poor person. You can do business over the cell phone. You can find out what prices are being offered in the city for your rice. You can find an inexpensive irrigation pump to replace the one that just broke. And you can find help for your sick child.

Just as we have seen cell phones and now netbooks proliferate, we will see smart phones and web-enabled tablets and the networks that support them proliferate across the "bottom of the pyramid" over the next decade with surprising speed. And healthcare apps of all kinds will proliferate with them. Access to real, reliable, applicable health information, and access to care are definitely of life-changing importance for the poor.

---

* Statistics from: http://mobithinking.com/mobile-marketing-tools/latest-mobile-stats.

Suddenly nearly every human on the planet will have access to medical information and, increasingly, to actual care in the palm of their hand (or in their neighbor's hand, or the hand of the guy down the block who sells minutes of connectivity)—in a device that can also take pictures ("show me the rash"), sense its own location, and compute information from other sensors. There is already a website dedicated exclusively to reviewing medical apps (iMedicalApp.com), including patient scheduler apps, charge capture apps, medical calculators, and patient trackers. The iTunes and Android App Stores are flooded with hundreds of apps for consumers and clinicians alike. Already some health workers are equipped with cheap sonograms, oxygen monitors, and microscopes that can be attached directly to a smart phone. The advent of mobile computing devices like smart phones and tablets, with the platforms they create for distributing inexpensive apps, will turn out to have been a major watershed event in the history of healthcare.

Extending the Clinic into the Home

In time, dedicated home medical devices will emerge to take the clinic directly into the home. One recent example arose from the work of the Worrell design firm, as shown in this video: http://vimeo.com/29485756. They took some insights from following ER folks around and charting their workflow, then used those insights to inform a design that would enable people to better interact with the health system from their homes. At about the four-minute mark in the video, the design team discusses what kind of home health kit/device would work. What follows is a demo of a mother consulting about her child's flu, and getting actual testing, care, and monitoring from a live nurse remotely, all from this kit, a kind of dedicated laptop with an attached home medicine kit. According to the member of the design team whom I spoke with, the kit shown is a real prototype, and all the technology used is currently available.

If the technology is all there, why don't we do this already? Because in a fee-for-service system there is no billing code for remote care. But, we are going to see this change. As healthcare providers take on more risk for the costs of the care for the family in the demo, treating them in the home through such a device (one device per family) could start to look like a better idea. It would be far cheaper, faster, and more effective than getting patients to come into an urgent care clinic—cheap enough that the healthcare organization would simply buy the devices and give them to the covered families.

So as major provider organizations move into risk-contracted relationships, actual medical care that would now be taking place in the built clinical environment would be taking place in the home, supported by a live nurse monitor in a dedicated environment at the clinic. The home becomes an extension of the clinic, not only for the chronically ill and frail elderly whom we now might tend with home care, but for the well family in primary care.

India and China: Globalization Cuts Both Ways

Increasingly, the competition for some parts of the U.S. healthcare system, especially pharmaceuticals, devices, and supplies, will come from beyond the U.S. borders. These include factors such as the growth of the Israeli company Teva into a dominant global force in generic drugs, now producing 60 billion tablets a year in 38 locations around the world, and a sixth of all prescriptions in the United States—along with the similar rise of the Indian generic companies, such as Sun and Cipla. These companies (especially Teva) have shown themselves to be smart, fast, Lean, and disciplined. They, and companies like them, will set the framework for much of the U.S. healthcare market for the future.

This runs parallel to another factor of vast importance, the growth of development and production of drugs, devices, and supplies in India and China. In the past, though firms based in wealthy countries happily exported manufacturing to countries with vast supplies of cheap labor, they would never have thought of exporting research and development. Today, that is reversing. In the last decade, multinational firms have built over 300 R&D labs in India alone.

The frame in which we have put this development in the past turns out to be completely wrong. We have called it outsourcing, exporting some of our capacity to the land of cheap engineers. Here's another lens to look through: these two nations, with together more than a quarter of the world's population, are rapidly developing their own capacity. Their primary concern will not be supplying the G8 countries like the United States, Europe, and Japan, but increasingly supplying, first, their own populations; second, the rising and increasingly urban and medicalized populations of the Islamic world, Southeast Asia, Latin America, Africa, and Russia; and third, the G8 countries.

How are they doing? They already manufacture over 80% of the active ingredients in medicines worldwide.

The competition that they inspire in all those markets will force G8 companies to radically reengineer their product lines to include quality products at price points far below the ones they are used to today. For any healthcare product or service that can be easily transported, this means the end of the world as these companies know it.

To understand the extraordinary force that this will have on the healthcare world that we know, we have to understand a few things about India and China and the growth state of their medical markets.

India

India is a very tough medical market. It is a competitive democracy with a broadly based economy, but it spends a lower percentage of GDP on public health than almost any other country,* and the majority of that is consumed by the well-off minority.† The entire healthcare sector costs only $75 billion, in a country with nearly four times the U.S. population. The really big potential market here is at the bottom because the billion poor Indians are very poorly served, when they are served at all, medically.

Though theoretically served by a universal free healthcare system, what they have in practice is a highly privatized system, more than any other major country, with 75% of all medical payments coming out-of-pocket. At the poor and rural level the system is rife with untrained quacks and *ohjas*, the folk healers.‡ Some 80% of rural doctors have no qualifications at all; many lack even a high school diploma.§ Doctors on the public payroll often shift patients to see them in their private clinics so that they can make more money off of them. The system is highly bifurcated between rich and poor. But like China, India has been on a rapid rise. Today, India's GDP is 2½ times what it was in 1980,⁵ the rate of rise is up, and the country has been less affected by the current downturn than many.

Even rural incomes are rising—a 27% increase is expected in the next five years—so that for the first time, marketing research companies are going door to door to ask what the people really want, and companies are tailoring products for them. The government is replacing a highly corrupt subsidy system for the poor with direct cash card payments, which should help create a stronger consumer market. The most ambitious database program in the world is deploying right now in India. Within a few years every Indian will be identifiable by a combination of fingerprints, an iris scan, and a number. This will enable direct contact for medical payments and help.

So there are huge structural problems in the Indian medical market—and at the same time a vast potential. It is this domestic Indian market that will engen-

---

* "India's poor need a radical package: Amartya Sen," The Hindu, 1/31/08.
† A Panagariya, "India: The Crisis in Rural Health Care," Brookings Institution report, 1/24/08.
‡ Amartya Sen, ibid.
§ A Panagariya, ibid.
⁵ M Wolf, "What India must do if it is to be an affluent country," Financial Times, 7/7/09.

der fierce competition to provide medical devices, supplies, and pharmaceuticals of acceptable quality at far lower prices than we have ever seen.

China

In China, people continue to flood into the cities of the east, looking for work. In Beijing and Shanghai, they are even renting out tiny rooms in former bomb shelters six stories and more underground with no sanitation or ventilation. They are coming from the west and the countryside, which until recently accounted for 80% of the population. The differences in income are enormous—as are the differences in resources.

Among the reasons people are on the move, besides looking for work, is looking for healthcare for themselves and their parents. In the countryside and the west, the healthcare system essentially does not exist. Clinicians have moved to where there is money to pay them. So the government has been rolling out a two-tier health insurance system across the nation, one for city residents and one for rural peasants (though even the extremely low cost for the peasant version has proven too expensive for much of the rural part of the nation). And the central government is on a tear to build the physical infrastructure and the healthcare workforce at a historically unmatched pace. The government plans to build at least one new hospital in every one of China's 2,000 counties, for a planned total of over 5,000 new hospitals, as rapidly as possible, within this decade—plus tens of thousands of clinics staffed by hundreds of thousands of newly trained clinicians. This will clearly mean a vastly larger demand for pharmaceuticals, devices, and supplies, but in a market in which the government is and will be fierce about holding prices down and controlling the supply chain.

Cheap Biologicals and Biosimilars

So we see combinations of Indian and Chinese companies building factories right now to supply not only the low-end generic pharmaceuticals we are accustomed to them making, but also generic versions of the high-end biologicals and biosimilars, such as Herceptin for breast cancer, Avastin for colon cancer, Rituxan for non-Hodgkins lymphoma, and Enbrel for rheumatoid arthritis. Cipla has recently announced that, working with Chinese partners, it will soon be able to provide these drugs for one-third of the cost for which they are currently available. But it won't stop there. Dr. Yusuf K. Hamied, Cipla's chairman, has stated, "Once we recover our costs, prices will fall further ... a lot further."[*]

---

[*] Harris G. "China and India Making Inroads in Biotech Drugs," NY Times, September 18, 2011. Available at: www.nytimes.com/2011/09/19/health/policy/19drug.html.

Should we credit his ability to carry out this promise? Ten years ago he promised that Cipla would be able to provide the basic cocktail of AIDS drugs for $1. At this point Cipla is providing that cocktail for 6 million patients worldwide for 20 cents.

There will be enormous patent battles over these attempts. These biologicals and biosimilars represent, for example, fully half of the income of Roche Pharmaceuticals. The price differences are so huge and the need so great that it is unlikely that the Western pharmaceutical companies will win these battles. Companies like Teva, Cipla, and others in India and China will eventually be supplying these high-end drugs to the vast populations of South Asia, Southeast Asia, Africa, and Latin America. India and China each have rising middle classes, but both of their populations still consist of more than 80% poor people who exist on less than a dollar a day. So the cost structure that they are developing and producing for, in their own and other countries, is vastly different than what we are used to. We're not talking discounts. We're not talking half price. We're talking 1/10 of the prices we are used to, 1/100.

And drugs are just the leading edge of this enormous shift in the healthcare supply market.

Reverse Innovation

We will see, over the coming decade, an efflorescence of low-cost, high-quality products designed and invented in the "emerging giants" for their markets and the markets of other bottom-tier countries, which will go on to disrupt markets in the G8 countries. Jeffrey Immelt, the CEO of GE, calls this phenomenon "reverse innovation." We are used to thinking that we in the United States and Europe and Japan will create products and sell them to the vast markets of the rest of the world. Now India, China, and other countries are creating innovative products and selling them to us.

The biggest impact of such reverse innovation will likely be in healthcare. For instance in May 2009, GE announced that GE Healthcare South Asia "would spend $3 billion to create at least 100 health-care innovations that would substantially lower costs, increase access, and improve quality." They accompanied that boast with the unveiling of a $1,000 handheld electrocardiogram device and a portable, PC-based ultrasound machine that sells for as little as $15,000, a mere 15% of the lowest-priced ultrasound machines marketed in the West. Both of these machines went on sale almost immediately in the United States and other G8 countries as well.[*]

---

[*] Immelt J., Govindarajan G., Trimble C. "How GE Is Disrupting Itself," *Harvard Business Review*, October 2009. Available at: http://hbr.org/2009/10/how-ge-is-disrupting-itself/ar/1.

ReaMatrix, an Indian company, has pioneered dry reagents to be used in diagnostic testing, a significant savings in a country with spotty access to electricity and refrigeration, driving the typical price of an AIDS test, for instance, from US$40 down to US$5—and the reagents are already FDA approved, making them ready for a world market. The same company is now pioneering an inexpensive, portable lab-in-a-box. Used with these reagents, it can be programmed to test for diseases such as HIV, malaria, arthritis, and diabetes—and it can work in the heat and dust of rural India, in a village clinic, or even on a patient's doorstep. It can operate on power sources that range from 80 volts to 230 volts of AC, or even 12 volts DC from a car battery.

Similarly, Perfint, a company in the Indian city of Chennai, has designed a low-cost, CT-driven robotic arm capable of doing biopsies, administering anesthetics, and ablating tumors with electromagnetic waves to diagnose and then treat lung, liver, and other soft tissue cancers. The company's CEO S. Nandakumar says, "The Indian market really pushes you to the edge. The procedures you look at are very different, very cost-effective, but when we do this, we find it is actually what the Western world wants."[*]

These devices are not "just as good as" the top-of-the-line expensive devices with which they compete. Rather, their makers describe them as being "just good enough" for many situations. According to Immelt and his coauthors in a 2009 *Harvard Business Review* article, they "deliver decent performance at an ultra-low cost—a 50-percent solution at a 15-percent price." At first these low-cost devices were marketed in the rich countries for niche markets, such as free clinics and mobile clinics, but they are already establishing a much lower-priced position on the product line. Over time, as U.S. and other G8 healthcare providers come under severe pressure to reduce their process costs, we will see low-cost devices like these used in mainstream medicine.

Smarter, cheaper, leaner ways of managing medical practices and healthcare systems; technologies that extend care into the home; evidence-based design for the built environment; "big data" analytics for patients, for systems, and for the whole society; low-cost drugs and devices built and designed in poorer countries—all of these are ways to rebuild the actual processes of healthcare to be less expensive, more widely available, closer to the customer, safer.

---

[*] Denver S. "From India, seeking simpler health-care products" Washington Post, Oct. 22, 2011. Available at: http://www.washingtonpost.com/world/asia-pacific/from-india-seeking-simpler-health-care-products/2011/10/11/gIQAo6Qy2L_story.html.
http://www.reametrix.com/.
http://www.perfinthealthcare.com/.

MAKING IT
ALL WORK

3

Chapter 11

Beyond Healthcare

You want to do something really big about health? You want fewer people to die, fewer to live crippled and in pain? You want to end suffering? You want to help more people live full, healthy, happy lives?

You want to do this as cheaply as possible, so that you can do it as much as possible? So you are looking for the biggest lever and place to stand to move the world?

I'm here to tell you that we have the lever. We know what it is. You can put your hands on it.

It's not easy, not by a long shot. In fact, it is a lot of hard work for a long time. But it does work. Here it is: Build healthy communities.

The cheapest healthcare investment with the highest return is to invest in making the cities and communities where we live and work healthier. The techniques are well studied, the examples are legion, the results are major, and the costs are tiny compared to the costs of treating people after they become sick.

Most of the work of building healthier communities has little or nothing to do with medicine. Many pieces do not even have anything obvious to do with public health measures like clean water. A healthier community, it turns out, means a community with better education, better jobs, more economic opportunity, easier small business credit, safer streets, stronger families, a stronger sense of mutuality and belonging. And these things are not just correlations, they are causative. If you help a community get better schools and adult education, it gets healthier. If more small businesses are able to start up and prosper, the community gets healthier. Create more education and more business opportunity for women, and women have fewer babies and are able to care for them better: fewer, healthier kids. Help rural families get clear title to the land and secure water rights, and you get more prosperity, better nutrition, and healthier people.

The difficulty with doing this kind of work is not whether it works. It does work. By now, the river of literature on the successes of the Healthy Cities/Healthy Communities movement is wide, deep, and incontrovertible.

The difficulty is simply that this is about the 99%. Health is about bodies, and bodies come, standard issue, one per person. No matter how rich you are, you can't buy a set of replacement bodies to use whenever the one you have stops working. You can't buy whole vast institutions, research to produce new drugs, clean air, or safe cities. For healthcare to support the care of our bodies, we need great institutions, research facilities, pharmaceutical efforts, massive supply chains, and hundreds of thousands of highly trained professionals. For public health, we need massive clean water systems and sewer systems, public safety organs like police and fire, disaster response systems, policies that insure clean air and food, and vaccination programs against infectious disease. For a healthy population we need an educated population, a population that can find work and economic opportunities that can support their families. We need strong community. In the broadest sense, we need each other.

We cannot achieve a healthy society—much less achieve it at low cost—without tending to the good of the whole society. Even the 1% cannot have the best, longest, healthiest lives possible for themselves and their families if the society as a whole is struggling. Their own prosperity depends on the health of the whole society, and on the infrastructure that nurtures that health.

One tiny business example of the linkage in the day-to-day nuts and bolts of healthy communities: I was brought in by an economic development commission to consult on the idea of the healthy community in a small town in Canada that depended on the tourist trade. They had the idea that it might be good marketing to promote their area as being a "healthy destination." I gave a talk, and had some good individual sit-down time with the mayor and some of the top local business people. I tried to impress on them that the healthy community idea was more than a marketing ploy, that it was about the fabric of their town.

One resort owner was having none of it. The whole "health" kick was a distraction from his business model. I asked him to tell me more about how his business was going, and what obstacles he was facing. His biggest problem was the workforce. He had a lot of turnover, and a lot of absenteeism. These problems are endemic, of course, to a low-pay service industry like tourism. But what was the main reason people didn't show up for work?

"Sick kids—mothers have to stay home to take care of sick kids."

"Are an unusual number of kids sick here?"

"Seems like it. There's only one daycare place in town and it's a terrible, under-staffed, wretched facility, overcrowded. Seems like a lot of kids get sick there."

"So a better daycare facility, with better staff, would likely result in less absenteeism among your workforce? How much do you think that would cost? Do you think you could get other business owners to invest in it? Is there a better spot in town for it?"

He had not thought of the possibility of acting like a CEO and securing his supply chain, in this case, the supply of mothers of young children able to come to work because their kids were well taken care of in a healthy environment. But it turned out that, smartly designed, there was a business model in the idea, a return on investment in health. He left the lunch with the sketch of a business plan, and a decision to talk to other business owners in town about it.

A tiny example, but it plays out in a thousand ways across all our communities: supporting a healthy community is good business.

Len Duhl, the Father of Healthy Communities

I first sat down with Dr. Len Duhl in 1993 at his home near the UC Berkeley campus. We talked in his cramped, book-lined, half-basement study with the laden plum tree bowing its fruit over the garden gate outside. He was gnomish, tweedy, and quiet spoken in a gravelly way, a university professor, a Menninger-trained psychiatrist with a warm and confidential manner. He didn't look like a world shaker, a cultural revolutionary. Yet Len Duhl had had more positive effect on people than any of us could ever hope for: one basic idea in a talk in 1984 had helped spawn a program of grassroots social change—the World Health Organization's Healthy Cities program—that was by 1993 growing in over a thousand cities around the world.

In a 40-year career in government and academia, in the Public Health Service, at the National Institute of Mental Health, at the Department of Housing and Urban Development, writing speeches for Robert Kennedy, organizing hearings on the health of cities for Senator Abraham Ribicoff, teaching at the University of California at Berkeley, consulting for WHO and UNICEF, Duhl had shaped and expounded that one idea: If you want healthy people, you have to build healthy cities, livable cities with decent housing, clean water and air, recreation programs, community organizations, and strong families. They must all knit together. To do this, you have to change things from the ground up. He told me, "The policies that run our society, and in fact run our health systems, are not health policies—they are business policies, they are profit policies, they are power policies."

Duhl's first insight into the intertwining of health and every other social factor came from being pulled out of his chosen field while he was still a young resident:

> In the midst of my psychiatric training, during the Korean war, Uncle Sam tapped me on the shoulder. I volunteered for the Public Health Service, and got assigned to Contra Costa County, California. Among other things, we did a massive x-ray screening survey for lung conditions. And we did a study on the people who didn't get x-rayed. The populations that needed it most didn't get x-rayed, and the ones that didn't need it, because they were pretty healthy, did get x-rayed.
>
> The ones who didn't were poor; they lived in north Richmond, an unincorporated slum. The health department had a hard time there, but the Quakers, the Friends Service Committee, did well. They ran the neighborhood house, and they were doing community organization and development. They were facilitating a process that got people involved, and suddenly the community started asking for services. During the two years I was there, we got involved in setting up daycare programs, well-baby clinics, housing programs, chicken dinners, and a legal service, all coming from the neighborhood house and the community organization. The more we worked, the more positive was the response of the people to the health department. I found that if we just did a health program by itself, we'd get little response from this population. But if we did community organization and got everybody involved, we got a lot more response.

The experience stayed with him, and he began a career as a doctor working to shape policies to help make cities better places to live. During the Nixon years, he returned to California and formulated the idea of the "healthy city."

Similar ideas were percolating elsewhere, as the field of "population health" took shape. In a long series of books and articles from the 1950s to the 1980s, the British physician and demographic historian Thomas McKeown argued that the great increase in population in Britain since the 1700s owed more to diet and lifestyle than to medicine or even public health measures like sanitation and vaccinations. His specific conclusions have not been borne out by subsequent research, but his general observation did: the "determinants of health" (a phrase he coined) extend far beyond medicine.* In 1974, the Canadian Ministry of

---

* Colgrove, J., "The McKeown Thesis: A Historical Controversy and Its Enduring Influence," *American Journal of Public Health*, Vol. 92, No. 5, 2002, pp. 725–29, available at http://www.ncbi.nlm.nih.gov/pmc/articles/PMC1447153/.

National Health and Welfare, under Marc Lalonde, published a groundbreaking report by Hubert Laframboise based on and refining McKeown's ideas, which first broached the idea of "health promotion." It grouped the determinants of health into four areas: human biology, healthcare systems, environment, and lifestyle. The Lalonde Report became enormously influential over time.

By 1984, Trevor Hancock, a young Canadian protégé of Duhl's, was taking Duhl's ideas beyond research and grand declarations to actual programs in a real city. He was organizing Healthy Toronto 2000. To celebrate the 10th anniversary of the Lalonde Report, Dr. Hancock organized a Beyond Health Care conference in Toronto with the Toronto Board of Health, the Canadian Public Health Association, and National Health and Welfare. Duhl came and spoke—and Ilona Kickbush, a young health promotions director from the World Health Organization's European office in Copenhagen, latched onto the idea with fervor.

Over the next five years, she organized a Healthy Cities secretariat for some 35 cities in Europe, with Duhl and Hancock writing the curriculum and designing the program. Cities elsewhere in the world asked for help, so Duhl and Hancock became a traveling global road show for how to build a healthy community. So many cities took up the idea and started projects that the WHO lost track.

By the early 1990s, Duhl and Hancock caught the eye of Kathryn Johnson, the visionary head of the San Francisco-based Healthcare Forum (then independent, today, as the Health Forum, it is an arm of the American Hospital Association (AHA)). The Healthy Cities/Healthy Communities rubric fit her large-scale, systems-thinking view of health and healthcare. And with the onrush of managed care, many hospitals were suddenly confronted with the possibility that they might be at risk for the health of populations. Johnson made Healthy Communities a central part of the Healthcare Forum's agenda and founded the Healthy Communities Fellowship, which continues to train organizers.

Involve Everyone

Dr. Duhl's words to me from nearly two decades ago seemed to ring with special prescience in the "occupy everything" fall of 2011:

> There has been a revolution in this country since 1954. The *Brown v. the Board of Education* court case was the turning point that began to say that people who had been oppressed can now speak up for themselves. Since that time, everybody speaks up for themselves to the point where we are all victims. We are all complaining. We are all saying that we have to get into the act. We all want to participate. We are all rejecting the top-down model of control.

Building a "healthy community" has to be a 360° project, involving stakeholders throughout a community and from the bottom to the top. People support what they help create. People own what they help create. This means that there is no cookie-cutter Healthy Community project and the variety can be rather amazing.

One healthcare organization asked homeless and unemployed people in Seattle, if there were only one thing they could provide for them, what would it be? The answer, by a large margin: dental work. If you have no money, you can at least go to an emergency room if you're sick, but you can't get a dentist to work for free. In New York, working with a different population, the answer was: cheap pagers, so that a potential employer could call them back.

Horsens, Denmark, has only a few minorities. One is a small, tightly knit group of immigrant Turks, few of whom speak any Danish. To protect their culture and religion, the men only allowed the women to go where the men went, which for the most part was not anywhere they would contact Danes. A Healthy Cities group concerned with children's health in that part of town realized that this was one group of children they could not reach. Rather than invent some bureaucratic answer to this isolation, they searched for something they might have in common with the Turkish women. They threw a few parties, got up a few bingo games, and got to know about 15 families. Then they hit on sewing. That was innocuous enough—the men would allow their women to go alone to a sewing class and sewing circle with Danish women. When the Turkish women showed up, they brought 50 kids with them. So daycare was arranged for the next session. After the sewing became routine, the Healthy Cities group introduced another idea: the women could learn Danish. By this stage, the men would even let the women do that. Bit by bit, the walls crumbled, and the Danes gained the confidence of the Turks.

Bethel New Life in Chicago has been building the community for decades on a shoestring, helping local people start businesses with micro-credit and training, building and rehabbing houses, teaching young people how to be good parents. It started with one white pastor and his sister in a very black neighborhood and was built piece by piece by the people of the neighborhood.

President Obama, in his days as a community organizer in the 1980s, was a protégé of some of the people involved in similar Healthy Communities initiatives in Chicago and other cities—and when his acerbic chief of staff Rahm Emanuel became the mayor of Chicago, one of his first priorities was an ambitious Healthy Chicago program.

By now, Healthy Communities projects are everywhere. The Robert Woods Johnson Foundation has, in the last two years, funded Healthy Kids Healthy

Communities projects in 50 locations across the country specifically to fight obesity in children—a particularly high-leverage goal.*

At the urging of the National Civic League, many cities over the last two decades have created civic indices that measure the quality of life in a variety of ways, from voter participation to local concerns, like the temperature of the water in the river downstream from a power plant. In many of these civic indices, people measure whatever they want to measure—different groups have different concerns. A rural community might be more concerned with pesticide runoff, while an urban group might measure the number of street arrests, or the availability of good grocery stores with fresh vegetables.

The health part of this kind of index is a health needs assessment or a community risk assessment. One clause of the Patient Protection and Affordable Care Act (PPACA) reform law mandates that all hospitals perform such an assessment of their communities: you can't improve what you can't measure. Seems like an onerous and costly task, but the American Hospital Association's Association for Community Health Improvement offers hospitals a risk assessment toolkit. And out in Berkeley, California, the Healthy Communities Institute is the brainchild of Deryk Van Brunt, one of Dr. Duhl's students and protégés. It offers a comprehensive plug-and-play package of software and databases that already knows all about your community—at least everything that can be mined from available data.†

We don't do healthcare to distribute medical services to people. We do healthcare to keep people healthy, to help them back to health when they are sick, and to ease their suffering in the process. Medicine is only one of the ways we can keep people healthy, and it is by far the most expensive, dangerous, and problematic. It is far cheaper and more effective to help people not get sick in the first place by planting a garden, organizing a hiking club, introducing young people to old people, starting a healthy cooking club, joining a Police Athletic League, becoming a Big Brother or Big Sister, testing the groundwater for arsenic and dioxin, getting the kids vaccinated, putting together micro-credit so that people can start businesses in their homes, any of the thousand and ten thousand ways that we can help knit our local communities, help them be more educated, wealthier, safer, and more of a real community. We can do this.

---

* Healthy Kids Healthy Communities, http://www.healthykidshealthycommunities.org/communities.

† http://www.healthycommunitiesinstitute.com/.

Chapter 12

The Evil Profit Motive and the Virtues of Competition

The great thing about working with changing healthcare is everybody's got an answer. Unfortunately, pretty much everyone thinks their answer is *the* answer, the one change that fixes everything. The world, especially the healthcare part of the world, is more complicated than that. It is a complex adaptive system, and no single tweak, no matter how fundamental, will set it on the right track.

Perhaps the largest set of single tweaks revolves around the idea of simply voting the insurance companies off the island and shifting the entire payment system to a single-payer (or "Medicare for all") model—and the related idea that, one way or another, all healthcare should be not for profit. As one friend put it, "Profit has no place in the business of healing."

Both of these questions are actually far more complex than they seem on the surface, and both go to the question of motive: What are the real goals of the organizations and people making up the healthcare system? Are they truly focused on their customers' health? Or is that just something else to manipulate to make money? These questions are worth giving some good, nuanced, informed thought to. What are the arguments for single payer?

Arguments for a Single-Payer System

Insurance Companies Are Evil

Proponents of a single payer point to common abuses by private insurance companies (which we discuss in some detail in the next chapter, "There Ought To Be A Law"). Some simply want punishment and revenge: "Health insurance companies are bad. Kill them!" One set of my friends can never seem to talk about ways to fix healthcare without using the phrase "lamp posts and rope"—and it is health plan executives that they picture swinging.

A subtler version argues not that health plans are morally evil, but that the profit motive necessarily drives them to do evil things: for-profit insurers have to return a profit to their shareholders to keep the stock price high and drive the value of their company. The more of the premium dollar they pay out in actual medical expenses (the higher the medical loss ratio (MLR)), the less that is left over for profit and bloated executive salaries. So health plans can't help it: they have to squeeze both the customer and the healthcare providers, and deny payments every way possible.

Yet for-profit health plans are not noticeably more evil than not-for-profit ones. There are plenty of horror stories and struggles over payment involving not-for-profit payers, and plenty of massive executive salaries.

These are actually arguments not for making the insurance companies commit *seppuku*, but for regulating them, specifically for setting a mandatory level of medical loss ratio (MLR). The Patient Protection and Affordable Care Act (PPACA) reform law does exactly that, requiring insurers (depending upon the type of company) to return 80% or 85% of premiums to the customers in the form of medical services paid for. Accomplish that, and executive salaries and profits are not taken out of the pockets of the customers.

Extra Transaction Costs

Historically, health insurance companies have intentionally made transactional friction—the extraordinary difficulty of simply getting paid by them for incurred medical expenses—an important part of the "risk mitigation" in their business model. The morass of denials, appeals, mistakes, partial payments, underpayments, and undisclosed fee schedules is designed to simply wear out the payee. For some fraction of the claims, the patient, doctor, or clinic will simply give up. Doctors, especially doctors in sole or small practice who may not have much staff to doggedly pursue claims, typically expect to just write off some percentage of their claims. It is hard to think of any other industry that so thoroughly and routinely messes with its principle suppliers and payees.

Aside from the cost of the dropped claims, the morass makes providers incur huge costs in just trying to get paid. As we have mentioned elsewhere, the cost averages $65,000 to $80,000 per physician per year, a total of about $30 billion per year across healthcare, or nearly a third of the added cost to cover all uninsured Americans.

Under a single-payer (Medicare for all) system, these costs would drop drastically. Medicare billing is complex, but nowhere near as arbitrarily complex and varied as private payer billing. But such costs could be pared dramatically without a single-payer system by regulating insurance companies more firmly, prosecuting patterns of contract breaking, requiring the use of common electronic codes, plus other legal changes that we discuss in the next chapter.

At the same time, changing from a fee-for-service system to risk-bearing bundled payments, as well as dictating a minimum MLR, will change the relationship between the payers and providers over time. When the insurer is paying for each item, it is far easier to challenge each payment. When every dropped claim can add to the insurer's profit margin, there is tremendous incentive to get the payee to drop the claim. When the insurer is paying for whole insured populations at predetermined rates, and when a set percentage of the premium income must be paid out for medical services, there is far less incentive to deny claims or try to get them dropped.

Extra Fundamental Costs

Some proponents of single-payer reform argue that single-payer systems are simply inherently cheaper, even aside from profit and bloated transaction costs. Many argue that this is *the* one change that would, by itself, drop healthcare costs dramatically. For proof, they point to other national systems, which do cost dramatically less. But would eliminating private health insurance, as Canada famously has for half a century, by itself solve the huge cost problem of healthcare?

The evidence suggests it would not, not by itself—and the evidence is massive and right in front of us. First, look at other countries. If a single-payer system were the method to drastically cut costs of healthcare in the United States, we could look at other systems and find that the low-cost systems were all single payer, and all the high-cost systems were privately insured. But that's not the way it is. In the political debate about healthcare in the United States, people generally assume that all of those other countries that pay half what we do for healthcare do it on a Canadian model: no private insurance allowed. But that assumption is wrong. Many (like the UK) allow supplemental insurance. Germany has a highly mixed public-private financing system. Some, like Switzerland and the Netherlands, have almost completely private health insurance systems that carry individual mandates and subsidies and are strongly regulated. Yet each of these systems provides healthcare for a much lower cost than ours. There is no lineup of low-cost single-payer systems on one side and high-cost private payer systems on the other. There is simply the United States and everybody else. Whatever their secret sauce, it's not government pay vs. private pay.

The second piece of evidence is right here in the United States: Medicare itself. Though Medicare reimbursements are almost always lower than those of private insurance, they are still far higher than medical costs in other countries. There is little evidence that, overall, Medicare's cost-cutting efforts have slowed the amazingly steady climb of healthcare costs. They have not, as the economists say, "bent the cost curve."

That's because neither traditional Medicare nor the imagined "Medicare-for-all" single-payer system subverts the commoditized insurance-supported fee-for-service business model. That model pays for activity, not outcomes. So what it gets us is lots of activity.

Going to a single-payer system would be one way to solve some of the problems of healthcare. But it would not solve nearly as many of them, or on nearly as grand a scale, as its proponents suppose. And it would not, by itself, bring us better healthcare that costs less for everyone.

I have many progressive friends who are passionate about the single-payer cause. To them I say, "Keep your eyes on the prize." The prize is not revenge on the insurance companies. The prize is not conforming to any imagined ideal structure. The prize is better and cheaper healthcare for everyone, whatever works to get us there. If we believe and act as if achieving a single-payer system is the only means in the United States to get us there, it is quite likely that we will never get there. If we believe and act as if achieving a single-payer system will solve the problem, then we will assuredly never get there, even if single payer becomes the law of the land.

Single payer is not the prize. The prize is better and cheaper healthcare for everyone. Keep your eyes on the prize.

For Profit? Or Not?

Some argue, more broadly, that it is simply morally repellant to make a profit from healthcare. "How can you be making a profit from people's suffering?" they ask.

But a question that seems at first obvious, on second thought seems nonsensical. Except for volunteers, free clinic staffers, and not-for-profit board members, everyone in healthcare makes a living at it. We hardly expect doctors and nurses to work for free.

The healthcare industry is vast, and most of it consists of for-profit corporations. Thousands of companies throughout the world are suppliers to healthcare, including some of the world's largest corporations, such as Apple, Google, Microsoft, GE, Toyota, Airbus, Siemens, and Philips. Suppliers also include lots of smart little start-ups coming up with things that could make healthcare a lot better and cheaper.

U.S. hospitals and health systems have a wide variety of structures. Most are not-for-profit in one way or another. There are self-organized and self-owned community hospitals, church-owned hospitals, district hospitals with elected boards, municipal general hospitals, and hospitals owned by for-profit or not-for-profit HMOs (such as Kaiser), or by multispecialty practices (such as Mayo, Scott and White in Texas, and the Cleveland Clinic). There are also for-profit chains, such as Columbia and Tenet, and private doctor-owned hospitals, specialty clinics, and ambulatory care centers. There are also for-profit/not-for-profit hybrids, such as not-for-profit hospitals that own for-profit subsidiaries, and not-for-profit hospitals managed under contract by for-profit chains.

It's complicated. The most egregious scandals over the years in the world of hospitals have come from the for-profit side, such as the heart doctor at a Tenet hospital in Redding, California, who, it seemed, would do a heart operation on you if you had a heart to operate on. And in the largest and most famous case, HCA, Inc. paid $840 million in 2000 and another $881 million in 2003 to the federal government in civil and criminal penalties for an admitted wide array of Medicare and Medicaid fraud, plus hundreds of millions more in settling private suits, all for widespread company practices under the leadership of Rick Scott, now governor of Florida.*

But the picture is actually more complex than that. If you watch healthcare as I have for decades, visit hundreds of hospitals, take the boards of scores of hospitals, systems, and chains through retreats and strategy conferences and visioning sessions, talk to thousands of healthcare executives in their offices, at conferences, at social hours, you see a lot of variation in behavior. You see not-for-profits whose business model is designed to ask how they can make money in the better part of town so that they can serve the poorer parts of town with free clinics. You also see not-for-profits shutting down services in the poorer parts of town and expanding into wealthier markets while sitting on a billion dollars or more in the bank. You see for-profits skirting the law—and not-for-profits as well.

---

* U.S. Department of Justice, "Largest Health Care Fraud Case in U.S. History Settled HCA Investigation Nets Record Total of $1.7 Billion" (press release), June 26, 2003, accessed online http://www.justice.gov/opa/pr/2003/June/03_civ_386.htm.

What you do not see is a bright line between for-profit and not-for-profit, with the for-profits acting evil and rapacious, and the not-for-profits acting like Mother Teresa.

How an institution acts seems to come from something deeper in its DNA than its for-profit or not-for-profit tax designation.

I noticed something interesting years ago. For some article or another, I was making a list of organizations that seemed to me to be the most advanced in their organization, and in their use of technology. I suddenly realized that the majority of the organizations on the list were Catholic, and several of the rest were religious. I thought: That can't be right. One would think of religious-based, especially Catholic, organizations as being more conservative, slower to change.

A little investigation and thinking revealed a different picture: most Catholic hospitals were founded quite a long time ago by orders of nuns. By the late twentieth century, being a nun was not such a popular thing. The average age of nuns had climbed to nearly 70. Many nuns felt that there would not be enough of them around to carry the organizations forward into the new century. Their solution? Merge their hospitals with others into new chains of Catholic hospitals, such as Catholic Health Initiative, Ascension, and Christus.

The result was a series of chains of old hospitals with brand new, young management teams who were eager to bring modern management techniques to bear on carrying out the missions of these deeply charitable institutions.

Other institutions are no longer church affiliated, but bear the community dedication in their DNA. For instance, Intermountain Health System, based in Salt Lake City, is independent of the Mormon Church. But its attitude of cooperation, particularly in Brent James's pioneering campaigns for better and more standardized medical quality, seems to derive directly from the fierce community orientation of Mormon tradition.

In the absence of a fierce commitment to community, patients, and the doctors and nurses who serve them, even not-for-profits can end up funneling resources to the bottom line, shaping the policies and structure and behavior of the organization to the comfort of those who run it, and of their affiliates outside the organization.

Kaiser, for instance, has gone through a number of struggles. Kaiser and its sister organization, Group Health of Puget Sound, were both born in strife. In the 1940s and 1950s, Kaiser and Group Health doctors were routinely called Communists, socially shunned and occasionally physically attacked. They were often kicked out of medical societies, or even had their medical licenses revoked for the simple crime of working for a prepaid healthcare system. They fought back with lawsuits that they had to take all the way to the Supreme Court.

By the 1990s, Kaiser was in a different fight, as for-profit arrangements calling themselves health maintenance organizations (HMOs), but with a completely different structure and organization, began to compete with it, in their own markets. These faux HMOs offered lower premiums for what looked and sounded like the same product, a unified payment-physician structure, but was not: unlike the Kaiser docs, the other HMO docs did not work together collegially in the same building, did not have a common governance structure or a common history. They and the hospitals and clinics and other services in these HMOs were united only by contract, not by a common identity. Contracts may seem the same as identity to investors, but they are not.

Kaiser felt it had to compete with these faux HMOs on price alone, and cut services and trimmed its operations to try to keep its premiums down. Members could feel it, as the organization seemed to become harder, not easier, to access, and the quality of service fell off. The effort triggered an identity crisis. To an outside observer (and longtime Kaiser member as well), Kaiser's history seems to have gone through a hinge point in the late 1990s, and it is this struggle and reaffirmation of identity in a shift in governance that seems to have made the difference.

This story goes to the heart of what it means to be not for profit or for profit, and what difference that distinction means in the real world of how a health system behaves.

What we call Kaiser is actually three large organizations with interlocking contracts: One is the health plan (Kaiser Foundation Health Plan). A second runs the facilities and operations (Kaiser Foundation Hospitals). The third is the physicians (the regional Permanente Medical Groups, under an umbrella Permanente Federation). The first two are separate not-for-profit organizations, but governed together with the same board and CEO.

The regional Permanente Medical Groups are multispecialty practices organized as partnerships or mutual benefit corporations; that is, they are for profit, but only for the profit of their member physicians, not for the profit of outside investors or stockholders. They do participate in profit sharing. Every year, under a 50-year-old agreement, the margins of income over expenses are split 50/50 between the not-for-profits and the 15,000 or so physicians in the Kaiser system. In 2007, for instance, the physician's share amounted to about $1 billion. How much of that goes personally to the physicians as profit, and how much simply to shore up the bottom line of the practices, or pay for needed growth, is not known, since they are not public corporations and do not need to report publicly.

The twist in the story is that it was the not-for-profit side of Kaiser driving the policy decisions to cut and trim in order to compete directly on price in the 1990s, while it was for-profit doctors that initiated the push to find a new direction. In the late 1990s, in reaction to the increasing competition and what seemed a fruitless effort to trim services to match other HMOs, the two sides of the organization erected a new umbrella structure embracing both the for-profit physicians and the not-for-profit foundation. The board and executive director of this Kaiser Permanente Partnership Group began to set the organization on a new path.

Kaiser has had many stumbles in its growth, and some big quality problems over the years. It has come under a lot of criticism. But it seems to have regained control of its rudder, and its sense of serving its member patients and its member physicians. In recent years it has consistently won high marks for overall quality and prevention.

In the end, the important yardstick is how a healthcare organization acts. That seems driven less by whether an organization is nominally for profit or not for profit than by its culture DNA, and by whether it has a fee-for-service business model, or other business models that tie its success to the overall health and healthcare of the people it serves.

The moral question, the real question, is not, Is somebody making money from healthcare? The question is, Are they making money from healthcare by providing greater value for lower cost? Or are they making money by strip-mining value out of healthcare? Are they making money by finding ways to relieve suffering, lower costs, and end needless deaths? Or are they making money by increasing the suffering, the deaths, and devastation?

Is Healthcare a Right?

If you want to get people going, ask this question. What we think about it is rife with philosophical assumptions and ideological framing, all of the lenses through which we see life.

Let's try to get some clarity on whether access to healthcare is a right, what we mean when we say healthcare is a right, and what the implications are for how we deal with healthcare. Let's start with a simple fictional story, a thought experiment:

Two men lying on emergency department gurneys. Same room. Writhing in agony, moaning, skin slick with sweat.

They are friends, Ralph and Brett. Firemen. Green Bay Packers fans. Married. Kids. They like to fish. They had been hiking in to their favorite hidden fishing hole when they had stumbled into a nest of the dreaded Great Lakes pit vipers. Both had been bitten. Stumbled back to the road. 911 on the cell phones. Ambulance rushed them to the hospital.

Doctor Keller bustles into the room, urgency in his movements. Consults the electronic chart on his tablet, moves to Brett's side, glances at the Brett's wrist ID band, and says,

"Brett Jones? We're going to take care of you. We have the antidote. The orderly here is going to wheel you into an operating room. We'll make a small incision and pump out as much of the venom as possible, then administer the anti-venom. You'll be good as new in a couple of days."

Brett says, "Thanks, Doc."

Doctor Keller turns to the other bed, consults his tablet again, looks at Ralph's wristband, and says, "Ralph Smith? You're going to die. We aren't going to treat you. We have the antivenom, but we're not going to give it to you. In fact, we need the bed space, so we called your family to come get you as soon as possible. And after you're dead, they'll be charged $7,000 for the ambulance ride and the time in the ER." He turns to go.

"What?" Ralph cries out. "Why?"

Doctor Keller turns at the door and says, "Well, obviously, because you're Black."

Now, wait, you say, that's a completely absurd story! The injustice, the immorality, is so obvious that the story doesn't ring true at all, not for America in the twenty-first century, not for any society that any of us want to be a part of. Come on!

Okay. But now let's try something. Let's back up and rerun that last sentence. The doctor turns at the door and says, "Well, obviously, because you're …"

What would make it okay? What word or phrase could we stick on the end of that sentence that would make most people say, "Oh, well, that makes sense. Nothing wrong there"?

Think about that for a while before you answer.

How about, "… because you're poor"?

Or, "… because it says here that you were laid off last Friday, and your friend wasn't"?

Or, "… because you don't have insurance"?

Or, "… because you both have insurance, but your insurance company considers the antivenom to be experimental and won't cover it. You could appeal, but of course, by then you will be dead anyway"?

What if his name was not Ralph Smith, but Rafael Gutierrez? Would this be a sufficient reason to just let him die: "… because you have a Hispanic name, and we can't treat you until you prove that you are in this country legally"?

Such possibilities shock the conscience. There seems to be no way that we can imagine letting one person live and another die, when we are standing at the bedside with enough antivenom to save them both.

This perhaps is a good definition of a right: we cannot find any line to divide those who have it or "deserve" it and those who do not. If we say, "Justice is a human right," we are saying that we cannot imagine any human being who does not deserve to be treated justly, to be given a fair trial, to be allowed to speak her views, to worship however he wishes or does not wish. It does not matter if he speaks Magyar and she speaks Quechua, to be human is enough to have a right to justice.

But wait, you say, come on, that's not realistic. These guys are in an ER, in a clearly life-threatening situation, and the ER has the capacity to treat them both. By law, they both have to be given the antivenom.

Sure, exactly. That is correct.

So let's change the story slightly. Let's leave the snakes out of the story. There is no such thing as a Great Lakes pit viper anyway. Instead, let's imagine something that actually exists. Let's imagine that they both have deadly cancers. Let's imagine that it's a cancer that they have an excellent chance of surviving with the right treatment, but they will both surely die quickly without such treatment. But at the moment, they are not in immediate danger of death. They are both stable. The hospital is not legally obligated to treat them.

Tell one that he will receive treatment, call a cab for the other one and wish him luck? It happens all the time in our system. All the time. Every single day across this great land of ours. Because one is well insured and the other is not, one is employed and the other has been laid off, one has an insurer who will stand by its contracts and the other has an insurer who will try to get out of its agreements whenever it can get away with it.

Now there is nothing hypothetical about our little story at all, nothing absurd. Yet it still shocks the conscience.

I am imagining that there may be some hard cases reading this, who are thinking no, my conscience is not shocked. Life is not fair. Suck it up. For those people and just those, let me add one more little twist to the story: imagine that they are both friends of yours. The doctor ushers you into the room, and tells you to choose which will live and which will die.

Don't be absurd. If randomly letting people die because of their insurance status does not register on your moral compass, you have none.

It's Not That Simple

Yet it's not that simple. Let's explore a bit of the complexities.

The first, most obvious complexity is the resource issue. In our story, I specified that the antivenom is right there, that the cancer treatments exist, are effective, are available.

We can only say something is a right if it is possible to imagine that we could have the resources to make sure that everyone can have it. Across the world, many things have been proposed as a universal human right. The ones that are generally accepted are those we can always make plenty of, if we decide to: freedom of religion, justice, freedom of opinion, freedom to associate. Other proposed rights are more problematic: a right to a roof over your head, for instance, or a guaranteed income, or a certain amount of land. Even where governments affirm these as rights, providing them can be problematic, since they require resources.

Or, as the online comic artist xkcd put it, "Given their annual marketing budget, Coca-Cola could afford to literally buy the world a Coke. However, singing lessons for every person on earth would be prohibitively expensive."*

Which kind of "right" is healthcare? It clearly requires great resources, but there is actually a lot of subtlety to the question.

Let's try another absurd thought experiment. Think about yachts. What if someone asserted a human right to have a yacht? Yachts are expensive, and the expense is expandable. That is, you can buy a yacht for $10,000 or $100 million or more. In fact, as anyone who has been around yachts can attest, you could pick a yacht for free—and spend $1 million restoring it. No matter how nice a yacht you have, there is no question that 10 times the expense would get you something like a 10 times bigger and better yacht.

Deciding, as a society, that having a yacht is a human right would seem kind of silly. But it could be done. Everybody could have a limited yacht allowance. Deciding that it is a human right to have as large and expensive a yacht as you like would not be silly; it would be meaningless and absurd. It would not be possible for everyone to have an infinite yacht allowance.

Justice is expensive. All those judges and their staffs, court buildings. All those lawyers for both sides, all those appeals. Proper training for police forces, proper jails, and other provisions to enforce laws without trampling on people's rights. There's a lot to it.

But unlike yachts, the expense of justice is not infinitely expandable. Ten times the expense might buy a society 10 times the justice, if what you start with is post-Qadaffi Libya. In any functioning modern state, no. Maybe the optimum amount to spend is more or less than you are spending now. But there is some amount that is enough, that does everything you need to do to secure justice for the citizenry. So it is possible to say, "We will be a just society. We will do what it takes to make that true."

If something is a commodity, and more is always better, it can't be a right. If consuming more resources always gets you more of something, it can't be a right. If there is an optimum amount that buys the society what it needs to enforce the right, then it can be a right.

---

* xkcd, accessed online at: http://imgs.xkcd.com/comics/money.png.

Healthcare is more like justice than it is like yachts. It is the argument of this book, in fact, that the optimum amount to spend on healthcare, in order to have the best healthcare available to all, is actually substantially less than we are spending now. The United States spends roughly twice as much as anyone else, and clearly does not get twice the results. We have overshot the optimum expense.

What about the outliers?

Let's go back to Brett and Ralph. Let's leave off the snakes this time, again. This time let's say they are both having some kind of cardiac event. It's been a long time since they used to go fishing together in high school because, while they are both 5 feet 10 inches, Brett weighs 175 pounds and Ralph weighs 375. This is Ralph's third time in the hospital this year. He has diabetes, arthritis, and atherosclerosis. He drinks too much, and has been addicted to painkillers. He smokes, and his doctor thinks he's developing chronic obstructive pulmonary disorder.

Now Ralph embodies one of the most commonly heard arguments against healthcare as a right: "Why should my taxes, or my insurance premiums, go to pay for these people who just refuse to take care of themselves?" I have heard more than one hospital executive say, "I wish I could just give some of these people a nice quiet room and a book on how to write your own will, and leave them to it."

Seems like a reasonable objection on the surface. But if you feel certain that we shouldn't have to help pay for Ralph's healthcare, let me propose a few questions for you to think about: What if Ralph only weighed 275? And he didn't smoke or have COPD? Would it be okay to pay for his care then? What if he only weighed 225? He's still overweight and having problems with diabetes and arthritis and his heart, but he doesn't drink excessively, and has never been addicted to pills. How about then? Where's the line? Who decides? How do they decide? Who's on this "death panel"? At what point does the patient fall off some kind of invisible edge and we can feel comfortable saying that he or she deserves no help?

The question assumes that Ralph is at fault for his condition, that he is refusing to take care of himself. After all, healthcare is not a commodity, it's a process. You have to be a good partner in a process—and Ralph clearly has not been.

But is it that clear? Do you have absolute control of your personality? Is it your experience of yourself that you make all the right decisions? And once you have made the decision, that you stick to your resolve? You say, "Okay, that's it for the nachos at bedtime," and that's it? Never again? "This is my absolute last cigarette." Have you never been addicted to anything?

Human beings, obviously, are flawed. If you think you're not, all I can say is I hope that works out for you. We are all on a psychological continuum over how our lives run. None of us can really know how easy or difficult it is for someone else to change his or her behavior and have better health. We may think we know, but we don't. A lot of our health problems spring from our behavior—but saying that is not to say that people could just change their behavior and be healthier, just like that.

We also live on a continuum in our knowledge about what really works to make us healthier. You may have had the experience of many Americans: you think you eat well, eating whole-grain organic breads, drinking only low-fat drinks, exercising regularly, yet you are still 20 pounds over your target weight and have trouble sleeping. The reality is there is not as much certainty and consensus as we might want to believe about what is best for you—let alone what would really work to get a seriously overweight or addicted person back on track. It is simply not that easy.

In the end, the right to healthcare means that we owe each other and our fellow citizens the help they need to get back to better health. The outliers need more help, not less. But fortunately, though there will always be some who can't get to better health, and can't stop costing so much, in the aggregate it costs less to give more help to the outliers. Clearly establishing that we have a right to healthcare is a path to lower costs, not higher.

Chapter 13

There Ought to Be a Law

Introduction

This book begins with the declaration that "most of the changes we need are not political or legislative at all."

Our theme here has been: How can the industry change itself to run leaner, faster, better, cheaper, for everyone? Our theme has been: Stop looking to Washington, to your state capital, to politicians to fix the industry. Politicians are unlikely to fix the industry, because they don't understand the industry, because they are in the thrall of various segments of the industry fighting for financial supremacy and ease, and because a problem is a political asset, while a solution is not.

But now we come to that qualifying word: *most*. Some needed changes do need legislative action. Some changes in the law are needed to allow these new business models and arrangements to take place. Current law in many details encases current practices in legal frames and effectively make it illegal to be more effective and efficient in healthcare. Other changes in the law are needed because any change that does not make such changes cannot call itself reform with a straight face.

Scope of Practice

In addition to licensing, most states have scope of practice laws that specify in detail who can do what. Must one be a registered nurse (RN) to give a vaccination, for instance, or can pharmacists and licensed practical nurses do that? These laws claim to limit each profession to what it is trained and licensed to do, but they are often far more restrictive than the license. In many instances, they serve more as guild restrictions, making sure that doctors, for instance, have enough work.

We are entering a period in healthcare in which making sure there is enough work for doctors is absolutely not the problem. In this coming period we will need far more clinicians than we have, and we need them working as efficiently as possible. We need everyone, whether nurses, nurse practitioners, physical therapists, or pharmacists, working at the "top of their license," doing everything that their training and license allow them to do. Scope of practice laws impede the new kinds of arrangements and organizational efficiency that the evolving Next Healthcare needs. They should be greatly loosened or eliminated.

Corporate Practice of Medicine

Most states outlaw the corporate practice of medicine. What they mean by that varies and includes any or all of:

■ General corporations can't employ physicians directly to practice medicine.
■ Corporations can't own medical practices, or can only hold minority interests.
■ Corporations can't even contract with medical practices to provide medical services to outsiders.
■ Corporations can't even contract with medical practices to provide medical services to their own employees (to staff in-house clinics, for example).

These laws, mostly hatched early in the last century, reflect a concern that corporations would come to dominate medicine and influence doctors' decision making, and that they would profit from medicine. The experience of the last 30 years suggests that corporations of all kinds do influence doctors' decision making, but they do it through the payment mechanisms: People do what you pay them to do. And lots of corporations and organizations profit hugely from healthcare, including the very doctor-owned multispecialty practices and specialty hospitals, as well as large-scale HMOs and managed care plans, that these laws specifically allow.

There is no sign that states with more stringent laws against the corporate practice of medicine have better, more ethical, or cheaper healthcare in any noticeable way. The laws complicate the entrance of new business models into healthcare in many ways.

In an environment in which the market is dominated by commoditized, insurance-supported fee-for-service medicine, the concerns about strip mining are very real, since the opportunities abound. In an environment in which most healthcare providers are competing on the basis of risk for providing the best health and care for the least amount of money, these concerns tend to disappear.

You won't get a lot of companies competing to provide shoddy, expensive healthcare if there's no money in it.

Certificate of Need

In 1964, in an attempt to keep healthcare costs down, New York State passed a law requiring anyone who wanted to build or expand a hospital to come before a commission and show that it was needed. In 1968, the American Hospital Association started plumping for such laws. By 1974, the federal government had gotten into the act, with legislation requiring every state to establish a certificate of need (CON) mechanism for any major capital project, including buying major new technologies. It also provided some federal dollars to make it happen. Most states complied, but when the federal law and funding were repealed in 1987, 14 states dropped most of their CON provisions. So today, 36 states plus the Commonwealth of Puerto Rico and the District of Columbia still have a CON program, and the other 14 have some CON provisions.[*]

In a system in which demand follows supply, there is some rationale for such legislation: suppress supply, and you suppress demand, and so save money. But it hasn't worked out that way. In such a system, it's hard to define *need*. The fact that you can fill the new beds, or that your doctors will use the MRI to capacity, does not mean anything. Certificate of need commissions have largely been another arena for political and bureaucratic jockeying for position by institutions. Even where there are strong laws, they only cover certain types of institutions, such as hospitals and convalescent homes, while others, such as freestanding surgery centers, specialty hospitals, and imaging centers, are free to compete with them without restriction. There is no evidence that states with stronger CON statutes and more vigorous CON commissions, in fact, have lower healthcare costs. There is no evidence that CON statutes have impeded the seemingly inexorable rise of costs in any noticeable way.

I have often heard the expression "Competition does not belong in healthcare." The expression is a bit baffling. Why is competition in healthcare no good, while it is fine in consumer electronics or architecture or poetry? Would I really want my doctor, or my hospital, or my insurer, to feel that no matter how bad a job they did, it would not affect their ability to make a living in any way? Would I really want them to feel that, if they come up with excellent new ways of doing things, they will not be rewarded in any way?

What the statement seems to express is that the biggest competition we have seen in healthcare is competition to extract money from the system, with little regard for whether it helps or hurts most of the system's customers.

---

[*] National Conference of State Legislatures, "Certificate of Need: State Health Laws and Programs," September 6, 2011, available at http://www.ncsl.org/default.aspx?tabid=14373.

In a system in which most of the healthcare market is at risk for the health and healthcare of its customers, the providers compete to provide health and healthcare in the most cost-effective way. In such an environment statutes like CON laws just get in the way of that competition, and should be set aside.

Anti-Kickback Legislation

States have vigorous laws against kickbacks, self-referral, and fee splitting. A doctor should not be able to refer a patient to a specialist practice, laboratory, or imaging center, for instance, which the doctor owns, or in which the doctor is invested (self-referral). Nor should the doctor receive a payment for such a referral, or a portion of the fee. These laws line up with the federal Stark laws and the federal anti-kickback statute.*

These laws have two problems. First, they don't work very well. Healthcare lawyers work very hard at finding the ins and outs of the laws and advising doctors how to get around their provisions. Many doctors do, in one way or another, make money off of their referrals.

The other problem is much bigger: they can easily be interpreted as outlawing accountable care organizations (ACOs; as in the Patient Protection and Affordable Care Act (PPACA) reform law), alternative quality contracts (Blue Cross/Blue Shield of Massachusetts' much touted AQCs), and indeed any structure in which doctors make money from anything other than directly treating the patient, fee-for-service style. A bonus for treating the patient so early and often that the patient never goes to the emergency department or is hospitalized? A bundled fee structure that includes all imaging and laboratory work? These all sound like, or could be interpreted as, violations of these laws.

State anti-kickback laws and the federal Stark and antikickback laws need to be clarified both to become more effective and to specifically allow the kinds of emerging organizational structures that have the breadth and financial heft to take on risk.

Transparency

Almost nobody knows what any healthcare purchase actually costs. Almost nobody, whether consumer, payer, or employer, can truthfully say exactly how much it will cost to have a given procedure or test done in hospital X, clinic Y, or physician-owned outpatient center Z. What information exists is elusive, fragmentary, estimates, averages, hand waving, smoke, reflections on the ripples in the pond. But when you, the consumer, payer, or employer, eventually pay

---

* Ibid.

the bill, all that insubstantiality somehow turns into very hard dollars and cents. Would you buy a car that way?

If we are going to "get what we pay for" in healthcare, we have to know at least two things: (1) what we will be getting and (2) what we will be paying for it. Since 2005 there have been myriad moves on the state and federal levels to promote price transparency in healthcare. Some states, for instance, have forced hospitals to publish average actual charges for specified procedures or tests for the previous six months or year. Clearly, though, these efforts are not enough, because they don't give consumers the basic information they need to make real choices: what they are getting, and what they are paying for it. Just as clearly, the industry will not willingly do more than it is forced to do by legislation.

"What we will be getting" means defining what's included: if I am paying for a cardiac stress test, will I get a separate bill for the disposable sensors used, or the tube of gel, or for the cardiologist's evaluation? It also means disclosing quality scores and patient satisfaction rankings.

"What we will be paying for it" means what we will be paying for it, that is, not some phantom charge, or a retrospective average of past amounts paid by other people, or a general nonbinding estimate, but how much money the consumer, the health plan, or both, will have to actually shell out. A prospective price list. "Ms. Burchard, if you have your baby in our birthing center, an uncomplicated birth will cost this amount. Complications are complicated, obviously, but here are the average amounts that various problems can cost. Here's how that will interact with your insurance coverage. Here's what the out-of-pocket cost to you will be. We guarantee that price."

Many things in healthcare are not easy to "bundle" and price. Getting patched up after losing a knife fight is not a bundle you can price. Nor is fighting pancreatic cancer. But even in such situations, smaller units that are needed, such as putting in a central line or closing a 10-centimeter wound, can be priced. Most things in healthcare, such as mammograms, an examination for strep throat, a transplanted hip, or arthroscopic reattachment of a torn knee ligament, can be standardized, bundled, and priced. And everything in healthcare, whether it is bundled or sold as an individual unit, eventually has a price put on it. Publish the price.

Healthcare providers object that publishing actual prospective prices will force them to enormously simplify their pricing structures. That is true, and is an excellent idea. They object, as well, that prospective pricing means accepting more risk. If you get the pricing wrong, you will cost yourself money. That is also true. Such risk is inherent in every business. True cost accounting (being able to establish how much it costs to deliver a given outcome, what are the independent and dependent variables and predictable range of variations) has been late in coming to healthcare, but it must come if the buyers of healthcare are ever going to be able to shop for value.

Fraud

Much of the fraud in healthcare would be much harder to pull off in a system with different incentives. Under a fee-for-service system, in which you are paid per procedure, small fraudulent clinics invent patients, or invent procedures done to real patients. Sometimes the patients are in on the deal and get a kickback.

Bundled arrangements such as an alternative quality contract, an accountable care organization, or any similar risk-based arrangements are by their nature large, and they must have electronic medical records in order to do the complex record keeping needed to support payments. Some such arrangements could include, by subcontract, small or even sole physician practices. But the fiscal agent (the entity actually contracting for and receiving money for patient care) must be large enough to bear risk for a population. The usual lower bound of size is considered to be an organization that has 5,000 patients under primary care. And the whole arrangement must be complex enough to encompass all the care these patients need, from flu shots to surgery, mammograms to cancer care, whether within the risk-bearing organization or outside it.

The clinic that actually provides care does not get paid per procedure, but for its share of the care per patient, including all the patients' care at all institutions, including all pharmaceuticals. To defraud the system, the clinic would have to invent whole patients—including faked histories with other institutions, a much more difficult thing to create or hide. Any faked patients would have to be backed up by medical records throughout the system. Patients don't just "fall off the back of the truck" like stolen appliances or computers. Nor is there any incentive in such a system to "upcode" procedures (billing for a more serious problem) or to tack on extra phantom supplies and tests, because you don't get paid extra for them.

The PPACA reform law contained strong anti-Medicare fraud provisions. For instance, it authorized the designating specialized accounting firms as recovery audit contractors (RACs). These RACs are authorized to go into any Medicare or Medicaid healthcare provider and audit the books in detail. They have a great incentive to root out fraud, since that is entirely how they make their living—they get a percentage of the recovered money. This is one part of the Fraud Prevention Initiative in the Center for Program Integrity of the Centers for Medicare and Medicaid Services (CMS), the federal agency that runs those federal programs.[*]

But the nature of the more complex risk-bearing entities envisioned in the Next Healthcare scenario make fraud harder to carry off in the first place.

---

[*] CMS Fraud Prevention Initiative, backgrounder, July 2011, accessed at https://www.cms.gov/Partnerships/downloads/BackgrounderFraudPreventionInitiative.pdf.

Insurance Regulation

ERISA Immunity

In December 2007, 17-year-old Nataline Sarkisyan of the San Fernando Valley, California, was in bad shape. According to her doctors, if she did not get a liver transplant, she would die.

Her insurer, though, called the liver transplant "experimental treatment," though it has not been experimental for decades, and refused to pay. Nine days later, after a storm of publicity and a public outcry, the company relented. CIGNA would pay for the transplant. Too late. Hours later, Nataline died.

Her parents filed a wrongful death suit against CIGNA, but in April 2008 the suit was thrown out. The judge cited the federal 1974 Employee Retirement Income Security Act (ERISA), which governs employee retirement funds and benefit plans. ERISA effectively immunizes most employer-provided health plans from any lawsuit over damages stemming from the health plans' interference in medical decision making. The company claimed that the failure of the suit showed that it was right all along, that the court "agreed with our position that the Sarkisyans' claims regarding Cigna's decision-making were without merit." The court had decided no such thing; rather, it had decided that the merits of the case could not be heard in any court.

Hilda Sarkisyan, Nataline's mother, persisted. In October 2008 she came to a CIGNA headquarters building in Philadelphia, entered the lobby, and demanded an apology from the company. None was forthcoming, but while she was there CIGNA employees jeered and heckled her from the balcony, she said, and one made an obscene gesture.

A month later, a CIGNA executive sent her a letter of apology, saying the harassment did not represent the views of the company or most of its employees, and expressing sympathy over her loss. But the following year she sued the company again, this time over the emotional distress caused by the incident. This time the court allowed the suit to go forward. Hilda's response: "They kill a beautiful 17-year-old girl, and I get to go after them for a finger? That's sick."*

The Sarkisyan case was only one of the most spectacular in a long string of such cases. A much longer list could be made of cases that were simply never brought because of the immunity in the ERISA law. In 2001, the late Senator Ted Kennedy (D-Mass.) was sponsoring ultimately unsuccessful legislation that would have plugged the ERISA loophole. He explained his reasoning:

> Patients should have the right to hold their HMO accountable in court when its negligence causes the injury or death of a patient.

---

* Girion, L., "Insurer's Agreement to Cover Surgery Comes Too Late," *LA Times*, October 8, 2009, available at http://articles.latimes.com/2009/oct/08/business/fi-cigna8.

No other industry in America enjoys immunity from accountability for its actions, and the insurance industry does not deserve it either. Few, if any, provisions will do more to guarantee that your HMO does the right thing than the knowledge that it can be sued if it does the wrong thing.*

If insurance companies make material decisions about therapy in individual cases, they should be legally liable for their decisions. The insurance industry argues that this would "kill" the industry. Robert Zirkelbach, a spokesman for America's Health Insurance Plans, said at the time of the Sarkisyan case that rescinding ERISA "will bankrupt these plans, and employers would no longer be able to offer coverage."

This is manifestly not true, since this protection does not exist in other countries, and is not universal even in this country. It applies only to employer-provided benefits, and not even to all employers. Plans for employees of church organizations or governments, for instance, do not fall under the ERISA immunity.† Yet health plans somehow manage to make a quite healthy market for church organizations and government employees. Spend time in the subways of the Washington, DC, metro area during the fall health plan renewal season, and you will see from the blizzard of ads how avid health plans are to cover government employees, from which they have no ERISA immunity.

It is not tolerable for doctors to be civilly and even criminally liable for the results of their decisions or neglect of the patient, while someone who is not the patient's doctor, and who has never seen the patient, can make material decisions about therapy that kill, injure, or impoverish patients without being liable for those decisions. ERISA immunity should be legislated out of existence.

End Fraudulent Rescissions and Claim Denials

So, there was this retired Canadian couple living on small government pensions. Artur and Anna Friesen lived in Abbotsford, British Columbia, and it gets cold in Abbotsford in the winter. But they did have a little motor home, so every winter they would pack up and drive down to California for a while. They had been doing this for 20 years.

They had some health problems, like most people their age, so they did the sensible thing and bought temporary health insurance for travelers from a company named PrimeLink Travel Insurance. They don't speak English well, and don't read it at all, so they did this through a broker, who carefully went over

---

* Congressional Record for June 19, 2001.
† U.S. Department of Labor, http://www.dol.gov/dol/topic/health-plans/erisa.htm.

the many-page form with them in the fall of 2010. Somewhere in the middle of the form there was a question about being treated for kidney disease: "In the last 36 months, have you received treatment for kidney disorder (including stones)?"

Anna thought that *treatment* meant treatment, like receiving treatment to cure or palliate a diagnosed disease or something like that. At least, that's what she thought the English word *treatment* meant. Her doctor had told her that she had weak kidneys, and they should keep an eye on the situation. But he had not diagnosed any kidney disease or prescribed any kind of treatment. So Anna said no.

The insurance cost them $694. It turned out that they had made a sensible choice to buy it, because while they were in California she developed a blood clot in her leg. She could have gone home, to a hospital in Canada, but she had health insurance, so she went to a California hospital.

The hospital staff did the sensible, prudent thing and called the insurance company to make sure that this elderly Canadian lady would indeed be covered for treatment in this hospital. Prime Link said indeed she would be.

She ended up spending five days in the hospital. The cost? US$51,125.49. Prime Link refused to pay.

After she had run up the bill, Prime Link had checked Anna's medical history and found a notation that she was being "monitored" for kidney disease. The insurance claim denial letter read, "You do have a chronic kidney disease for which you have undergone investigations which is considered treatment." So, in the special English used by U.S. insurance employees, a potential problem apparently means the same as diagnosis of a real problem, and finding out that you might potentially have a problem is the same as treating the real problem. If my doctor says to me, "We should keep an eye on your heart," that means I am being treated for heart disease.

The letter contained a check giving them back their $694. It explained that the contract was null and void because of "misstatements during the application period." The company was saying that Anna Friesen, who is not fluent in English, had lied on an official form.

According to a CBC report in November 2011, the Friesens were not planning on returning to California. For the first time in 20 years, when their neighbors packed up, they did not. They were afraid to travel to the United States. They were afraid of their great, welcoming neighbor to the south. They didn't know what might happen to them there.

Several Canadian doctors had written to the insurance company, attesting that there had been no diagnosis of chronic kidney disease and no treatment. The company did not budge.

By the fall of 2011, the Friesens were no longer even picking up the phone if it showed an "outside" number, since they were being hounded by a U.S.

collection agency. "We are stressed out. Really stressed," Artur told the CBC. "We are not the same people [as we were] last year when we came home."

As a result of the CBC news item, and prodding from the CBC's Go Public advocate, the Friesens finally were promised relief. Michael May, a spokesperson for the policy's underwriter, Manulife, told the network, "I understand a decision on the appeal of this case will be made shortly and should be communicated to the individual in the next couple of days."*

Argument from anecdote is no argument at all. If the Friesen case, pitiable as it is, were a fluke, or even an outlier, there would be no reason to even mention it. But it is not. It is one in a constant, appalling stream of stories of rescission as an ordinary tool of risk mitigation for insurance companies. In fact, this is how common these stories are: The Friesen story is in this book because it popped up in the news on the day I was writing these pages. It was simply the health insurance horror story of the day. It is useful to note that this case took place after the PPACA reform law made the practice of rescission illegal for the U.S. health insurance industry, except in the case of fraud, and many months after the industry announced that it would voluntarily end the practice early. Maybe they had their fingers crossed when they made that announcement. Maybe the spokesperson muttered, "Except for Canadians." Maybe the word *fraud* has a different meaning for the industry than for the rest of us, a meaning that would reveal to us the full ghastly face of Anna Friesen's criminality. Maybe the word *rescission*, as used by health insurance industry spokespeople to denote the practice they would stop, does not mean the same as the word *rescission*, which denotes the practice outlawed by PPACA.

I have a libertarian acquaintance who is very concerned about government power. He believes that only government power is coercive, and is dismissive of the power of corporations in our lives. Next time we have a chance to talk, perhaps he can describe to me in more detail, in a way that will convince me, how this couple freely and with full knowledge engaged in this contract that put them in this difficult situation. Perhaps he can describe to me how it is that a pattern of such practices over time is considered the ordinary course of business, and not evidence of a criminal enterprise.

An industry spokesperson in the article about the Friesens was dismissive of the idea that denial of claims was a problem since, by his estimate, less than 5% of claims were denied. Industry spokespeople in the United States routinely point out that, before the passage of the PPACA reform, rescissions only happened in

---

* Tomlinson, K., "Retired Couple Billed $50,000 Despite Travel Insurance," CBC News, November 14, 2011, accessed at http://www.cbc.ca/news/canada/british-columbia/story/2011/11/11/bc-travelclaim.html.

individual plans, and only to less than 7% of those.* One searches in vain for any other industry in which companies can enter into contracts, and then simply tear up 5% or 7%, or any percent of them, after their counterparty has already spent the money that the contract promised them, and that they were assured by company representatives would be paid before they committed themselves to the expense.

Health plans should not, in fact, be able to interfere in the clinical process of an individual case in any way. Like credit cards and other financial instruments, health plans cover some things and not others, some people under some circumstances and not others. When I pull out my wallet at the market, it is quite clear whether I can use my American Express or Visa card, or a bank debit card. It is quite clear that I cannot put my home mortgage payment on a credit card. I am not going to be sued for fraud, or hit with some charge larger than my yearly income, for making some tiny mistake in the transaction, or for believing what a representative of the credit card company says.

The rules for what is covered by a health plan and what is not should be clear enough that no one has to guess, and no one has to ask for an interpretation or preauthorization by someone at the end of a long telephone tree at the insurance company. Any communication the company makes about whether some person or some procedure will be covered should be binding, just as in any other industry.

The industry will and does argue that this level of clarity is simply not possible. This is simply false. If there exist areas of coverage in which it is not possible to be clear, then the insurance companies should not write rules limiting coverage in that area. It really is that simple. It is not tolerable, for any reason, for anonymous insurance company employees in a call center to be making life-and-death decisions about patients they have never examined, or for insurance adjusters to remake the coverage decision after the fact.

Swiss Rule

Even for legitimate claims that are ultimately paid, billing a health insurer can be a morass. Any doctor's staff or hospital billing department can tell you the story: many health insurers routinely deny some large fraction of claims, forcing the provider to go through a lengthy appeal process or drop the claim. Insurers often sit on claims for months for no reason except their internal cash flow needs. Some insurers are like the Bermuda Triangle of healthcare, a sea of claims lost under mysterious circumstances.

---

* Japsen, B., Ban on Retroactive Cancellations of Insurance Policies Approaches," *Chicago Tribune*, July 6, 2010, accessed at http://www.chicagotribune.com/health/ct-biz-0706-rescissions-health-reform20100706,0,7052695.story.

During the 2009 debate about healthcare reform in the United States, a number of articles showed up in the press about the Swiss healthcare system as a possible model. The Swiss system is private, with an individual mandate and heavily regulated private insurance companies, which are only allowed to make a profit on supplemental insurance, not basic insurance.

There was one detail that most writers missed. Swiss doctors' offices and clinics look much like American ones, except for one thing: there is no billing department. Swiss doctors typically do all the billing themselves, because there is no complexity to it. There is no preauthorization, no claims denial, no argument about preexisting conditions. The doctor bills the insurance company at preset rates. And the insurer, by law, must pay every bill within 10 days or face large fines.*

If the insurance company truly believes the claim is fraudulent, it has the same legal recourses as any other company to recover its money. But it has to pay the claim first, and it has to pay it fast.

Adopting a "Swiss rule" for claims payment would go a long way toward making the health insurance industry a reliable partner for financing healthcare, and greatly reduce transaction costs in the industry.

The health insurance industry would likely complain that 10 days is an absurd amount of time to set for paying out billions of dollars in claims. And they would be correct: most of the trillions of dollars of financial market and banking transactions worldwide are settled overnight. For a well-run accounting system operating on agreed contracts with preset rates, a 10-day float would be a luxury of time.

Direct Primary Care

In Chapter 6 ("1: Explode the Business Model") we talked about direct primary care, in which doctors take a set amount per month, and in return offer a set menu of primary care services. The amounts are low, such as $49 per month and $10 per visit, or $30 per month per employee and $5 per visit as a package deal for small employers.

This growing movement has one problem: some states contend that such services are, in fact, insurance companies, and need to be regulated as such, including the hefty reserves and underwriting mechanisms of insurance companies. This would make any such practice impossible.

The physicians argue that they are not operating as insurance companies, but are simply offering prepaid services. Unlike a health insurer, they are not taking on any unpredictable financial risk. They offer only primary care; if a patient

---

* McManus, D., "Switzerland's Example of Universal Healthcare," *LA Times*, October 18, 2009, accessed at http://articles.latimes.com/2009/oct/18/opinion/oe-mcmanus18.

develops a more complex problem, they do not provide care, but send the patient to a specialist or hospital.

Direct primary care needs to be defined clearly as not coming under the purview of insurance regulators.

Transparency

Healthcare providers should establish real fee schedules and stick to them. So should healthcare insurers.

Surprisingly, this is a radical proposal. Healthcare insurers typically negotiate discounted fee schedules with hospitals and health systems in great detail, then embed those fee schedules in contracts that include nondisclosure agreements. The healthcare providers are forbidden to disclose just how much the insurer is paying them for each procedure or test, or just how deep the discount is off of their "master charge list." They are especially forbidden to tell other healthcare executives who might be negotiating with the same insurer.

The health insurance industry has consolidated over the last few decades. In most markets today there are only a few insurers available for healthcare organizations to work with. In many markets only one or two insurers effectively control the private market. The insurers that control the vast majority of the private healthcare market in the United States, especially the for-profit companies, are national or regional. They can move into and out of markets, and drop whole states or industry segments if they prove unprofitable. Most hospitals and health systems are not national or regional. They cannot get up and move to a different city. Unlike the insurers, they can't simply abandon any significant part of their market that proves unprofitable. Even if they are part of a chain, for the most part a hospital needs to make its budget where it works, with the populations in its catchment area. The healthcare providers can object and discuss, but eventually they simply must sign the contract or they will be cut out of a huge portion of their business. This puts enormous quasi-monopoly market power in the hands of the insurers.

In many markets, physician practices have to sign contracts that have no fee schedules in them at all. They are forced to simply accept what the insurer decides to pay them. They find out what the insurer pays for an office visit by sending in a claim and seeing what the numbers are on the check when it comes back. But they can't use that number for their financial planning because the insurer typically reserves the right to change the amount at any time.[*] It is not

---

[*] Personal discussions by the author with doctors in a number of different markets in recent years.

tolerable for providers not to know what they will be paid. No other business would be expected to operate that way.

Health plans, understandably, consider the fee schedules proprietary. They like the extra bargaining power that secrecy gives them. That's why they force secrecy on providers. But if there is virtue in competition, such secrecy is clearly anticompetitive, and not in the public interest. As in banking, "too big to fail" is too big, and does not help establish healthy competitive markets. Just as healthcare providers should publish fee schedules and discounts, so healthcare insurers should publish all fee schedules in all markets all the time.

Competition

The PPACA reform, much reviled as a "government takeover," was in fact a serious effort to preserve the private insurance system, and at the same time take advantage of the virtues of competition. It recognized, at the same time, that the consolidation in the insurance market had deprived many markets of the very competition that is the great virtue of private enterprise. The "insurance exchange" section of the law stipulates that insurance companies' participation in the exchanges is voluntary. But every state's insurance exchange must have at least two health plans competing for the exchange's customers, including at least one not-for-profit health plan. If two health plans (including one not for profit) do not step up, then the government will charter a new, independent, not-for-profit health plan to enter the competition.

Operating across State Lines?

A consistent conservative healthcare talking point in recent years has been that we should allow healthcare insurance companies to operate across state lines.

This may seem confusing, since many companies obviously do operate in multiple states, whether for-profit or not-for-profit. The call to allow companies to operate across state lines is actually a call for something different: to allow companies to operate in any state, but only under the rules of the state they are chartered in. Today every state has an insurance commissioner. Some, like California, have two: one for insurance companies, and another for HMOs. Every state has different regulations, and different levels of enforcement.

Conservatives usually campaign for the rights of states to run things the way they see fit, without interference from the federal government. But the conservative call for companies to operate across state lines is a call to gut all those state insurance regulations and commissions. Such a change would allow any company to shop for the state with the loosest regulations, take out a charter there, and do business under those loose regulations in every state. It would effectively make the United States one giant national insurance market under the weakest possible regulation, with state regulators rendered helpless by federal law.

This would not only greatly weaken the protections of state regulation, but it would also deprive us of the virtues of competition in another very important way: today we have 52 experiments going on (50 states, the District of Columbia, and Puerto Rico), demonstrating different ways to regulate insurance markets. Hawaii, Utah, Texas, Massachusetts—these states deal with health insurance in very different ways. We can have some insight into what works and what doesn't. Insurers have said, for instance, that forcing them to take all comers, but without an individual mandate forcing everyone to buy insurance, would be a disaster for them and force premiums sky high. Yet five states have mandated exactly that situation for years now already, with no obvious disastrous consequences.

We should continue to allow states to manage their own insurance regulations.

Malpractice

People get hurt in healthcare. People make mistakes. Patients die. Some are disabled and need lifelong care. There are careless clinicians, thoughtless systemic practices, even some "bad doctors."

Malpractice law is a highly complex problem. There is no easy solution. Unlike many areas of healthcare that we have discussed, there is no model that really works—but most other systems work better in one way or another. As in other areas of healthcare, all other methods cost less than the U.S. method.*

Looking at malpractice law with an eye schooled in looking at systems dynamics reveals some deeper problems. Start with the question: Why do anything? Why do we not just "put this behind us," as scandal-plagued politicians like to say, ignore the problem, and hurry forward into the future? The answers are obvious: You have an injured patient, with possibly major medical and care expenses that could last a lifetime. Or you have a bereaved family. And you have a system capable of injuring or killing a patient, and no feedback into the system to correct the problem.

The purposes of the malpractice claims process should be three:

■ Help the injured patients out with their care, or compensate the survivors to the extent possible for their loss.

---

* Some examples in Library of Congress Reports (all dated September 23, 2011):
  United Kingdom (England and Wales): http://loc.gov/law/help/medical-malpractice-liability/uk.php
  Germany: http://loc.gov/law/help/medical-malpractice-liability/germany.php
  Canada: http://loc.gov/law/help/medical-malpractice-liability/canada.php

- Provide a deterrent to poor practice of medicine, and an incentive to excellence.
- Provide the system with some corrective feedback so that it can find those excellent best practices that will prevent such problems in the future.

Malpractice law, as practiced in the United States, fails massively at all three. Under our adversarial system, in order to receive any compensation for the injury done to you, or even acknowledgment of that injury, you must be able to prove your case in court, with an opposing attorney bringing in a stack of experts to prove that you are wrong. And you have to know whom to blame, which is not always easy in such a complex system. Since malpractice attorneys work for a share of the award, you have to have a pretty open-and-shut case to get an attorney to take it on.

This means that malpractice cases are rare, compared to the number of injuries done to patients. The great majority of patients injured by the healthcare system have no chance of being helped at all, or even acknowledged.

At the same time, the threat of malpractice suit does not prod physicians toward excellence. Almost all physicians already strive mightily to do their best not to injure a patient, but the malpractice process in no way assists them in doing that.

Understandably, physicians' traditional attitudes toward malpractice have been, for most of the existence of malpractice law, purely defensive. Authors of two journal papers pictured the attitude vividly:

> For over a century, American physicians have regarded malpractice suits as unjustified affronts to medical professionalism, and have directed their ire at plaintiffs' lawyers ... and the legal system in which they operate.

> Physicians revile malpractice claims as random events that visit unwarranted expense and emotional pain on competent, hardworking practitioners.*

Once you've been sued, the standard practice is called "deny and defend." Your and your attorney's entire effort is bent toward building a massive defense that can prove that nothing went wrong. Or if something went wrong it was trivial, or it could not possibly have caused this specific injury, or it was not due to your actions, or if it was due to your actions it was unavoidable. Or the injury

---

* Sage, W.M., "Medical Malpractice Insurance and the Emperor's Clothes," *DePaul Law Review*, Vol. 54, 2005, pp. 463–64.

Studdert, D.M., Mello, M.M., and Brennan, T.A., "Medical Malpractice," *New England Journal of Medicine*, Vol. 350, 2004, p. 283.

Both quoted in Boothman, R.C., et al., "A Better Approach to Medical Malpractice Claims? The University of Michigan Experience," *Journal of Health and Life Sciences Law*, Vol. 2, No. 2, 2009.

is not as bad as the plaintiff says it is. This is not a method designed to find the problem and correct it. It's a method designed to avoid accepting any responsibility for the problem. It is rare that either individual physicians or healthcare systems learn anything from malpractice cases. To learn anything, they would first have to admit there was a problem.

In any system designed for learning, course corrections and feedback have to be frequent and minor, not rare and massive. Walking into a forest and getting mauled by a tiger does not teach you how to handle tigers, it just teaches you to stay out of forests. And to be of any use, feedback needs to be as immediate as possible, not years later.

To the physician, malpractice suits seem random, disconnected from daily practice. Whatever the doctor got sued for, such as a failure to monitor anesthesia correctly, or amputating the wrong leg, the failure arose out of a process that the doctor has gone through hundreds or thousands of times before without getting sued—and without being forced to examine the process for potential problems. The massive but relatively rare and seemingly random intrusion of malpractice suits does not push physicians to do better. It pushes them to do more. It pushes physicians to throw in every possible test and procedure, just so that they can say that they did their best, they did everything that could be done, whether or not the test or procedure was really called for. This is a significant contributor to wasted medical resources.

And the process itself is costly and damaging to both physicians and patients. As the authors of a University of Michigan study put it:

> The "deny and defend" strategy was born of these fears and continues to thrive, fed by them. Given the medical community's well-publicized loathing of litigation, it is ironic that over the past 30 years, litigation remains the dominant response by hospitals, healthcare providers, and insurers to patients with complaints about their medical care.*

The authors describe deny and defend as "incredibly inefficient and costly" in all ways from dollars to emotions. A *New England Journal of Medicine* study of the "exorbitant" overhead costs of malpractice law shows that "for every dollar spent on compensation, 54 cents went to administrative expenses (including those involving lawyers, experts, and courts)." Even at that, not all the claims even involved medical errors: 37% of the claims (accounting for 13 to 16% of total costs) were over some other fault than a medical error.†

---

* Boothman et al.
† Stewart, D.M., et al., "Claims, Errors, and Compensation Payments in Medical Malpractice Litigation," *New England Journal of Medicine*, Vol. 354, 2006, pp. 2024–33.

It's Not Greedy Patients

When a patient sues, most of the time it is liability insurers who defend or settle the case for the individual physician. When doctors complain vociferously about "the cost of malpractice," they are complaining about rising insurance premiums. Over the recent decades, we have seen continuing rounds of premium increases, which the insurers blame on huge payouts to patients, followed by ever-louder demands from physicians and insurers for reform that would put a stop to those huge payouts. These have been accompanied by claims from politicians that tort reform that would simply suppress the payments to patients decreases the cost of healthcare, and causes physicians to migrate in large numbers to states with the most severe tort reform laws.

There is a problem with the logic of these demands, though, and it goes to the heart of the question of what will fix malpractice. The problem is this: It is certainly true that there have been large increases in premiums, and fewer companies have been willing to offer medical liability insurance. But the assertions and assumptions about why this has happened, and how it has affected medicine, are not necessarily so. In 2003, the U.S. Government Accountability Office did a set of studies of these assertions and found that the facts did not fit. The premium increases were not due to any surge in ever-higher payouts to patients. That surge did not exist. On the other hand, outside influences such as the falls in the stock market, which affected the insurance companies' investments, and natural disasters, which caused them to pay out more money, had a much larger effect than malpractice payouts. The supposed great migration of doctors never happened. The lower cost of healthcare in states with severe tort reform laws is not true.*

The political advocacy group Americans for Insurance Reform (AIR), totals up every year how much liability insurers have taken in and paid out, in inflation-adjusted "constant dollars." The conclusion of these studies matches that of the GAO:

> Payouts have been stable, tracking the rate of medical inflation, but premiums have not. Rather, premiums that doctors pay rise and fall in sync with the state of the economy, reflecting profitability of

---

* U.S. General Accounting Office, GAO-03-702, "Medical Malpractice Insurance: Multiple Factors Have Contributed to Increased Premium Rates," 2003, available www.gao.gov/new.items/d03702.pdf.
U.S. General Accounting Office, GAO-03-836, "Medical Malpractice: Implications of Rising Premiums on Access to Health Care," 2003, available www.gao.gov/new.items/d03836.pdf.

the insurance industry, including gains or losses experienced by the insurance industry's bond and stock market investments.*

A look at the maps showing variation in healthcare costs proves false the idea that suppressing patient claims has much impact on lowering healthcare costs. There is no pattern showing that states with more severe tort reform laws have lower costs. In fact, some of the states that have led the charge, such as Texas, are noticeably high-cost states.

There are a lot of problems with malpractice law in the United States, but greedy, demanding patients and their lawyers driving up insurance premiums are the least of those problems.

Fixing Malpractice

All of the attempts to fix the malpractice mess focus in one way or another on backing away from the adversarial nature of the process. Politically, this has predictably devolved into two battling strategies: Republicans, backed by physicians and insurance companies, campaign for tort reform. What they mean by this is largely two things. The first is to make it harder for the plaintiffs to bring and prove a claim. The second is to limit the amounts that the plaintiffs can recover, especially for noneconomic claims, such as compensation for pain and suffering. Malpractice should be a method of righting a wrong and being assisted in your suffering, they argue, not a method of getting rich because some poor doctor made a mistake. Democrats, backed by trial lawyers and claiming to represent the needs of patients, resist such limits, and instead propose ways of settling claims faster and less expensively.

These goals are not incompatible, but rather than meld them into a comprehensive solution, the two parties have consistently fought each other to a standstill over them. The PPACA reform law, for instance, has provisions to establish special health courts with independent expertise designed to move cases swiftly toward just resolution rather than years of expensive trial. At this writing, though, the Republicans in Congress have not allowed any funding to implement these courts. At the same time, the Republicans' tort reform bill, passed by the Republican House, has been blocked by the Democratic-controlled Senate.†

Some parts of the system, though, have found ways of reducing malpractice costs while using it to learn something. For instance, New York State has insti-

---

* AIR is a project of the Center for Justice and Democracy, available at http://www.insurance-reform.org/about/index.html.

† Norman, B., "Medical Malpractice Reform Efforts Stalled," Politico.com, November 8, 2011, available at http://www.politico.com/news/stories/1111/67780.html.

tuted experimental health courts of a sort by separating medical malpractice suits from other injury suits, and giving them to judges who have become specially trained in medical matters. Instead of waiting until the case is ready to come to trial, these judges convene the two sides early, bringing the lawyers, the doctors, even the patients, for a meeting in chambers, to work through the issues and the evidence. After three or four meetings, over a period of six to nine months, most suits come to an agreeable settlement, some 95% in fact since the program began in 2002 and was expanded in 2010.[*]

Over the past 15 years, an emerging body of evidence and analysis has shown that getting sued is at least as much the result of mistrust and miscommunication as actual technical fault. The patient or family is angered at being stonewalled about the reason for the injury or death. Most people understand that medicine is risky; they don't understand being lied to and shut out. Only a minority of cases involve actual negligence, but all seem to involve a breakdown of communication and trust between the doctor and the patient. Malpractice attorneys commonly estimate in studies that half or more of malpractice cases could have been avoided by full disclosure and apology.

The classic advice from attorneys and insurance companies has been admit nothing, never apologize—because anything you say can be used against you in court.

Some 35 states have passed laws that to one degree or another shield clinicians from having their disclosures and apologies used against them in a lawsuit. These laws are not consistent or complete, though. In some states, the apology and disclosure, such as "I am so sorry that we lost your mother, due to the drug interaction ...," cannot be used against you. But the rest of the sentence can, if you admit fault: "... which happened because I failed to check the chart to see what anesthetics she had already been given."

Still, a number of large institutions have pressed forward with a different strategy. Rather than "deny and defend," the new strategy is "disclose, apologize, settle." When a claim is filed, the hospital will conduct an in-house investigation, talking to the clinicians involved and reviewing the records, asking other physicians to give input, to determine what parts of the claim have merit and which don't. For instance, maybe the patient was hurt by a wrong early diagnosis that missed a cancer, but her chances of future recurrence are not as great as she fears (or as her outside experts are saying). When they have gathered their material, the hospital will schedule a meeting, or sometimes several of them, with the patient and the attorney. In these meetings, they will lay out what they found about what actually happened, and work their way toward a settlement.

---

[*] Gallegos, A., "Medical Liability: Cutting Costs from the Bench," amednews, October 31, 2011, available at http://www.ama-assn.org/amednews/2011/10/31/prsa1031.htm.

It's not simple, and it's not magic, but it seems to work. Though some critics have been concerned that such an open, transparent attitude would open the floodgates to more and more nuisance claims, that has not happened. Organizations that have used these different strategies typically report lower overall malpractice costs, sometimes as low as half of previous trends. And the transformation of the relationships can be quite powerful.

In the study of their "disclose, apologize, settle" program, the researchers from the University of Michigan Health System included a study of the case of a woman, J.W., whose cancer had been misdiagnosed at first. She made a claim for $2 million in compensation and prepared to sue—in part because she thought that she would not be able to return to work, and would not live to be able to support her two sons through college. The hospital found that she had indeed been misdiagnosed, but that her chances of permanent remission were better than she feared. After the meetings, she agreed to a $400,000 settlement, which included a college fund for her boys. She pressed the university to make a training video about her case, and they agreed. In the video, her feelings about the experience were quite vivid. What was most powerful for her was not the money but the sense of having a voice:

> After that night [of the meeting], I left there like I was on a mountaintop. I felt like I had finally been heard, they listened.... If that had been the end of the legal pursuit, that would have been fine with me. I was perfectly satisfied after that night.

Perhaps even more interesting, certainly more surprising, is the change in her lawyer's attitude. The same University of Michigan video features her lawyer, and his comments show that the university's shift in attitude to "a principled approach based on evidence and substance, not hyperbole" had forced him to change as well.

> Instead of adversarial, it was conversational. Instead of trying to figure out what the claims and defenses needed to be, I found myself trying to figure out some higher calling: What's the right thing to do here? What's the best thing to do here?

The university's shift forced him to reevaluate his role in a fundamental way:

> [My role] changed from advocate and warrior to counselor. We are attorneys *and* counselors, and the counselor part got emphasized, in fact became the dominant, ascendant part just as soon as it became clear the University hospital was going to take a different approach to this case.*

---

* Quoted in Boothman et al.

Systemic Effects

The evolving Next Healthcare reduces the malpractice problem by its very nature.

One of the large trends we are seeing is that more and more physicians are going on salary to some large institution or system. These huge systems are more commonly self-insured for liability; that is, they pay out malpractice claims directly. This is a very different situation from individual physicians covered by a liability insurance firm. Here the institution that is directly at risk for malpractice claims is the same one that employs the physician and can impel cooperation with a different way of dealing with malpractice—and is the same one that is driving quality through all of its medical services, and might be able to learn something from each malpractice claim.

All of the new arrangements and business models that we have discussed necessarily have much higher demands for tracking quality (because, in one way or another, that's what payers are paying for in these models)—and at the same time they tend to standardize medical care and reward higher-quality, evidence-based practices. We can expect, over time, to see less actual malpractice, as doctors adhere to best practices, guidelines, and checklists. We can expect to see fewer malpractice claims, as we see lower rates of hospital-acquired infections, fewer adverse drug events, and fewer of what clinicians call "never events," events that should simply never happen, like amputating the wrong limb.

We will also see malpractice suits becoming easier to defend. Following the best-practice guidelines provides a physician a better defense in a malpractice suit than following his or her own judgment at variance with best practices. Imagine a doctor on the stand, with the plaintiff's attorney asking, "So you decided not to take the CT scan, which our experts have argued would have revealed the tumor. Why not? What would it have hurt?"

Imagine the doctor replying, "I just didn't think it was necessary." The plaintiff's attorney turns to the jury, arches his eyebrows, and repeats the words: "You just didn't ... think ... it was necessary."

Imagine another doctor replying to a similar question, "Given the presenting symptoms and the results of the previous tests, according to the evidence-based standards of our specialty, there is no reason to do a CT scan at that point. Had I decided to order a CT, just because I felt like it, I would have been going against the standard best practices of my specialty, as laid out in the guidelines. I don't do that without very good reasons, and there were no such reasons in this case."

The new arrangements and business models are also inextricably tied up not only with quality standards, evidence, and careful control of processes, all of which will reduce actual malpractice, but with accountability and transparency, which will reduce patients' and families' desire or need to sue.

Malpractice, and malpractice law as we have been practicing it, is a huge problem. But it is not a problem of greedy patients and their lawyers. It is a problem of systemic quality and transparency. It will be solved by methods that drive the system toward reducing real medical problems and "misadventures." Such methods acknowledge problems when they occur, seek out the system reasons why they occurred, and eliminate the potential for problems at the source while they make the victim or their survivors as reasonably whole as possible. Malpractice and malpractice law have been a giant pain for the medical profession. What they can be, instead, is an enormous opportunity for systemic learning.

Fixing the Pharmaceutical Industry

Drugs have transformed our lives, and we would like them to transform them more by, for instance, curing cancer. There is little doubt that the development over the last century of antibiotics and antivirals, vaccines, anesthetics and analgesics, and a wide range of disease-specific drugs, have allowed many more people to survive into old age, and to live more productive, pain-free lives.

There is no question that biotechnology and other research directions offer tantalizing possibilities of new pharmaceuticals that could tame cancer, heart disease, diabetes, AIDS, new viruses, and a host of other scourges.

Yet the path to developing and deploying those drugs seems broken, difficult, and obscured.

Over the past several decades, as drug development became increasingly risky and technically complex, a new development model arose in the United States. Small start-ups became the "farm teams" for the large pharmaceutical firm. Researchers, often university based, would come up with a promising avenue of exploration. They might gain some insight, for instance, into how fatty plaques form in the wall of a coronary artery, enlarge until they are closing the artery down, grow unstable, and burst, sending clots downstream to lodge in the next narrowing, causing a heart attack. They might think that they see a way in which a chemical compound of a certain shape or activity could interfere in this process, so that the fatty plaques never form, or stay small. They might attract venture capital to this idea and found a small company to research the compounds that might work.

The goal of the start-up is not to develop and market a drug. The goal is to develop the idea far enough that some big pharmaceutical company will buy the firm and its compounds and patents, with the twin benefits of making the original researchers and investors rich, and introducing a fine new therapeutic drug into the world. The advantage for the pharmaceutical companies is that these thousands of small farm teams can do an exponentially wider range of risky research down many more blind allies than the big companies ever could do in their own labs.

Buoyed by its venture capital, the firm plunges forward with research, develops several compounds, testing them first in the lab and then in animals, and then enters the long and expensive phase of human testing. There are four stages of human testing, each more expensive and complex than the last. Stage 0 is a micro-test on a few paid volunteers at a very low dose, just to see how the drug acts in the body, and how the body metabolizes the drug. Stage I tests the drug on a small number of volunteers at slowly increasing doses to assess its safety, how well the body tolerates it, and again how the drug acts in the body, and how the body metabolizes the drug at these higher doses.

Stage II is a big step up. Now the researchers are working with several hundred volunteers, at the doses that they determined in stage I. Now for the first time (in most cases) they are testing the drug on people with the target disease to see if it actually has the effect that they think it should. This is the stage at which most compounds fail: After years of work and research, the researchers try the drug on people with the condition it's supposed to improve, and they don't get the effect they hoped for. The fatty plaques don't shrink, or the subject group has more heart attacks rather than fewer.

If the compound survives stage II, actually showing the desired effect, and not too many side effects, it is ready for stage III: giving the drug to hundreds or thousands of actual patients in multiple medical centers under the guidance of outside physicians, in real clinical circumstances.

The results of each stage are submitted to the FDA. Its expert panels of physicians and pharmaceutical researchers can allow the compound to go on to the next stage, or can ask for that stage to be repeated with some variation. Only when the compound has successfully completed all three stages can the drug be certified by the FDA for medical use.

Anywhere along the development and testing track, the little start-up may be sold to a large pharmaceutical company. The closer to a real, marketable drug they are, the higher the price. The whole process can take as long as 15 years, and billions of dollars, for a single compound. The great majority of promising compounds fail along the way. Developing a drug is a vastly difficult and risky business.

Pharma Runs into a Wall

Over the past three decades, the pharmaceutical industry exploded to become a behemoth, possibly the most profitable industry in history, attracting enormous investment capital and proliferating business models.

It also "hit the wall," as long-distance runners would say. The tremendous promise of new genomic discoveries proved slow to produce workable drugs. The flood of investment into the long, difficult development cycle addicted the industry to the next "blockbuster."

Think like a pharmaceutical company executive for a moment: What would be the characteristics of your favorite drug, the drug you would want to snuggle up to in your dreams? It would be a drug for a lot of people, not some small group of people. The people who take it would either like its effects a whole lot, or they would have to risk sickness and death if they didn't take it. They would have to take it often, preferably every day. They would have to take it not for three days or a month, but for years, maybe the rest of their lives. It would be patentable, not just a repackaging of something already known. And it would be expensive.

Most of the big drugs introduced in the last 20 years fit that profile: selective serotonin reuptake inhibitors (SSRIs) and other drugs for depression or anxiety; Viagra, Cialis, and other sex drugs; Ambien and other sleep drugs; Ritalin for attention deficit; statins for cardiovascular conditions; and so on.

Not that these drugs are not valuable, or do not help solving some problems for some people. But of all the potential problems out there, and all the potential solutions, this is the kind of solution our current business model for drug development throws up: aimed at a broad audience, must be taken regularly for long periods, expensive, patentable. Existing compounds that could find new uses are passed up. So are the thousands of "folk" remedies from throughout history and around the globe that actually have therapeutic effect: they are not patentable, and so are not of interest.

The pharmaceutical companies even discovered a new and highly effective technique: condition branding. Suppose you discover that some compound you are working with has an interesting effect, maybe even a side effect, that some people might find useful. Like maybe it helps people sleep. Or maybe it helps people be less anxious and shy at parties. You could just develop it, get it approved, and sell it. But that might not pay off the huge investment you've put into it. So you do something else first: You market the condition. You found an institute all about sleep disorders or situational anxiety. You pay medical researchers to write papers that show that huge numbers of Americans are troubled by this terrible disorder. You get journalists to do stories on these papers in typical scary fashion: "Millions Lie Sleepless—Scared of Parties—Lives Ruined."

Then you produce your drug—voilá! A solution to this problem hounding Americans! Sound familiar? It's a well-established practice defined most vividly by Vince Parry in a 2003 article, "The Art of Branding a Condition," in *Medical Marketing and Media*. Perry argued that, to guarantee big sales for a pharmaceutical, you only had to accomplish any one of three things:

- Elevate the importance of an existing condition
- Redefine an existing condition to reduce a stigma
- Develop a new condition to build recognition for an unmet market need

Condition branding is very effective. It's a good way to make more money by selling drugs. It's not a great way to find the best and least expensive ways to meet the real needs of the nation for better health and healthcare. In fact, condition branding has nothing to do with that goal.

At the same time, the steam is running out of the big pharmaceutical company's development engine. Increasingly, patents on their best sellers are running out, and new replacement "blockbusters" are not showing up. The biggest event in the industry over the last decades has been (as we have discussed) the explosive growth of the generic companies, which now supply over 75% of all pharmaceuticals used in the United States.[*]

The model is not working for the public good, and it is even showing a decreasing ability to keep the industry in beer and skittles.

But unlike the other parts of healthcare, there do not seem to be large-scale working models for fixing the pharmaceutical business model. There are, though, some intriguing possibilities. One way to think about it arises from an earlier time in U.S. history when the government needed to harness the genius of the private sector for a truly pressing national need.

Burying Germany in Jeeps

The United States and its allies won the Second World War, the Axis lost.

There was nothing actually inevitable about that victory. It could have gone the other way. Germany could have ended up holding onto much or all of the continent, and Japan much of China and the Pacific. The question of why the Allies won is a complex subject for analysis. But one piece of that analysis is worth thinking about here: the Allies, and especially the United States, outproduced the Axis in war materiel by a huge margin.

The numbers are staggering. The war began, for the United States, on December 7, 1941, with the attack on Pearl Harbor, Hawaii, by the naval forces of the Empire of Japan. It ended in Europe 3½ years later on May 8, 1945, with the collapse of the Third Reich, and a few months after that in the Pacific with the surrender of Japanese Imperial forces on September 2, 1945. So for the United States, World War II lasted only 46 months, a far shorter time than the United States has spent making war in Afghanistan.

Both Germany and Japan had been gearing up for war, and at war, for a long time by 1941. They both were huge, thriving economies commanding the resources of vast empires, and both were highly organized for war in the industrial age.

---

[*] Cook, J.P., et al., "Generic Utilization Rates, Real Pharmaceutical Prices, and Research and Development Expenditures," National Bureau of Economic Research, February 2010, accessed at http://www.nber.org/papers/w15723.pdf.

U.S. war production started a bit earlier than the start of the war, with the Lend-Lease program to aid the United Kingdom and the Soviet Union. But the huge surge in production happened during the brief war. In a little over four years, the United States manufactured 88,000 tanks, 250,000 pieces of artillery, nearly 3 million machine guns, 10 million M1 rifles and carbines, 2.4 million trucks, 325,000 planes, 34 million tons of merchant ships, and 650,000 jeeps.* Despite truly astounding production achievements during the war in Germany and Japan, every number dwarfed the Axis numbers. The Allies fairly paved Europe and the islands of the Pacific in equipment.

All sides, except for the Soviet Union with its nationalized industries, depended on the private sector for war production. But there was a key difference between the way the United States and the Axis handled that production. In Germany and Japan, the government would say, "We need a new light truck for infantry support," for instance. It would put out a request for proposals. Different companies would submit their designs and cost estimates. The government would choose one design and award the contract to that company.

The Roosevelt administration, in contrast, would say, "We need a new light truck for infantry support," and put out a request for proposals. On the basis of very quick first-draft design proposals, the government would pay a number of companies to come up with a full design and cost estimate. A war resources board of production and design experts would gather the designs together and, rather than picking the best one, would meld them. Perhaps one had a better engine design and another a better suspension, while a third had some great ideas on how to build a truck that could be dismantled for shipping. They would have the designers from the different companies make one common design, specifying every measurement—then contract with all the companies to crank out thousands of the exact same model.

The companies got paid for their design abilities, creative genius, and manufacturing capacities. But the nation made use of the capacities of all of the companies to design and build what the nation needed.

Apparently, when the nation really needs something done fast, it has figured out how to use the genius of the private sector to get 'er done.

What would this look like in pharmaceutical development? It would look like a greatly expanded program of grants in which the National Institutes of Health designates pharmaceutical priorities (say, drugs that would better fight diabetes). The NIH would sign large research contracts with companies that had promising avenues to pursue, and some of the companies would come up with compunds worth testing. The NIH would then let a second set of contracts, with the same

---

* Selected equipment production figures of World War II, http://www.taphilo.com/history/WWII/Production-Figures-WWII.shtml.

companies or others, to do the hard work of translational research that would turn the promising compound into testable, and eventually marketable, drugs.

In January 2011, Dr. Francis Collins, head of NIH, set his stamp on the agency in a striking way. As head of the Human Genome Project in the 1990s, he had trumpeted the enormous benefits that would flow from genomic research. In the years since he had become increasingly frustrated as pharmaceutical companies failed to turn the explosion of genomic findings into useful drugs. Repeatedly, he had watched as drug companies withdrew from encouraging lines of research because they did not have the will or resources to take the risk of investment. So Collins founded a new center, the National Center for Advancing Translational Sciences (NCATS), starting with $700 million of existing NIH funding and hoping, against the tide of budget cutting, to expand it to at least a $1 billion per year program. The NCATS is not designed to replace the private sector, but rather to fund development of ideas to the point at which the private sector would be willing to invest in them.*

In May 2011, Senator Bernie Sanders of Vermont reintroduced a proposal that, if passed, would dwarf the NCATS. His Medical Innovation Prize Fund Act would eliminate all legal barriers to the manufacture and sale of generic versions of drugs and vaccines, and create a prize fund for drug development set at 0.55% of the U.S. gross domestic product, about $80 billion in 2011. The prize would be jointly funded by the federal government and the health plan industry. The bill languished in committee. Being a good idea that could solve a problem of pressing national importance is not enough to garner enough votes to pass.

Why We Don't Get Legislation That Works

Each of these discussions highlights ways in which laws on the books today hinder the rapid development of the Next Healthcare, a thriving, learning industry bent on providing the best health and healthcare for the lowest cost to everyone, or fail to support that development. The problems in this complex industry are never simple, and rarely admit to simple solutions. Yet a problem, and the ability to claim a simple solution for it, is a valuable political tool with which to hammer the other side and to garner campaign contributions. An actual solution, subtle, complex, intelligently fit to the problem and the resources that can be brought to bear on it, does not make for good grandstanding, and does not rake in the campaign money. It just helps the nation.

---

* Harris, G., "Federal Research Center Will Help Develop Medicines," *New York Times*, January 22, 2011. accessed online at: http://www.nytimes.com/2011/01/23/health/policy/23drug.html.

Chapter 14

The X Questions

The questions have changed. The key strategy questions that the C-suite of any organization in healthcare must be asking—and getting actionable answers to—are different now from what they were in the past, even from what they were last year. Most of today's healthcare CEOs and C-suite leaders are missing many of the key questions they need to ask to drive strategy now, this year, this budget, in order to survive the next three to seven years. Which ones are you missing?

A New Mind-Set

When I work with organizations and leaders, the next question is always: What do we do now? How does all this translate into a program of new action? In the case of organizations that are already well into the changes I've described here and who may now be in danger of foundering in the weeds, the question is more: How do I get back or stay on track? How do I know if I'm getting where I need to go and whether a course correction is necessary?

These questions are what leaders do best. It is their job to ask them. Some years back I conducted an extensive series of interviews of 60 thought leaders on the subject of change and leadership. (For more information about this project go to http://www.ImagineWhatIf.com/MastersOfChange.) One of the most popular interviews was with Ronald Heifetz of Harvard University's Kennedy School of Government. His seminal book *Leadership Without Easy Answers* pointed out that the core job of real leadership is not to come up with solutions but to pose the tough, creative questions, the way Martin Luther King Jr. managed to juxtapose the grand declarations on which this country is founded ("all men are created equal") with images of African Americans being fire hosed, beaten, and attacked by dogs in the act of marching for their rights. The hard questions you ask are key to planning for a proximate future with such huge disruptive potential.

Today and for the next few years the weather of the healthcare industry will be dominated by pervasive, discontinuous change. Structures, revenue streams, relationships of every level: all are shifting in fundamental ways. As we have been discussing, the weather will be driven by:

- Invention and propagation of *new business models*
- Shifting *risk* onto both the clinical provider and the patient, accompanied by building of new risk-based relationships, contracts, and alliances
- *Smart primary care* coming to the fore as the foundation of healthcare, driving most business models
- *Digitization and automation* going wall to wall and beyond the walls—accompanied by powerful new info-capacities, from "big data" strategic analysis to new ways of reaching and bonding with customers
- A striking new need for *efficiency and effectiveness* in response to rapidly rising demand as the baby boomers age, the baby boomer healthcare workforce ages and disengages, and the newly insured increase their use of healthcare facilities

Most of these factors, except the very last, are not dependent on the healthcare reform act, and will not change much if the act is altered or set aside.

Here are 10 strategic questions for the healthcare C-suite. There are lots of questions you can ask at the strategic level, but these 10 stand out as existential questions, the ones that, unasked or poorly answered, could cripple your organization, narrow your options, and threaten your continued viability. So we will call them the X questions—X for the Roman numeral 10, for the existential nature of the answers, and for the key "X factor" role they will play in your future. If you are not asking these questions, asking them seriously, not rhetorically, in a venue that searches for answers that result in actions, you and your organization are flying blind into unknown territory.

The X Questions

1. *Smart primary care*: What would it take to derive the majority of your income and profit from primary care in three to five years? What would that look like? What capacity would you have to buy or build or ally with to do that? What structure would make primary care a profit center

instead of just a source of patient flow for the real profit centers? Do you recognize the elements that make a primary care practice "smart," Lean, effective, and a true medical home?

2. *Risk*: Are there definable populations in your market whose health costs could be driven down by improving their health status? While there are thousands of examples out there, think about one that we mentioned in the "Getting on the same team with the docs" section of Chapter 8 ("3. Put A Crew On It"): in the last 10 years, through basic, conservative preventive measures, Kaiser drove down the incidence of heart attacks in its members by 24%; it reduced serious heart attacks requiring hospitalization or surgery by 68%. Those are big numbers. That's a lot of suffering and premature death to prevent. Kaiser is financially at risk for the care of its members. You can probably imagine how the return on investment for preventing all that suffering and death looked on Kaiser's bottom line.

   These definable populations could be populations defined by payer (all the Blue Cross/Blue Shield members in your area, for instance, or all the members of your own health plan). Or by disease process (anyone with diabetes), by living situation (everybody in a particular retirement home), by income level (all the lower-income people in a particular part of town), by life stage (all the mothers of young children), or even by occupation (all those dock workers with the bad backs). How could you put your organization at risk—therefore at profit—for those particular health costs? Who might pay you to care for them? In what way might they pay?

3. *Hotspotting*: Think of the "Pareto Principle in healthcare" discussion in Chapter 9 ("4. Swarm The Customer"), of the top 1% and 5% of healthcare spenders. These are typically the long-term chronic patients who are not getting the real care and attention they need to stabilize their condition and keep them out of the ER or the hospital. If you are going to be at risk for some population, do you know who that top 1% or top 5% of resource spenders are? Do you know how to find out? Do you have a clear idea how you could lower their costs by serving them better?

4. *Alliances, customers, partners*: Who is going to work with you? Who will share the risk and the benefit of these new risk environments? Are there competitors—such as physician groups, specialty clinics, urgent care clinics, or retail clinic chains—that are now potential allies? Are there employers in your area with whom you can work directly, to be at risk for some aspect of their employees' care (behavioral health, for instance, or spine care, or all primary care in a workspace clinic)?

5. *Teams*: What sort of clinical teams will you need to build to take on this kind of risk? What will make those clinical groups into teams and not mere collections of clinicians with their own agendas? In what ways can

the way you pay those clinicians tie them directly into the organization's goals for each group of patients? How will the business structure, patient flow, and workflow have to be different from what you have now?

6. *Definition*: How will the definition of *care* expand beyond your traditional inpatient and outpatient "sick care" concerns when you take on such risk? For instance, how can you affect outcomes and costs by putting behavioral health professionals into the care flow early and often? Consider this: The two top predictors of an individual's healthcare costs are not physical. They are not body mass index, blood pressure, or blood sugar level. They are stress and depression. Are you going to put yourself at risk for those healthcare costs without trying to do anything about those factors?

7. *Setting*: Where will such care have to be delivered? Through what kind of channels, and in what kind of environments? If your survival depends on managing the health risk and costs of populations, how do you bring the care to them? How do you snuggle up to your customer? What are the technologies that could put your relationship to your customer in her purse, on her desk, in her house?

   How will your physical plant and building environment have to change? As you contemplate building, renovating, and repurposing in a new risk-based environment, you will have to focus not only on getting closer to your customers, but also on building a safer, more efficient and effective environment where your clinicians can work with them. How conversant are you and your executive team with the principles of evidence-based design championed by the Center for Health Design and encapsulated in its certification program? Are your architect and interior designer certified?

8. *Benchmarking*: Are there organizations of your size and level of complexity, in markets like yours, that have done something like what you are navigating, that you could benchmark? How could you best find them? How could you best work with them?

9. *Digitizing*: Everyone is getting digital at once, but there is no mantra that makes it all work. It can be done badly, even when working with market-leading companies. You can cripple your organization's workflows, cut efficiencies, and make your clinicians hate you—at the same time that you pay out checks as much as 10 times larger than you need to.

   How much do you and your executive team actually know about the changing horizon of information capacities? How seriously have you studied it? Does that knowledge simply pad out your strategy, or does it drive it? How satisfied are you that the strategy and the company you are choosing to lead your drive toward computerization and automation are the best for you? Or are you and your CIO simply buying the security of a major company's imprimatur? How aware are you of the new technological capacities arising and being showcased in the Health 2.0 environment, in the open-source movement, or in primary care, in the ideal medical practice movement?

In your enterprise-wide digitization, are you using OpenVista and the Resource and Patient Management System (RPMS), the open-source software suites available for free from the Veteran's Administration, one of the oldest, most tested, and largest digital implementations in healthcare? If you are not, how good are your reasons?

In taking your smart primary care practices and other physician practices electronic, have you considered the free or cheap software-as-subscription packages, such as Practice Fusion or Doctations? How strong are your reasons for spending money you don't have on systems that cost far more?

Kaiser recently rebuilt its entire electronic system (and by all reports quite successfully) to the tune of $4 billion. Top managers involved 160 physicians from all parts of the system in the redesign, not just once, but repeatedly, as a task force. This really helped not only in building a good system that actually works for the clinicians, but also in getting the doctors to actually use it to advantage once it was implemented. How much have you involved your doctors in designing your system? Or is it just, "Oh, we have a doc on the committee"?

Ask yourself some functional questions from a doctor's point of view, such as: Are the accounts and records transaction-based or patient-based? When an ED patient is admitted, does that become a new record? Or is all the clinical information on that patient brought forward as part of a continuing, longitudinal patient record? Can it display, for instance, variations in blood albumin level over time as a single graph? Or does the clinician have to burrow through dozens of transactional records to write down the data, then visualize it in her head? Can the system accept data from other hospitals' systems or from legacy data sources within your own system? If not, why not, when translational software is available?

If you don't know the answers to these questions to a close approximation of on-the-ground clinical reality, you need to find them. They could be killing you.

10. *Healthy communities*: If you are at risk for the health of a population, what could you be doing to help members of that population be healthier? The least expensive way to deal with disease is to prevent it. Many prevention methods range far beyond the medical environment. They have involved everything from a bicycle helmet campaign to better daycare centers to traffic lights, community gardens, yoga classes, and healthy cooking clubs. Do you know what the key leverage points are in the community

you are at risk for? Have you asked the community? Have you done the community health risk assessment mandated in the reform law?

The amount of actual funding involved in partnering to build a healthier community can be so low that the chief financial officer of one healthcare system described it to me as "lost in the noise" of the budget. In a risk environment, the return on investment can be very high.

Confronting Your Risk

In the environment that is developing right now, with the shift in underlying economics, demographics, technologies, and business assumptions, every organization in healthcare is at risk of slowing its development, crippling itself, or even falling by the wayside. At the same time, tremendous new opportunities are opening up, often in directions we have never had the possibility of even thinking about.

This is the time to ask and answer the fundamental strategic and tactical questions, the X questions.

Chapter 15

It's the System

So let's review the five-part formula, the combination of ingredients that will reshape healthcare to be leaner, faster, higher quality, less expensive, and more available:

Explode the business model, that is, in one way or another overturn, subvert, supplement, or rework the commodity-based insurance-supported fee-for-service model that dominates the healthcare market in the United States. Share risk in much more measured ways across healthcare, putting some financial risk on the customer, and some on the medical provider. Not all of it should be on the payer.

Build on smart primary care. Every example where healthcare works better and cheaper is tightly organized around smart, efficient, well-incentivized primary care.

Put a crew on it. Every example that works in every part of healthcare is a true team effort, not part of the siloed, blinkered, uncommunicative past of medicine.

Swarm the customer with help, information, advice, resources, hand-holding, early, often, and as close as possible. Target special help for those who are costing the system the most.

Rebuild every process. The processes of most parts of healthcare are still archaic. Every process must be rebuilt—and the data to drive it must be derived from a massively digitized and transparent healthcare that is ready to become the most massive learning organism in history.

Add to that the sixth part, which is outside the healthcare system itself: *build healthier communities.*

Wait. Half?

We started out talking about cutting healthcare costs by half. The examples we have explored show costs dropping by 15, 20, or 25%. Even if all of healthcare switched to these new, leaner models, how can we imagine that would result in costs dropping by half?

To see that, we have to think about the system dynamics. Healthcare is an extraordinarily complex system—and its dynamics are shifting in a historically unprecedented way.

Our Shaky Equilibrium

Systems get stuck. In economic game theory, the technical term for this particular way of getting stuck is a Nash equilibrium, named for the mathematician who formulated it, John Nash (portrayed in the 2001 film *A Beautiful Mind*). Systems consist of a number of different interacting players. In the healthcare system, for instance, there are hospitals and health systems; doctors and physician groups; and other providers, health plans, employers, government payers, politicians, pharmaceutical companies, various suppliers and manufacturers.

In any system, individual players seek what is best for them, to survive and grow and do what they are there to do. But we can't think about them in isolation, because individual players think about, and act on, what they think the other players' strategies will be. They fight to a position that is the best they can do with the information they have, against the strategies of the other players as they understand them. What that means is that the best position they can fight to is not their best possible position; in fact, they are usually far from the best possible due to actual and perceived limitations.

Players may well be able to imagine a much better situation for themselves, they may be able to see other, more profitable, more moral, more helpful solutions. However, they feel unable to strive for those because, as they see it, any move toward them will at least temporarily take them away from what they believe to be the best they can do right now. It will take them down from the height they have achieved and into the valleys of uncertainty, poorer performance, or lower returns.

So they are doing "good enough" to stay where they are, but they are stuck there. Because each player is watching the others and reacting to their strategies, everybody is doing only good enough and no one is striving for their best possible.

So doctors being paid fee-for-service may know that their patients need and deserve more of their time and attention, and the insurance companies less of their time and attention, but if they do this unilaterally, they will make less money and will likely be driven out of business. Insurance companies may know that there are less expensive ways to fund healthcare, but they are paid a percentage of the healthcare market. If they truly drive their customers to better, cheaper healthcare, they cost themselves a chunk of their market.

Hospitals are in the same position as doctors: they have to take the good enough funding that they can get and keep begging for more, because to do anything seriously different would so undermine their position that they might have to close their doors, and what good would that do?

This position holds as long as the status quo does, even as it may slowly become less tenable for every player. A Nash equilibrium changes only if something causes the ground under everyone's feet to shift.

That is what is happening right now.

Beyond the Tipping Point: Rapid System Change

Healthcare is a complex adaptive system—every part of it adapts to every other part and the system as a whole adapts to new inputs of energy, ideas, and money, and new outflows of its products and services and capital.

Each of the examples we have talked about (such as the Alaska Natives Health System or Boeing's Intensive Outpatient Care Program) exists mostly in isolation, so destabilizing systemic effects have not kicked in for them or for the system as a whole.

Imagine, for instance, that you are a device manufacturer or other vendor to healthcare, and you dominate your market segment. Imagine that you are hearing from your sales force that some 1% or 2% of your market is demanding a much lower-cost product, or saying that they are finding a way to do without your product entirely. If it's only a few percent, you can safely ignore them.

But what if that becomes 15%, 20%, or 25%? It is hard to say just what the tipping point is, but it's there. At some point, you can no longer ignore them. You may have competitors, whom you fear will steal this low-cost part of the market from you. This becomes a matter of existential importance. A wrong choice could kill the company or greatly reduce its market share. One strategic argument would be to stick it out at higher price ranges by offering only the finest products with the most features and the best design, and be happy dominating only the upper end of your market. This is the strategy of companies like Apple and BMW.

But this works only if you can very clearly differentiate your product line from the disruptive competitors, which may ultimately become very hard to do. Eventually, you must find a way to accommodate the low-cost part of the market, and produce products at a broader range of price points. But when you do that, you can't segregate your market, and sell these lower-cost products just to that 15% that is demanding it. Your other customers may go for them as well.

In a disrupted market, you can anticipate a rush to some lower-cost equilibrium between price and value. You can't help but disrupt your own market with lower-cost, higher-value products.

I remember a shocking conversation a few years back with the CEO of a major manufacturer of artificial legs and other prosthetics. Business was booming, largely due to the two wars the United States was fighting in the Middle East. I asked him about pricing. He said an artificial leg costs in the range of $10,000, but the whole process of bringing a person from amputation to being healed, going through fittings and rehab, and moving forward in his or her life with an artificial limb, cost about $100,000.

"How do you work out pricing?"

"We start with the reimbursement we can get, then work our way backward to what we could engineer and manufacture for that, with a reasonable profit margin."

I asked him his opinion of Jaipur Foot.

"Who are they?"

"Largest maker of artificial legs in the world."

"That can't be right. I've never heard of them."

"Big charity organization in India. They make legs for about $30 each and give them away. Materials cost about $12.50. Custom-fitted. Plastic. They give you the mold so you can make more in your home oven."

He was skeptical that they could ever affect his market. And he was probably right, at the time. And these artificial legs were certainly not of a quality that an American market would want.

But imagine for a moment that kind of manufacturing genius, combined with the ferocity to keep the price down, applied to his market. If Jaipur Foot can produce a workable, custom-fitted leg for $30, what could they (or some for-profit start-up) produce for $300, or even $3,000?

Imagine a market in which the incentives were flipped, in which, for instance, the provider, the payer, and the end customer all stood to gain by paying for the highest quality at the lowest possible price. Could such an organization disrupt the market at a seriously lower price point?

Similarly, Narayana Hrudayalaya (NH) cardiac care center, located in Bangalore, is one of the world's largest providers of heart surgery and other forms of cardiac care, known for high medical quality. It provides heart surgeries at $1,500, 1/30 of the average U.S. cost for such surgeries. But a lot of that cost difference is due to factors that cannot cross national boundaries, such as costs of labor, land, and facilities. What is perhaps more interesting is that Narayana Hrudayalaya charges one-third as much as the typical Indian top-end hospital with the same costs for labor, land, and facilities. That difference comes largely from Narayana Hrudayalaya's devotion to Lean manufacturing principles. As one example: It has its own sutures for heart surgery made locally for $90 each, at world-class quality, custom-made for each surgeon's preferences, instead of paying $200 each for imported mass-produced sutures.*

Another Indian organization, Aravind Eye Care, is the world's largest provider of cataract surgeries. It does over 250,000 eye procedures and treats 1.6 million out-patients a year. The intraocular lenses it uses cost $60 to $100 each on the world market, so they took to manufacturing their own for $3 each. They are already exporting over half of their production to the United States and other countries.†

Imagine this scenario across all the millions of transactions in this vast industry: a competition to provide real value at competitive prices to produce provable outcomes.

Each transaction that drives some part of the system toward greater value at lower cost—better and cheaper—sets up a positive feedback loop that drives other parts of the system to do the same. You have individuals, government, employers, and health plans paying for healthcare; physicians buying supplies, pharmaceuticals, software; health systems paying for those things as well as massive specialized buildings, equipment, devices, and labor; and on and on throughout the massive $2.5 trillion U.S. healthcare economy. Nearly all of these buyers at each step and level of healthcare tend to think of themselves more in the role of procurement managers. They try to control unit costs (the cost of each item), but are not in the frame of mind to look at the big picture. They do not ask how they can dramatically drive down the cost by increasing the quality and breadth of their service at the same time. In a universe of flipped incentives and crushing twin pressures for lower cost and greater efficiencies, all of these buyers at each level truly become shoppers, and systemic shoppers at that.

This set of positive feedback loops will feed into one another. A lower-cost, portable sonography machine working through a laptop makes it possible, for instance, to offer lower-cost services in retail clinics, or in the home, leaving primary care practices and clinics searching for ways to compete in those services. Hospitals, in turn, search for better ways to compete with the clinics and large physician practices. As these positive feedback loops interact, the price for various services will drop.

But if the buyers at all levels and in all sectors become systemic shoppers, this will not trigger a positive feedback race to chaos like a bank collapse. Rather, it will drive all healthcare products and services toward lower price points that are more truly supported by the value received. "You get what you pay for" works as a rule of thumb in most industries. You pay a lot more for a new Mercedes or Mini Cooper than for a used Kia, but you get more and better car for your money. A room at the Ritz in Manhattan costs several times what a room at a

---

* Prahald, C.K., "The Innovation Sandbox," *Strategy and Business*, August 28, 2006.
† Ibid.

Days Inn out by Newark Airport costs, but it is a far nicer experience. In today's healthcare, that rule of thumb fails. Today, whether you are an individual paying for a back surgery or a hospital paying for software, it is easy, in fact common, to pay wildly more and get less. We will know that we have arrived at the Next Healthcare when "you get what you pay for" works as a rough rule of thumb most of the time.

True Shoppers

We can try to imagine what healthcare would be like if all of its buyers became true shoppers. One way to imagine that is to compare mainstream healthcare with parts of healthcare that are not covered by insurance, but are paid for almost completely by the end customer, such as laser eye surgery and cosmetic surgery.

These are minor parts of healthcare, but what they sell are medical procedures, performed by doctors and nurses and technicians, requiring the same standards of care as any other medical procedure. The general cost inputs of these clinics are much like those of other medical practices or clinics: office space, nurses, other clinicians, office assistants; specialized medical machines and software; and so on. The only real difference is that a much higher percentage of their practice is optional for the patient, and paid for out of the patient's own pocket. The patient is clearly the shopper.

So comparing the patient's experience, and the business profile, of these two optional services to the rest of the industry might be instructive. What do we see? We see that the two market segments, LASIK and cosmetic surgery, show very similar patterns. Over the last two decades, the costs for cosmetic surgery and LASIK eye surgery have not risen nearly as fast as the costs of the rest of healthcare, even as both fields have added new, more refined techniques. In both fields, we have seen a proliferation of products. Cosmetic surgery, especially, has expanded its product line to include low-end offerings, such as chemical peels and Botox treatments.

Despite offering products that can result in problems or, as with breast implants, have a limited life span, both fields offer warranties of one kind or another on their work. Both fields offer actual medical procedures, with the nuances and caveats of any medical procedure: What are the limits of the procedure? What are the possibilities for failure or infection? Practitioners of both LASIK and cosmetic surgery offer a lot of information about how best to use their services, how to be a smart shopper, and how the cost can be financed over time. A visit to a clinic to ask about prices and options is more like a visit to Nordstrom's, or a BMW showroom. Compare that experience to phoning local hospitals, health systems, and clinics to ask for a price on, say, a cardiac stress test, or minor hand surgery.

This is what happens when the person choosing the service acts as if he or she is spending his or her own money.

Automatic Cost Reductions

Some costs will drop out automatically with different incentives and structures. People do what you pay them to do. People do exactly what you pay them to do. Look down the list of wasteful practices we discussed earlier. No one is going to do the estimated 35 million unneeded scans we see in this country if they aren't getting paid fee-for-service to do them. No one is going to use computer-aided mammography, with its zero greater effectiveness rate over human-read mammograms, if they can't get reimbursed for the higher cost by a fee-for-service system. An enormous amount of insurance processing cost just goes away when you are not billing for, and having to argue over, every single item, but are just paid bundled rates per case or per life. Change the incentives, change what you are paying for, and the world of healthcare changes.

Chapter 16

Beyond Reform—The Next Healthcare

The future is already here—it's just not evenly distributed.

—*William Gibson**

The Next Healthcare beyond reform is not one thing. It is no monolithic system designed by some committee of experts. One size does not fit all. The Next Healthcare is a fertile landscape, lush with the growth of new types of businesses, new relationships, innovations, payment systems, delivery modes, all focused on the ultimate customer: the individual with a body that is aging, getting pregnant, having accidents, getting diseases, getting fit, having pleasure, having pain; the individual, the individual's family, the individual's community.

The Next Healthcare is not one thing, but all of its parts have adapted in a thousand ways to these five prime vectors: exploding the fee-for-service business model, building on smart primary care, working in teams, swarming the customer with help, and continually rebuilding processes for greater quality, efficiency, and effectiveness. Just as the lushness of a jungle is driven by the thousands of ways in which plants and animals compete for a few common factors, such as sunlight, moisture, and nutrients, the lushness of the Next Healthcare is driven

---

* Gibson often quotes himself as having said this "many times." One example accessed online is in this NPR recording, "Talk of the Nation: The Science in Science Fiction," November 30, 1999, at http://www.npr.org/templates/story/story.php?storyId=1067220.

229

by its multitudinous participants competing through these five vectors to serve customers of all different economic levels, life stages, states of health, genders, body types, education levels, personalities, and social environments.

It will be unevenly distributed. Like all real, growing, adapting systems, the experience of it from any one vantage point will seem lumpy, inhomogeneous, arriving differently in different geographic areas, socioeconomic classes, and parts of the economy.

Employers

It is likely that the early adopters will be employers. We already see large employers leading the charge on incentivized wellness programs, in-house clinics, direct-pay primary care, and a number of other innovations. Employers have the strongest incentives: unlike the health plans, they do not make a percentage of the costs as profit; the cost of healthcare is pure cost to them. If they are self-funded, any money saved goes directly to the bottom line. They have the flexibility to experiment, they have a defined population of employees to work with, and they have far more control over the employees' environment and communications. It is far more possible to build a culture of health with people who work together and have the same incentives and communication structure than with people who don't.

Big employers will design and experiment with their own systems, as have such companies as Boeing, Disney, Qualcomm, American Express, Cisco, and Pitney Bowes. But these programs are quite scalable. Smaller companies will use consultant firms like Orriant to set up their programs. We are likely to see firms in the insurance broker/consultant market put together packaged incentive programs for small businesses that duplicate the experiments of the largest companies.

We will see providers that specialize in providing team-built wellness/health/primary care packages in direct-pay contracts with employers. These will be special projects of established large medical practices, or hospital systems, or small medical start-ups that set up to work with certain employers, the way the Permanente Medical Groups set up to service the employees of Henry J. Kaiser's various companies starting in the 1930s.

The Poor

Don't go with the assumption that innovation will come quickest to the rich, or those with the most generous insurance. In fact, it may come at least as swiftly to the poor. Why? Because they need it the most, and any organization at financial risk for their care needs it the most. As sets of innovations prove that they can actually lower the cost of care and make it more efficient, we will see them adopted as rapidly as possible by free clinics, federally qualified community health centers, and clinics run by health systems that are overwhelmed by the uninsured, the undocumented, and the poorly insured—and especially by systems overwhelmed by the newly insured under the Patient Protection and Affordable Care Act (PPACA) reform law.

Medicare

Medicare will not be an early adopter. A massive system whose administration is constantly in the political spotlight will of necessity be less nimble. A shift that an employer can do almost instantaneously will take Medicare far longer. The Medicare shift is already beginning, in pilot programs and grants and demonstrations under the PPACA reform law. But it will really pick up speed only after much of the private market has shifted, and major providers in many parts of the country are used to working under a different set of incentives, and costs have actually begun to fall in parts of the market.

States

Different states have such different attitudes toward healthcare that some of them may as well be different countries. Texas and Florida have been overtly hostile to any healthcare market reforms, and instead cling to malpractice tort reform as the key to lower-cost healthcare. Florida, of course, elected ousted for-profit healthcare executive Rick Scott to the governor's mansion. On the other hand, Massachusetts famously passed "RomneyCare," which became the template for "Obamacare," and is attempting to upend the fee-for-service model by making risk-based healthcare contracting the law of the state. Vermont has installed the Vermont Blueprint across the state and is attempting a state single-payer finance system. Hawaii (called by some the People's Republic of Hawaii) has 26 hospitals, of which 24 are owned and operated by the state, and has long had far lower rates of uninsured than any other state.

With so many state-level experiments going on, and so many declarations of success or accusations of failure by various political figures and presidential candidates, wouldn't it be nice if we could ask, "So how's that working for you?" In fact we can. What would you want to compare? Not just the price of private insurance. You would want to compare the quality of medical care: Do people in that state have better outcomes? Do they get more preventive care? You'd want to know what percentage of people are covered. Since wealth and poverty correlate strongly with health status, you would also want to see how the cost compares to the relative wealth of the state population, that is, what percentage of income do people have to pony up for healthcare? How affordable is it for people in that state?

It turns out that someone has done the calculations. Al Lewis, president of the Disease Management Purchasing Consortium, worked through reams of publicly available data to give every state a Health Insurance Success Score. By this measure, which includes affordability, coverage, outcomes, all of the above, the list of top states reads like a list of the states that have been most aggressive in pursuing solutions: Hawaii, Vermont, New Hampshire, Massachusetts, Minnesota, Wisconsin. The bottom end of the list includes states that are not only low income, but have just as aggressively resisted any new solutions involving greater regulation of insurance, or better coordination of care, or greater coverage, such as Montana, Louisiana, Oklahoma, Mississippi, Arkansas, and firmly ensconced in last place, Texas.*

We can expect that these multiple new possibilities for the future of healthcare will unfold with similar unevenness. Healthcare is functionally organized in regional markets made out of hospital catchment areas, that is, areas defined by where you are likely to go when you need to go to the hospital. If you fall ill in Longmont, Colorado, you will likely go to Longmont United. You might go to Avista Adventist down in Superior, or Exempla Good Samaritan in Lafayette, or Banner McKee up in Loveland, or even the big medical centers in Denver, but you are unlikely to head to Salt Lake City or Omaha for treatment. Many of these changes will unfold in those regional markets, as providers and health plans compete against each other, and large employers aggressively seek solutions. Many changes will be enabled, encouraged, or stymied by state regulation and legislation. Those states that have shown the flexibility and political will to try to work with the problem so far, and with some success, are likely to remain the states that deal with it earliest, and most effectively.

How Fast?

Remember 1995? No Google, no Facebook, no iPods, iPads, iPhones, iMacs, iTunes, apps or appstores, smart phones, e-books, Skype, netbooks. If you were to name the giants of the publishing and music industries, you would never think to name Apple

---

* Lewis, A., "Massachusetts and Hawaii Offer the Most Cost-Effective Health Insurance Coverage," The Healthcare Blog, November 23, 2011, accessed at http://thehealthcareblog. com/blog/2011/11/23/massachusetts-and-hawaii-offer-the-most-cost-effective-health-insurance-coverage/.

and Amazon. No always-on connectivity, immersive online games, 3D TV. Think through the pace of change in the last 17 years or so in the interconnected worlds of computing, information, entertainment, music, movies, and gaming, as one innovation after another has surged to the fore. New hardware played a big part, from the laying of thousands of miles of optical fiber to bring us high-speed Internet, to the seemingly ceaseless creation of new gadgets. But the hardware fed on and fed into a rapid unspooling of new business models and entire new business sectors.

Contemplate that pace of change—jerky, lumpy, but rapid, sometimes breathtakingly rapid. Now think about healthcare, with its traditionally glacial pace of change. Flip the image: imagine healthcare unfolding innovative business models, technologies, ways of connecting with its customers, with the stunning speed we have come to expect from the info-world.

As the logjam of healthcare's Nash equilibrium breaks up, things will begin to move very quickly. Every organization in this vast industry will feel it has lost its footing, will feel existentially threatened and desperate to find new footing, solid ground, a place from which to build. They will be constraints, but the constraints will not be primarily in the market. The pace will be dictated first by the time that it takes for people to come to a new understanding of the situation, and then by the amount of time it takes for companies to form, for legislation to be passed, and for people to make career changes.

The most intense period of change will be in this decade.

The Next Healthcare

Rick wakes up, rolls over, and his wife says, "What's that?" She is poking at a spot on his back.

"What? What's what?"

"What's that spot? You've got a new spot on your back."

"Ah, criminy!" Rick's in his 60s, and has had a history of melanoma. Weird skin spots are a concern. In the old days, the routine would have been: Book an appointment with his primary care doctor in a week or so. Have the doctor give his opinion, and a referral to a melanoma specialist. Make that appointment, at least a couple of weeks out. Deal with the insurance billings for each, and the month or more of anxiety before hearing the specialist pronounce him safe.

But that was then, this is now. Rick goes into the bathroom and tries to see the spot in the mirror. He can see it's there, but he can't get a good look at it. He sets the timer on his smart phone, props it against a shelf, and takes a picture of his back. Too far away. Tries again. Better. One more try and he has a good picture of the spot. He emails it directly from the camera app to his doctor. An hour later, a message pops up on his phone: he should log into the system's secure website for a note. The note is from his doc: looks like nothing to worry about, but the doc has forwarded it to the system's melanoma specialist. Two hours later, another note: the specialist confirms that it is nothing to worry about. "But send me another picture in three weeks." A reminder inserts itself into Rick's calendar.

Total time of anxiety: Three hours, instead of a month or more. Out-of-pocket cost: zero. Rick is a customer of a system that is at risk for the health of its clients.

At his offices at the clinic at Next General Health System, Rick's primary care doc is sitting in a morning meeting with his team, going rapidly through checklists of the patients on their panel: Who is in the hospital? What's their situation? What's the next step? How will their care be handled on discharge? Who's in charge of the contact? How are the contacts going on the patients on the diabetes register? Who still needs to be contacted and scheduled, if necessary? Who is working with each of their half-dozen outliers with multiple problems? What's next for them? How are they each responding?

The meeting takes an hour out of the day for the whole team, but everyone on the team considers it the single most valuable hour in the day—and their pay and bonuses are hooked to the health and health improvement of the panel of patients they talk about every single day.

In the operating room at Next General, the charge nurse goes over the checklist prior to an operation: Who's in the room? Name of the patient? What is the operation (confirm with notes made on the patient's body the day before)? Amount of blood plasma on hand in case of hemorrhage? All down the list. They've been doing it for years now. This operation, a "robo-cabbage" (robotic cardiac artery bypass graft) is one that has a warranty: any problems or infections, and any extra hospital time or do-overs are on the house. They have never had to pay out. So far, their rate of infections and do-overs has been zero in three years. This surgical team has worked together consistently for years with minimal changes. They meet regularly outside of surgery to go over results and to refine their processes. Like other teams at Next, their pay and bonuses are partially linked to their clinical outcomes and error rates.

Around a boardroom table in the offices of Next General, a lively discussion is turning around the question of how to respond to the announcement of a new Gizmo International distribution facility on the northside. The planning staff is presenting their idea—propose to Gizmo a package that has three parts: a general on-site primary care clinic, a dedicated team to track and help the top 5% of their users of resources, and a specialized clinic for back care for all those warehouse workers.

"Who else do you think is going to hit them with a proposal?" the CEO asks. "Who is our competitor here?"

"Probably not Traditional Memorial. They are not quick to reach out like we are. Probably Ebbingdon, the for-profit over in Forestville. And the Rampart Clinic guys, multi-specialty clinic. But we don't think they have the breadth to pull it off. And Charter Health might make a bid."

"Charter Health?"

"A new virtual group. They'll low-ball the contract, then try to put together providers once they get it."

The CEO laughed. "Good luck with that! This business is all about relationships. So what's our strong point?"

"We have the breadth to take the risk, we've got a track record on similar projects with Caton Tractor and the Monster Chip Cookie people. We know how to streamline these things to keep our costs down, which means we can probably give Gizmo a very good ROI picture."

"But how would we staff it?"

"You know, we think we could get Rampart to come in with us. They staff it, we cut them a deal based on our managing it, they have to keep up the outcomes markers we set. We take the bigger risk, they get a steady income with no insurance hassles, just pure doctoring."

"Okay, let's see if we can set up a meeting with them."

In Forestville, Randall Kotter, MD, takes his time listening to a patient complain about getting older. It's such a pleasure being a doctor these days. He has a steady stable of clients, who pay him directly $40 per month, plus three small companies that pay him $35 per month per employee for a set roster of primary care. He operates on his own, and trades off with a half dozen other doctors in town and a live medical help line so that their customers can get to a live trained human any time of any day of the year—and to their own doctor if it's an emergency. Bookkeeping is simple. He never has to deal with insurance companies, though some of his customers get their monthly fee paid by health plans, most through their HSAs—and some of those HSAs are funded through Medicaid or the federal children's fund, SCHIP. He makes heavy use of medical apps, secure email, and scheduling programs to ease contact with his patients. In fact, he's happy to talk with them at home or to message with them, because he is no longer paid by the visit. All this frees up a lot of the time he used to spend on running the business, and lets him spend more time with patients, and keep some looseness in his schedule for people who need to see him right away—and he knows this makes him more popular with his customers and earns him good online reviews. He earns his money not by getting health plans to pay for tests and procedures but by keeping his customers happy.

Patsy Barnsill is pretty down and out. She has difficulty coping. She's clinically depressed and sometimes suicidal, and tonight is one of those nights when she is afraid. Her counselor at the county mental health center would call it an event. She used to cut herself when she felt like this, mainly just so she could go to the emergency department at Traditional Memorial, where at least they would pay attention to her, because they had to. And she had Medicaid, anyway. But her counselor had given her a card a few months back. It worked like a debit card, but just for healthcare. Her counselor had explained that if there was money left over at the end of three months, she would get to keep the rest—and she could go to the new federally qualified community health center instead of the ED, and it would be a lot cheaper. It was good the first time she went there. They did see her, even though she wasn't bleeding. But they had turned her over to an even better place. It was called the Living Room, and that's what it looked like. They listened to her, gave her a safe place to be until the darkness passed. They talked to her doctor and made sure she was on her meds. And it was cheaper even than the community health center. Maybe she would have some money left on the card this time and be able to get something nice.

Across the country, hundreds of companies, from small start-ups to "skunk works" of Fortune 100 companies, are competing hard to create better, cheaper ways of delivering healthcare. They are inventing new gadgets, new apps, new support systems for clinicians, new building systems that leverage the latest clinical knowledge about the built environment, all manner of new techniques—because the healthcare market has burst wide open. Traditional healthcare providers, new entrants to the marketplace, health plans, and employers are all vying for any advantage in the competition to keep people healthy and fix what ails them as efficiently and effectively as possible.

Over time, each segment, each section of the system, infuses, nourishes, and pushes the others in lush, fructifying interactions to grow more efficient, more effective, more fine-grained and close to the customer, and year after year the whole system gets leaner, smaller, smarter, cheaper, better, at half the percentage of GDP, half the cost per person. Half the cost. Better.

Appendix A:
Stupid Computer Tricks: How Not to Digitize Healthcare

The digitization of healthcare—making everything electronic, computerizing all processes—does not in itself make anything more efficient or more effective. Make a stupid workflow electronic, and it's still a stupid workflow. And in healthcare, a stupid workflow doesn't just cost money and waste people's time, it kills people.

Ask doctors about their experiences with using electronic medical records, and you'll get an earful. Enterprise software for healthcare systems is enormously complex. Most big healthcare systems buy from a big vendor, and have it customized to their own specifications. Some EMR installations are great, once the doctors get used to them. Others get in the doctors' way. It is not uncommon for doctors to refuse to use them, for sound clinical reasons.

One doctor detailed for me in email how seemingly unremarkable details of computerized record keeping can so frustrate physicians that the software becomes a danger to patient safety. In reproducing her emails here, I have redacted the physician's name, the name of her institution, and the names of the programs and the vendors who built them, for two reasons: so that she can speak freely, and because her complaints are not peculiar to her institution or to these suites of software. They are, in fact, similar to what I hear from many doctors working with different software suites in healthcare systems across the country. She works in two major academic institutions, and the several different vendors she mentions are among the top companies selling healthcare software systems right now, as the great majority of healthcare systems are attempting to "go digital" over the next few years:

> *Encounter-based records*: My favorite asinine stupidity related to the EMR, that dominates and dramatically limits the usefulness of both the systems at my present hospitals, is that they are built around "encounters." "Encounters" are each time you set foot in the hospital, and what happens after that; they're designed for billing purposes. I have no problem with encounters as a necessary evil for someone to be aware of and monitor. But both of these systems parse the results for patients by "encounters" so that I have trouble correlating the data across "encounters," graphing lab results, reviewing which medications were given, and following trends in vital signs.
>
> A decent system would make the "encounter" part of things invisible to me, and give me a seamless, longitudinal patient history—because I treat patients and not "encounters." These encounter-based systems are built for the billers who buy them; their use in the clinical environment is indecent and unconscionable.
>
> Similarly, I can review orders in the computer and sort them several ways, but they only come up one encounter worth at a time. So imagine that I want to enter a complex set of orders—say, someone receiving chemo for severe lupus kidney disease. I want to remember which version of a saline solution I used last time vs. the time before that, and what the flow rates were each time, and which time they needed an extra boost of Lasix because they didn't handle it as well. To do this I have to repeatedly go back and forth between encounters so that I can see the different orders in each encounter.
>
> *No way to input approximate or variable information*: In [this widely used software system], I must enter an order in the right encounter, or the lab or pharmacy cannot find it. My outpatient lab wants all orders entered in the computer. They will not accept a script that says "please draw a CBC with diff one time between 5/6 and 5/9/11," which is what I want for someone who received a dose of cyclophosphamide on 4/25/11 and whose white blood cell count will reach its nadir between those two dates. I cannot create encounters, only my administrative staff can do that, because an "encounter" is a billable session, not a clinical definition. The encounter must be

created for the exact day on which the patient will come in for the lab draw, and only then I can finally enter my order into that encounter.

Inflexible careset workflow: The software contains predefined care-sets, that have the basic set of orders that a given diagnosis would usually have, which is helpful. But once I start to enter the orders in a predefined careset, I cannot change encounters or review the last labs or anything else. I must finish the entire careset without looking anything else up, or cancel it. My workaround is to keep a separate window open so I can view and review orders and labs. [The other widely used software system at the second institution] does not allow me to keep two separate windows open into the chart, but it is at least a little more flexible about allowing me to pause midway through doing something, check something else, and come back to my previous work in progress.

Cannot update earlier records: If I have a patient who has an encounter on a particular day, I write or dictate a note on that day, edit it a few days later, and sign it. Suppose six weeks later I finally get some labs back that change my interpretation of what is going on with the patient in an important way. I want to write an addendum on the previous note with the better interpretation—but I can't, because the "encounter" it was entered into is closed.

Encounters in [the other widely used software system] are really a mess, because my ability to view certain data as a flow-sheet or graphically is limited to the present encounter. As a visually oriented person who has had a lot of experience with graphical data, that is by far the fastest and most accurate way for me to understand trends in cell counts and creatinine and other important things. This is the worst when I am dealing with vital signs, because I can only view blood pressure read-ings from a previous hospitalization as a list, not a flowsheet or graph, and certainly not as part of the same flowsheet or graph as those from the present encounter. ER visits and hospitalizations are different encounters, so I cannot see the blood pressure readings taken in the ED on my patient who seized shortly after transfer to the floor—were they hyperten-sive in the ED or not?—without going back to the previous encounter, lots of time, frustration remembering how to navi-gate there, and viewing a list. I frequently care for kids who are in and out of the hospital several times over their first month or two after diagnosis for control of hypertension. It's not an insignificant problem, and if I were not persistent in tracking this stuff down, I would not be doing right by the patients.

Not good with long-term chronic problems: In [one widely used software system], I can view lab results over multiple encounters on a single graph while logged into their present encounter, but by using a set of options that allow me to set the beginning dates for only up to one year in the past. But most of my patients have chronic diseases and I want to review their lab results over two or five years to see whether the present values are a new low or pretty close to where they were at the beginning of their disease. Having to flip back and forth between the present encounter chart and the "old chart" gets old quickly.

I would like the system to be seamless, so that I can view results and orders by dates, by order or test, enter orders for a particular date, and the system automatically puts them into encounters without my having to know about the encounters that are so vital to the bean counters. I would like to put in flexible orders and not tie patients to returning on a particular day and not have it be a fiasco requiring five phone calls and three pages to complete.

Compartmentalized, can't search: All of the systems I've worked with suffer from a lot of compartmentalization, and lack of searchability. I can sort things this way and that, and work my way through long alphabetized lists, but can't type a patient's name into a search box and immediately pull up all the notes I have entered on that patient, or enter "ulcer" to see whether anyone else ever documented the presence of oral ulcers on that patient (which might be key to confirming a diagnosis of lupus).

Can't work with other information systems: When I get records from patients seen at [another system in the area, highly computerized], I get pages and pages of [bleep] that have the order, and lab title, and lab result interspersed with telephone calls and visit notes. It's all nicely chronological, but not in the least useful for me as a consultant. I want to track what their lab values were over time, so I can figure out how they responded to the various medications they were being given. Theirs may be a wonderful system when you're in it, but it's a terribly disorganized core dump of data to muddle through when they try to extract data for outside use.

Stupid and inflexible navigation: At my old hospital, they redesigned the system to give over half of the screen space to a
   cute little "remote control" with buttons to allow you to
   switch functions, because we were too dumb to use the simple
   drop down menu, presumably. This made the screen about
   half as useful for finding data, because the smaller space
   available meant that all the information was truncated. And
   when I complained to them vigorously about the stupidity of
   this gimmick, they defended themselves by saying that they
   did have a resident and an attending on the committee that
   okayed the changes. One resident. One attending physician.
   For a system used by hundreds or thousands of doctors.

Index